REA's Test Prep Books Are The Best!

(a sample of the <u>hundreds of letters</u> REA receives each year)

" I did well because of your wonderful prep books... I just wanted to thank you for helping me prepare for these tests."
Student, San Diego, CA

" My students report your chapters of review as the most valuable single resource they used for review and preparation. "
Teacher, American Fork, UT

" Your book was such a better value and was so much more complete than anything your competition has produced (and I have them all!) "
Teacher, Virginia Beach, VA

" Compared to the other books that my fellow students had, your book was the most helpful in helping me get a great score. "
Student, North Hollywood, CA

" Your book was responsible for my success on the exam, which helped me get into the college of my choice... I will look for REA the next time I need help. "
Student, Chesterfield, MO

" Just a short note to say thanks for the great support your book gave me in helping me pass the test... I'm on my way to a B.S. degree because of you! "
Student, Orlando, FL

" The gem of the book is the tests. They were indicative of the actual exam. The explanations of the answers are practically another review session. "
Student, Fresno, CA

(more on next page)

(continued from front page)

" I just wanted to thank you for helping me get a great score on the AP U.S. History... Thank you for making great test preps! "

Student, Los Angeles, CA

" Your Fundamentals of Engineering Exam book was the absolute best preparation I could have had for the exam, and it is one of the major reasons I did so well and passed the FE on my first try. "

Student, Sweetwater, TN

" I used your book to prepare for the test and found that the advice and the sample tests were highly relevant... Without using any other material, I earned very high scores and will be going to the graduate school of my choice. "

Student, New Orleans, LA

" What I found in your book was a wealth of information sufficient to shore up my basic skills in math and verbal... The section on analytical ability was excellent. The practice tests were challenging and the answer explanations most helpful. It certainly is the Best Test Prep for the GRE! "

Student, Pullman, WA

" I really appreciate the help from your excellent book. Please keep up with your great work. "

Student, Albuquerque, NM

" I used your *CLEP Introductory Sociology* book and rank it 99%– thank you! "

Student, Jerusalem, Israel

" The painstakingly detailed answers in the sample tests are the most helpful part of this book. That's one of the great things about REA books. "

Student, Valley Stream, NY

(more on back page)

Research & Education Association

REA's
TESTBUSTER™
for the
SAT

with CD-ROM
for both Windows & Macintosh
REA's Interactive SAT TEST*ware*®

Robert A. Bell, Ph.D.
SAT Skills Consultant
Mathematics Professor
The Cooper Union School of Engineering
New York, NY

Suzanne Coffield, M.A.
SAT Preparation Instructor Aurora, IL

George DeLuca, J.D.
SAT Skills Consultant
New Rochelle, NY

Joseph D. Fili, M.A.T.
Director
Verbal "PrepSAT" Program
English Department
Christian Brothers Academy
Lincroft, NJ

Marilyn B. Gilbert, M.A.
SAT Skills Consultant
Hampton, NJ

Bernice E. Goldberg, Ph.D.
SAT Skills Consultant
Former Adjunct Professor
Seton Hall University, South Orange, NJ

Leonard A. Kenner
SAT Preparation Instructor
Math Instructor
Island Trees Junior High School
Levittown, NY

Marcia Mungenast
SAT Preparation Instructor and
Educational Consultant
Upper Montclair, NJ

Sandra B. Newman, M.A.
SAT Skills Consultant
Research Associate
Queens College / CUNY, Flushing, NY

Richard C. Schmidt, Ph.D.
SAT Skills Consultant
Instructor, Department of English
Roosevelt University, Chicago, IL

REA • 61 Ethel Road West • Piscataway, New Jersey 08854
http://www.rea.com

REA's TESTBUSTER™ for the SAT with CD-ROM for both Windows & Macintosh–REA's Interactive SAT TESTware®

Printed in the United States of America

Library of Congress Catalog Card Number 99-74658

International Standard Book Number 0-87891-294-0

Research & Education Association
61 Ethel Road West
Piscataway, New Jersey 08854
Email: info@rea.com

About Research and Education Association

Research and Education Association (REA) is an organization of educators, scientists, and engineers specializing in various academic fields. Founded in 1959 with the purpose of disseminating the most recently developed scientific information to groups in industry, government, high schools, and universities, REA has since become a successful and highly respected publisher of study aids, test preps, handbooks, and reference works.

REA's Test Preparation series includes study guides for all academic levels in almost all disciplines. Research and Education Association publishes test preps for students who have not yet completed high school, as well as high school students preparing to enter college. Students from countries around the world seeking to attend college in the United States will find the assistance they need in REA's publications. For college students seeking advanced degrees, REA publishes test preps for many major graduate school admission examinations in a wide variety of disciplines, including engineering, law, and medicine. Students at every level, in every field, with every ambition can find what they are looking for among REA's publications.

Unlike most Test Preparation books that present only a few practice tests which bear little resemblance to the actual exams, REA's series presents tests which accurately depict the official exams in both degree of difficulty and types of questions. REA's practice tests are always based upon the most recently administered exams, and include every type of question that can be expected on the actual exams.

REA's publications and educational materials are highly regarded and continually receive an unprecedented amount of praise from professionals, instructors, librarians, parents, and students. Our authors are as diverse as the subjects and fields represented in the books we publish. They are well-known in their respective fields and serve on the faculties of prestigious universities throughout the United States.

Acknowledgments

In addition to our authors, we would like to thank the following:

Dr. Max Fogiel, President, for his overall guidance which has brought this publication to completion.

Carl Fuchs, Director of REA's Testbuster Series, for his guidance and management of the editorial and graphic arts staff through every phase of development, from design to final production of book.

John Paul Cording, Manager of Educational Software, for overseeing the development of the software for this book.

Gary J. Albert, Project Manager of REA's Testbuster Series, for his substantial editorial contributions.

Nicole Mimnaugh, New Book Development Manager, for her editorial contributions and meticulous proofreading.

Ilona Bruzda, Senior Graphic Designer, for the design, illustrations, and graphic layout of text and cover.

CONTENTS

About Research and Education Association v

Acknowledgments vi

About REA's TEST*ware* for SAT 1

Installing REA's TEST*ware* 2

CHAPTER 1

Introducing REA's SAT Testbuster™   3

Busting the SAT 3

What is the SAT? 4

Who Makes the Test? 5

Beating a Multiple-Choice Test Like the SAT 5

The Math and Verbal Sections of the SAT 6

The Verbal Section 9

The Mathematics Section 10

How is the SAT Scored? 11

How Should I Study for the SAT? 12

Two-Month Study Schedule 13

CHAPTER 2

The Most Important Strategies for Beating the SAT   15

Don't Be Intimidated! 15

Your Best Friend: The Process of Elimination 16

The SAT's Greatest Weakness: Order of Difficulty 19

Guessing on the SAT—Yes! 21

Use Your Time Wisely 24

Don't Look at the Directions 25

You Paid For It, Use It! 26

Summary of "Must Do" Testbusting Rules 27

CHAPTER 3

SAT Practice Test   29

SAT Practice Test 31

Answer Key 63

Detailed Explanations of Answers 65

CHAPTER 4

Building Your Vocabulary for the SAT   117

The SAT Vocabulary Builder 118

How to Use the SAT Vocabulary Builder 119

The SAT Vocabulary Builder 121

Verbal Drills Answer Key 161

CHAPTER 5

Attacking Sentence Completion Questions   163

About the Directions 165

About the Questions 165

Points to Remember 166

Answering Sentence Completion Questions 168

Dealing with Positive Value Words 171

Dealing with Negative Value Words 174

Dealing with Mixed Value Words 177

Dealing with Neutral Value Words 181

Sentence Completion Drill 186

Sentence Completion Drill Answer Key 190

CHAPTER 6

Attacking Analogy Questions   191

About the Directions 194

About the Questions 195

Points to Remember 201

Answering Analogy Questions............................... 203

Analogies Drill 207

Analogies Drill Answer Key................................... 210

CHAPTER 7

Attacking Critical Reading Questions   211

Critical Reading Passages and Questions 213

About the Directions... 214

About the Passages 215

About the Questions 221

Points to Remember 224

Answering Critical Reading Questions 225

Critical Reading Drill 240

Critical Reading Drill Answer Key 250

CHAPTER 8

Attacking Regular Multiple-Choice Math Questions   251

Multiple-Choice Math.. 252

Working from Easiest to Hardest 253

Calculators and the Regular Multiple-Choice
     Math Section 256

About the Directions... 258

About the Questions 259

Attacking SAT Arithmetic Questions 260

Points to Remember for Busting SAT
     Arithmetic Questions 288

Attacking SAT Algebra Questions 291

Points to Remember for Busting SAT
     Algebra Questions 309

The Fundamental Rules of SAT Geometry................. 311

Contents

Points to Remember for Busting SAT
Geometry Questions 338

Regular Multiple-Choice Math Drill 341

Regular Multiple-Choice Math Questions
Drill Answer Key 348

CHAPTER 9

Attacking Quantitative Comparison Questions   349

About the Directions 352

About the Questions 353

Points to Remember 358

Answering Quantitative Comparison Questions 359

Quantitative Comparisons Drill 375

Quantitative Comparisons Drill Answer Key 380

CHAPTER 10

Attacking Grid-In Questions   381

Scoring Grid-Ins 383

About the Directions 383

Taking Advantage of the Format of Grid-Ins 385

Entering Your Answers Into the Grid 386

About the Questions 388

Points to Remember 414

Answering Grid-In Questions 415

Grid-In Drill 416

Grid-In Drill Answer Key 425

ANSWER SHEETS   431

About REA's TEST*ware*® for the SAT

Just by buying this book, you are one step closer to busting the SAT. Our TEST*ware*® will give you a further advantage on the test. The software offers two complete exams under actual exam conditions with controlled timing and question order. It automatically will score your test performance, provide you with analysis, and give you directions for further study. Here are some other benefits:

- A quick, on-screen tutorial will get you started right away.

- The on-screen text is superior in quality. The graphics and mathematical symbols are sharp and clear, and reading passages are easy to read and scroll.

- The pause button will allow you to use your study time efficiently.

- You can suspend the test and resume it at any time.

- The TEST*ware*® displays a list of questions featuring their answered or unanswered status, and allows students to mark questions for later review.

- The TEST*ware*® has the ability to display multiple windows simultaneously, allowing you to view a list of questions, exam directions, questions, and explanations while testing.

- There is an unlimited toll-free number and technical support via phone, fax, Internet, or America Online.

For further review, we have also provided you with REA's Verbal Builder Software. This software includes games and crossword puzzles that will help you build your SAT vocabulary, verbal, and reading skills while you are having fun! The puzzles and games are created by the computer with our dictionary of must-know SAT words. You can also add your own words to the dictionary. Improve your reading comprehension with our special speed reading software.

REA's TEST*ware*® is extremely user friendly, easy to install, easy to learn, easy to use, and exceptionally helpful.

Software Installation Instructions on following page...

INSTALLING REA's TEST*ware*®

System Requirements: 14" Monitor or larger

Windows: Any PC with 4 MB of RAM memory minimum. At least 5 MB of hard disk space available.

Macintosh: Any Macintosh with a 68020 or higher processor or Power Macintosh, 4 MB of RAM memory minimum, System 7.1 or later. At least 5 MB of hard disk space available.

MACINTOSH INSTALLATION

1. Insert the SAT TEST*ware*® CD into the CD-ROM drive.

2. Double click on the REA SAT Installer icon. Follow the on-screen installation process.

3. Start the SAT TEST*ware*®, or SAT Verbal Builder applications by double-clicking on their icons.

WINDOWS INSTALLATION

1. Insert the SAT TEST*ware*® CD into the CD-ROM drive.

2. From the Program Manager's File Menu, choose the Run command. When the Run dialog box appears, type D:\setup (where D is the letter of your CD-ROM drive) at the prompt and click OK.

3. Follow the on-screen installation process.

4. Start the SAT TEST*ware*®, or SAT Verbal Builder applications by double-clicking on their icons.

TECHNICAL SUPPORT

REA TEST*ware*® is backed by toll-free customer support. For problems with **installation or operation of your software**, contact Chariot Software Group. Questions about the book should be directed to REA.

Chariot Software Group
Phone: 1-800-242-7468
World Wide Web: http://www.chariot.com
Email: csg.support@chariot.com

Problems with installation or operation of your SAT Verbal Builder software, or the SAT Testbuster book should be directed to REA.

Introducing REA's SAT Testbuster

Busting the SAT

REA's SAT Testbuster is the result of a massive effort to provide you with the best possible preparation for the SAT. The techniques, strategies, tricks, and tips you'll learn from this book have been tested and proven to work on the SAT. They are the techniques and strategies used by the leading national coach and review courses. Why use a Testbuster? Because our testbusting techniques are proven, they work, and they will help you get the best score you possibly can on the SAT.

Bust it!

If you follow the strategies we teach you, you will do better on the SAT than you ever thought possible. "But," you may ask yourself, "won't that mean I have to spend every spare moment I have studying the same boring stuff that I'm studying in school?" No. The techniques we will teach you have nothing to do with school or verbal and math skills. We will teach you to beat the SAT. That means we will teach you ways to beat the people who write the SAT at their own game. There are ways to use the structure of the SAT to your advantage. We will teach you these methods. Armed with them, you will go to the test center, sit at a desk, and take the SAT knowing you will not be intimidated. In fact, the SAT should be intimidated by you because you will know its weaknesses! We will teach you how to "outsmart" the SAT.

What is the SAT?

Important Information!

The SAT I, which most people refer to simply as the SAT, is usually taken by high school juniors and seniors. As you probably already know, colleges use the SAT as a way to judge students who apply for admission. Since there are many different grading systems in high schools across the country — a teacher in Oklahoma will grade differently than a teacher in Maine — colleges use the SAT to place prospective students on equal ground. Your SAT score, along with other information (such as your high school grade point average, extracurricular activities, and references) are supposed to help colleges predict how well you will perform at the college level.

Who Makes the Test?

The SAT is developed and administered by the Educational Testing Service (ETS). ETS is a very large "non-profit" organization that not only develops and administers the SAT, but hundreds of other tests. You might have heard that ETS is a government agency or affiliated with Princeton University. Neither of these statements are true. ETS is an organization that makes a lot of money developing and administering tests. The company is based in Princeton, New Jersey (which is why some people assume that ETS is affiliated with Princeton University).

ETS is hired by another organization called the College Entrance Examination Board to write the SAT and a number of other tests. Now that you know what ETS is — a company selling a product, no different than McDonald's or The Gap — we hope you won't be as intimidated by their best-selling item: the SAT.

Important Information!

Beating a Multiple-Choice Test Like the SAT

Most of the SAT questions (except for some of the math questions) are multiple-choice questions. **The significance of a multiple-choice test is that the correct answer is always given**, in contrast to "fill-in-the-blank questions" or essays where you have to come up with the answer yourself. Of course, finding the correct answer among the multiple choices is what the test is all about.

Bust it!

Look!

Important Strategy

Testbusting will teach you that sometimes it's easier to find the incorrect choices than the correct answer. By eliminating the incorrect choices you can hone in on the correct answer. There will be a lot more about that later.

The Math and Verbal Sections of the SAT

The SAT is broken into two subjects: verbal and math. You will be given three hours to complete seven sections. The sections are broken down as follows:

Important Information!

VERBAL SECTION
(Skills covered: Vocabulary, Linear Thinking, and Reading)

Question Type	Number of Questions
Sentence Completions	19 multiple-choice questions
Analogies	19 multiple-choice questions
Critical Reading	40 multiple-choice questions

MATHEMATICS SECTION
(Skills covered: Arithmetic, Algebra, and Geometry)

Question Type	Number of Questions
Regular Math	35 multiple-choice questions
Quantitative Comparison	15 multiple-choice questions
Student Produced Response (Grids-Ins)	10 non-multiple-choice questions

The seven sections can appear in any order. There is one "experimental" section that ETS uses to try out new questions. You will not be scored on the "experimental" section, nor will you be told which section it is. So do your best on all seven sections.

The breakdown of questions may appear as follows:

Important Information!

Section 1
(30 minutes)

9 Sentence Completion questions

6 Analogy questions

Reading passage #1 with 6 questions

Reading passage #2 with 9 questions

Section 2
(30 minutes)

25 Regular Math questions

Section 3
(30 minutes)

10 Sentence Completion questions

13 Analogy questions

Reading passage #3 with 12 questions

Section 4
(30 minutes)

15 Quantitative Comparison questions

10 Grid-In questions

Section 5
(15 minutes)

Double reading passage with 13 questions

Section 6
(15 minutes)

10 Regular Math questions

Section 7
(30 minutes)

Experimental (ETS "tries out" new questions). An additional section of one of the above mentioned sections can appear in any order on the test. You will not know which section this is and you won't be scored.

Important Information!

Don't worry about the types of questions too much right now. We'll go into further detail about each type of question you'll encounter on the test later on in this book. For now, let's just take a quick glance at the question types.

The Verbal Section

There are three types of verbal questions on the SAT:

- **Sentence Completion:** *(19 questions)*
  A sentence will be given with either one or two words omitted. You will be required to choose the word or words which best fit the meaning of the sentence.

- **Analogies:** *(19 questions)*
  These questions test your ability to identify the relationship between two words and choose a pair which shows a similar connection.

- **Critical Reading:** *(40 questions)*
  There are four reading passages on the SAT, including one double passage consisting of two related selections. The questions are designed to test your critical reading skills, such as analyzing and synthesizing material.

Important Information!

The Mathematics Section

In the mathematics sections, you will encounter the following question types, which test your arithmetic, algebra, and geometry skills:

Important Information!

- **Regular Math:** *(35 questions)*
  These are mathematics questions in the standard multiple-choice format.

- **Quantitative Comparisons:** *(15 questions)*
  You will be asked to compare the quantities in column A and column B in terms of the four statements presented.

- **Student-Produced Response (Grid-ins):** *(10 questions)*
  These questions require you to solve a problem and enter the solution into a grid. These are not multiple-choice questions.

How is the SAT Scored?

The SAT gives you one point for each multiple-choice question you answer correctly. You lose a quarter of a point if you answer a multiple-choice question incorrectly. Leaving a question blank does not affect your score; you neither lose nor gain points. The Student-Produced Response (Grid-In) questions in the math section are graded a little differently and we'll discuss them in that review later in this book.

The number of points you earned in each section are then added together to reach your raw score. This raw score is then converted to a scaled score. The scaled score is set on a scale of 200 to 800, with 800 being the best possible score. You will receive one score for the verbal section and one score for the math section. The average score per section on the SAT is about 500.

Scoring the Test

About four or five weeks after you take the SAT, you'll receive a score report from ETS.

Your SAT scores are a very important factor when you apply to colleges. But we want to make it very clear that your SAT scores are not the only factor in getting into a college. Some schools put a lot of emphasis on your SAT scores, while others will also give strong consideration to your extracurricular activities or your essay response on your application. There is no absolute rule when it comes to the SAT and college admission. The best way to look at your SAT scores is to think of them as the first impression you give a college. And, as you know, first impressions can be very important, but once a school gets to know you through the application process, the SAT become less important in deciding your admission.

How Should I Study for the SAT?

It is very important for you to choose the time and place for studying that works best for you. Some students will set aside a certain number of hours every morning. Others may choose to study at night before going to sleep. It doesn't matter when you study, it only matters that you study every day. You will not help yourself by trying to read this entire book the night before you take the SAT!

The study schedule that we provide on the next two pages is designed to help you prepare for the SAT in a flexible time frame. The schedule presented is for an 8-week study course. However, you can condense it to a 4-week program by combining two weeks of studying into one. Remember, the more time you spend studying, the more prepared and relaxed you will feel on the day of the exam. If you choose to follow the 8-week schedule, plan to spend about an hour a day studying for the SAT.

It is very important that you give yourself the best possible chance to learn the techniques that this book offers. This means studying in a distraction-free environment. You should not have a radio or TV on while you are studying. Try to find a space where no one will interrupt your studying. Give yourself lots of light and space to spread out. A poorly lit room will strain your eyes and make you tired before you finish studying for the day.

Study Schedule

Two-Month Study Schedule

Week	Activity
• **Weeks 1 & 2**	*Read and study chapters 1 and 2 in this book. Then, take the Practice Test to determine your strengths and weaknesses. Carefully study the detailed explanations for the questions you answered incorrectly. Make sure you understand why you got each question wrong. If you need to refer to textbooks to refresh yourself on certain topics, please do. Pay attention to sections where you missed a lot of questions. You will need to spend more time reviewing these sections.*
• **Week 3**	*Study the review on Attacking Sentence Completion Questions and answer the drill questions. Review any material that you answered incorrectly in the drills. Study the reviews on Attacking Analogy Questions and Building Your Vocabulary for the SAT and answer the drill questions. Review any material that you answered incorrectly in the drills. Use the Verbal Builder software provided for further review.*
• **Week 4**	*Study the review on Attacking Critical Reading Questions and answer the drill questions. Review any material that you answered incorrectly in the drills. Study the review on Attacking Regular Multiple-Choice Math Questions and answer the drill questions. Review any material that you answered incorrectly in the drills.*

*Study
Schedule*

Study Schedule

- **Week 5**   Study the review on Attacking Quantitative Comparison Questions and answer the drill questions. Review any material that you answered incorrectly in the drills. Study the review on Attacking Student-Produced Response (Grid-In) Questions and answer the drill questions. Review any material that you answered incorrectly in the drills.

- **Weeks 6 & 7**   Take the Practice Test again. Compare the score you received on this practice test to the first test you took. Then take Diagnostic Software Exams I and II. Review carefully all incorrect answer explanations. Be sure to look for areas where you missed a lot of questions. Use this book and other textbooks to review the areas where you missed questions.

- **Week 8**   Go back and re-read the first few chapters of this book. Refresh your understanding of the structure and format of the SAT. Be sure to pay special attention to the Most Important Strategies for Beating the SAT. Review any material that has proven difficult to master during your studying.

2

The Most Important Strategies for Beating the SAT

Don't Be Intimidated!

The single most important strategy you can use to beat the SAT is **NOT TO BE INTIMIDATED**. Test-taking anxiety, a very common factor when students sit down to take the SAT, can absolutely ruin your score. You've already learned that there are ways to beat the SAT by using its weaknesses against itself. You've already learned that great SAT scores are not absolutely necessary in getting into the college that you want. You've already learned that ETS is not a huge, government-run monster that was created to make you feel stupid. And you've already learned what types of questions to expect to see on the SAT. **You already know a lot about this test and you haven't really even begun to study for it!** So just remember, knowledge is power. **DON'T BE INTIMIDATED!**

Bust it!

Your Best Friend: The Process of Elimination

The process of elimination will teach you that it's often easier to find the incorrect choice on a multiple-choice test than the correct answer. By eliminating the incorrect choices you can hone in on the correct answer.

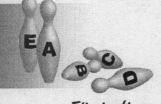

Eliminating Answer Choices

You probably already know how to use the process of elimination, but you may not realize it. More than likely, you've been taking multiple-choice tests for years. And you've been using the process of elimination to help yourself out while taking those tests. Let us show you:

Say you've been asked the following question on a history test (lucky for you there are no history questions on the SAT!).

Who was the 12th president of the United States of America?

(A)   **Bill Clinton**

(B)   **Zachary Taylor**

(C)   **Gerald Ford**

(D)   **Thomas Jefferson**

(E)   **Franklin D. Roosevelt**

Now, you may not know the order of presidents, but we bet you could still get the correct answer. Let's look at the answer choices. You know that Bill Clinton is definitely not it. You probably even know that he's the 42nd president. So you know this choice is incorrect.

(A)   **Bill Clinton**

Answer choice (B) may be tough for you, so we'll go on to the next choice.

Gerald Ford, answer choice (C), was president pretty recently and you probably know that. There have definitely been more than 12 presidents before Ford, so you can safely assume that answer choice (C) is incorrect.

(C)   **Gerald Ford**

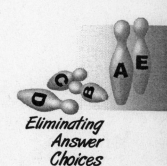

*Eliminating
Answer
Choices*

You probably know that Thomas Jefferson was one of the United States' first few presidents. In fact, it is likely that you know that Jefferson was the 3rd president. You can easily label answer choice (D) as incorrect.

(D)   **Thomas Jefferson**

The final answer choice, Franklin D. Roosevelt, may give you some difficulty. You may know that he was president during World War II. You probably can say with confidence that Roosevelt couldn't have been the 12th president just by knowing he served during the 1930s and 40s, but a bit of math will tell you for sure. If World War II was fought in the 1940s, that means about 150 years had passed since the first president in 1790. Dividing 150 by 4 (the number of years in a presidential term) and you get a little over 37. There is no way that Roosevelt could have been the 12th president. This is an incorrect answer choice.

(E)   **Franklin D. Roosevelt**

(A)   Bill Clinton

(B)   Zachary Taylor

(C)   Gerald Ford

(D)   Thomas Jefferson

(E)   Franklin D. Roosevelt

This question, at first glance, may have appeared a little more difficult than it was. By using process of elimination you were able to figure out that Zachary Taylor was our 12th president without knowing the exact order of presidents.

Eliminating Answer Choices

"But," you're probably thinking to yourself, "that's not the way we've been taught in school to get the answers." You're absolutely correct. Your teachers want you to work through each question very carefully, using all your knowledge. But guess what? The SAT doesn't care how you got the right answer, it only cares that you filled in the correct oval on your answer sheet! And using the process of elimination will help you fill in the right oval more times and faster than if you tried to work through every question like your teachers want you to.

Now, we don't want to make you believe that every question on the SAT is going to be as easy to answer as the one we just showed you. Because they aren't. But by using the process of elimination, you can usually eliminate 3 of the 5 answer choices. This means you've taken a 1 in 5 chance, or 20% chance, of getting the correct answer and turned it into a 1 in 2 chance, or 50% chance, of getting the correct answer! That sounds pretty good, doesn't it?

But wait! Say you use the process of elimination on 20 questions. That means you have a 50% chance of getting the right answer for those 20 questions (if you've eliminated 3 of the 5 choices). If you get 50% of the questions right, that means you've earned 10 points for the 10 correct answers (50% of 20 is 10). "Yes," you're probably saying, "but what about the 10 questions I got wrong?" Well, you lose a quarter of a point for getting the 10 questions you answered wrong. Which means you lose 2.5 points. But that means you've earned more than you've lost! The process of elimination gave you 7.5 points.

The SAT's Greatest Weakness: Order of Difficulty

Now that you know about the process of elimination, we'd like to introduce you to a variation on that method which works so well it may feel like cheating!

Many people for many years have known that the SAT presents the easier questions first and the harder questions later. Knowing this and knowing how to use the process of elimination gives you the tools to beat the SAT in a very advantageous way.

Just imagine that you are a question writer for ETS. You've been asked to come up with 40 easy questions, 40 medium-difficulty questions, and 40 hard questions. How would you make some of the questions easy? Some medium in difficulty? And some hard? The answer usually lies in the choices. It's not so difficult to write a question, but to come up with four incorrect answer choices is pretty hard. In fact, a lot of the time the wrong answers will stick out like a sore thumb because they are so silly or obviously incorrect.

Easy to Difficult

Like our example asking who the 12th president was, the easy questions can usually be answered by looking for the obviously correct answer choice. This enables the majority of test-takers to reach the correct answer. The medium-difficulty questions are designed so some people would get it right and some people would get it wrong. To do this, the correct answer choice wouldn't be so obvious, but there would still be one or two choices that could easily be ruled out. The harder questions would want almost everyone to get the wrong answer, so they usually try to trick the test-taker by giving you a lot of answer choices that look right but are actually wrong and the correct choice would look wrong but be right! **In fact, on difficult questions, the obvious choice is an "answer trap" and almost always wrong.**

Knowing this, and to take advantage of the SAT's biggest weakness, you must do two things: 1) know exactly how many questions you have answered in a section and 2) be able to recognize the "obvious" answer choices.

Here are some examples:

Say you are working on question 3 in a series of 10 Sentence Completion Questions. You know that this must be an easy question because it is in the first third of the series of questions. To beat the SAT, you should look for the obviously correct answer choice and choose it. You can do this with confidence because you know that the SAT will want the majority of people to get this answer right. They want to make the correct choice obvious to everyone.

Now imagine that you are working on question 5 in a series of 10 Regular Math Questions. You know that this is a medium-difficulty question because it is in the second third of the series of questions. To expose the SAT's weakness, you should remember that a medium-difficulty question is designed so some people get it right and some people get it wrong. To achieve this goal, the correct answer choice will not be obvious, but there will be some choices that are obviously wrong. Using the process of elimination, decide which answer

*Easy to
Difficult*

choices are obviously wrong, and then choose the correct answer from the remaining choices.

Finally, put yourself at the end of a series of questions, say 12th in a series of 13 Analogy Questions. You know this must be a hard question because it is in the last third of the series of questions. To use this technique in this situation, you must look for the answer choice that seems obviously correct and *eliminate it*. This is the correct way to approach a hard question because the SAT will want almost everyone to answer the question wrong. To do this, the question must be written in a way to trick people into choosing an answer that looks right but is really incorrect. So, you should eliminate the seemingly obvious correct answer and make your choice from the answers that remain.

Eliminating Answer Choices

Using this strategy will take some practice, and it may feel strange at first. But remember, all the SAT coaches and test experts have been teaching this technique for years. They wouldn't keep telling people to do it unless it worked. **And this one works incredibly well!**

Guessing on the SAT - Yes!

Another very important strategy in beating the SAT is to guess. Of course, the more answer choices that can be eliminated with the process of elimination the greater your odds of guessing correctly. You certainly have a better chance of guessing the right answer when you have eliminated most of the answer choices for a question and can pick between only two choices (50% chance of guessing correctly) than when you have to guess between five choices (only 20% chance of guessing correctly.)

Should I Guess?

But even when you can't eliminate any answers, you should still guess. That's right, if you can't answer the question, and can't use the process of elimination to reach the correct answer, just pick a letter and fill in the oval!

"How can this be true?" you're probably asking "Don't I lose points for getting the wrong question?" You're absolutely right — you do lose a quarter of a point for a wrong answer. But you gain a whole point if you get a question right! What ETS calls the guessing penalty can really be seen as the guessing reward. Let's look at this in more detail:

You remember that you earn a point for getting the correct answer and lose a quarter of a point for answering a question wrong. Looking at it this way makes it appear that the SAT is designed to penalize blind guessing. But that's not true! To better understand this, imagine that you are betting on your answers: If you answer the question right you get 1 point; if you get it wrong you lose a quarter of a point. Say you get the first question correct, that means you've earned a point. Now you can get the next 4 questions wrong before you lose any points (since you would have to lose 4 quarter-of-a-points to equal the 1 point you've earned). So, for every question you get right, you can get 4 incorrect before you start losing points!

Should I Guess?

Now, let's apply this idea with the law of averages in mind. Since there are 5 answer choices given for each SAT question, you can expect on average to guess the correct answer 1 out of 5 times (read up on your mathematical probability if you don't believe us!). This means that by guessing 5 times you'll get 1 question right. Let's go back to our betting game: if you get 1 answer right, you can get 4 answers incorrect before you start losing points. Make the connection yet? That's right, the law of averages says you'll earn a point and lose a point if you blindly guess on 5 SAT questions. (By blindly guessing we mean you don't even look at the question and answer choices!)

So you now see that blindly guessing will not affect your score on the SAT. If you get 1 answer out of 5 correct, you'll be back where you started: with no points. If you had left those 5 questions blank you would also have no points.

By now, you've probably already reached our next conclusion: "We're playing the law of averages, if we guess blindly along with using the process of elimination we'll beat the odds." Right! If you guess blindly you have a 1-in-5 chance of getting the question right. As you already learned, if you eliminate just 1 answer choice you increase your odds of getting the right choice from 1-in-5 (20%) to 1-in-4 (25%). This means that if you blindly guess on 20 questions, you can expect to get 4 answers correct. If you eliminate just 1 answer choice from those same 20 questions and blindly guess from the remainder of answer choices, you can expect to get 5 questions correct. So, when used together with some process of elimination techniques, guessing on the SAT will actually raise your score!

Should I Guess?

We'd like to show you another reason guessing at a question is better than leaving it blank (as if getting a better score isn't enough!). Some students wrongly believe that if you answer a dozen questions correctly and leave the rest blank they will receive a perfect score. This is absolutely wrong. While it is true that you don't lose points for leaving questions blank, you don't gain points either.

"How does this apply to guessing," you're probably asking. Well, you need to answer every question on the SAT correctly to earn a perfect score of 800. If you leave one question blank, you can only get a 780 or 790. If you leave 20 questions blank, the best score you can get is a 600. This means there is a penalty for leaving questions blank. And once you lose those points, you can't make them up later on in the SAT where you're skills are stronger. So guessing an answer will also help you to avoid losing points on the SAT!

Use Your Time Wisely

Watching the Clock!

The SAT is a timed test. You'll be given 15 to 30 minutes to work on each section. You'll need to work steadily, concentrating very hard on the questions. You don't want to spend a lot of time on any particular question. If you find yourself stuck on one problem, mark it in your test booklet and go on to the next question. If you have time left over, go back to it. If you're running out of time, just fill in the blank ovals on your answer sheet because you know that guessing will only help your score.

You know that the SAT gives you easier questions first and then the harder questions. You also know that you get the same amount of points for answering easy questions correctly as you do for getting hard questions correct. So why not answer all of the easy questions first? This will give you more time to spend on the medium-difficulty and hard questions.

After you've answered all the easy questions in a series (the first third), go on to the medium-difficulty questions (the second third). Finally, attempt to answer the hard questions (last third). This technique will save you a lot of points and time.

Why? Well, lets look at one of the sections that the SAT will give you:

Section 3
(30 minutes)

10 Sentence Completion questions

13 Analogy questions

Reading passage #3 with 12 questions

If you were to answer the questions in order, you might run out of time before you get to the Reading passage because you spent valuable time on the hard questions in the Sentence Completion and Analogy sections. You know that there are going to be about 4 easy questions for the Reading passage. That means you missed out on answering 4 questions that you would have probably answered correctly. That's 4 points.

Watching the Clock!

Now let's look at the hard questions that you did answer in the Sentence Completion and Analogy sections. You know that there are about 7 hard questions in these sections. If you answered half of them correctly (and that is being generous), you would have only earned about 3.5 points. You would have earned less points than if you had just skipped the hard questions and gone straight to the 4 easy points at the beginning of the Reading passage! And we're not even considering the possible points you could have gotten on the 4 medium-difficulty and 4 hard questions in the Reading passage!

So as you can see, answering the easy questions first is a **MUST** strategy for the SAT.

Don't Look at the Directions!

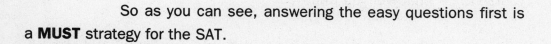

The SAT is a standardized test. That means the directions and the types of questions will be the same from test to test, person to person. If you learn the directions and how to approach each type of question before your test day, you will save valuable time by NOT reading the directions before beginning to answer the questions. And as you've already learned, time is critical on the SAT. Also, knowing

Important Information!

what to expect and how to handle all the question types on the test will enable you to avoid test-anxiety and nervousness.

You Paid for It, Use It!

Our final tip for your first set of strategies in beating the SAT is to write in your test booklet. We're sure you're tired of hearing teachers drone on about not writing in your textbooks because they are school property and will have to be used again next year. Well, here's your chance to write all over your test booklet. You've paid to take the SAT and your test booklet will be thrown away as soon as you hand in your answer sheet. So scribble in it, mark it up, make notes to yourself...do whatever you want!

One of the best ways to use your test booklet is to mark questions that you've spent some time on but decided to skip. By marking these questions, you can go back to them if you have time left over.

Look!

Important Strategy

For medium/hard questions, cross out answer choices you know you're not going to select. If you have time to return to those questions, you won't waste time eliminating answer choices again.

Also, working out math questions will be much easier if you can write them down. So use the margins of your test booklet. No one will see that you had to use long division to figure out 100 divided by 5! Besides, it wouldn't matter if someone did see it. The only thing that matters is that you chose the right answer!

Summary of "Must Do" Testbusting Rules

✔ **Don't Be Intimidated**

Fear is your worst enemy. Studying this book will enable you to approach the SAT with confidence and poise.

✔ **Use the Process of Elimination**

Possibly the easiest and quickest way to increase your score. Eliminating answer choices will lead you to the right answer almost every time.

✔ **Take Advantage of the Order of Difficulty**

The proven technique that let's you use the SAT against itself. Knowing where you are in a series of questions in terms of difficulty level and knowing the strategies for dealing with easy, medium, and difficult questions will help you beat the SAT at it's own game.

✔ **Guess, Guess, Guess**

Can't seem to get the answer? Pick a letter and fill in that oval! If you blindly guess you'll get 1 answer in 5 right. If you can eliminate just 1 answer choice, you'll get 1 answer in 4 right. Either way,

On Target!

On Target!

you'll raise your score because you do lose points for leaving an answer blank (even if ETS says you don't!).

✔ Use Your Time Wisely

Working quickly is important, but knowing which questions to answer first is even more important. Answering the easier questions before the harder ones will earn you more points faster.

✔ Don't Look At The Directions

Why waste valuable time reading what you already know? Learn the directions beforehand and ignore them during the test.

✔ Write In Your Test Booklet

You've paid for it, now use it! Make notes to yourself and mark questions that you want to return to. Work out math problems. It doesn't matter what you write, but write in your test booklet. It's there for you to use.

3

SAT
Practice
Test

Now that you have some background information concerning the SAT, you are ready to take the practice test. This test is designed to help you identify where your strengths and weaknesses lie. This will help you make more effective use of your study time.

This is a full-length test, so you should try to simulate actual testing conditions as closely as possible. Allow yourself three hours to complete the test. Situate yourself in a quiet room so that there will be no interruptions and **keep track of the time** allotted for each section.

*SAT
Practice
Test*

After you complete the practice test, identify your strengths and weaknesses by scoring each section of the test. The next step is to study the reviews and answer the drill questions in each chapter. Then, after studying the reviews, take the practice test again and see how well you score.

There are other options, however. The first option is to take the practice test and study only the reviews in your weaker areas and then retake the test. A second option is to study all the reviews and answer all the drill questions first. Then take the practice test and go back and review your weaker areas. You may already know where your weaknesses lie and might want to read the reviews and answer the drill questions for those sections and then take the test.

Remember to employ all of the Most Important Strategies for Busting the SAT which we introduced in Chapter 2. Begin using these strategies now so you can become comfortable with them before taking the actual SAT.

It is a good idea to photocopy the answer sheets for the practice test, even if you do not plan on retaking the practice test. By photocopying the answer sheets, you will ensure that you will have clean answer sheets no matter how many times you take the practice test.

SAT
Practice Test

Section 1 – Verbal
Section 2 – Math
Section 3 – Verbal
Section 4 – Math
Section 5 – Verbal
Section 6 – Math

(Answer sheets appear in the back of this book.)

TIME: 30 Minutes
30 Questions

For each question in this section, select the best answer from among the given choices and fill in the corresponding oval on the answer sheet.

DIRECTIONS: Each sentence below has one or two blanks, each blank indicating that something has been omitted. Beneath the sentence are five lettered words or sets of words. Choose the word or set of words that BEST fits the meaning of the sentence as a whole.

Example:
Although the critics found the book _____, many of the readers found it rather _____.

(A) obnoxious . . . perfect
(B) spectacular . . . interesting
(C) boring . . . intriguing
(D) comical . . . persuasive
(E) popular . . . rare

(A) (B) ● (D) (E)

1. The frightened mother _____ her young daughter for darting in front of the car.

(A) implored   (D) reproved
(B) extorted   (E) abolished
(C) exhorted

2. People who drive when they are drunk put themselves and others on the road in _____.

(A) guile   (D) distress
(B) discord   (E) dissonance
(C) jeopardy

3. The salesperson's _____ voice was exceptionally annoying. Potential customers avoided going anywhere near her product.

(A) exorbitant   (D) strident
(B) uproarious   (E) egocentric
(C) docile

4. Everyone avoided Pete at the party after his _____ comments insulted the hostess.

(A) tenacious   (D) pessimistic
(B) rancid   (E) sagacious
(C) sarcastic

5. Perhaps one reason for the lower number of female writers is that women traditionally have lacked the _____ independence and the _____ necessary to permit them to concentrate their efforts on writing.

(A) literary . . . talent
(B) intellectual . . . ability
(C) social . . . reputation
(D) emotional . . . intelligence
(E) financial . . . leisure

6. After carefully evaluating the painting, the art critics unanimously agreed that the work had been done by a _____ and should be _____.

(A) progeny . . . refurbished
(B) charlatan . . . repudiated
(C) neophyte . . . qualified
(D) prodigal . . . nullified
(E) fanatic . . . purchased

7. _____ swept the crowd when the natural _____ suddenly occurred.

(A) Infirmary . . . dispensation
(B) Pandemonium . . . catastrophe
(C) Vehemence . . . iodides
(D) Rectification . . . cravenness
(E) Turbulence . . . atmosphere

8. Rather than trying to _____, one should try to _____.

(A) abolish . . . destroy
(B) instigate . . . change
(C) demolish . . . enhance
(D) hurt . . . harm
(E) console . . . comfort

9. Despite the fact that they believed in different political philosophies, the politicians agreed to _____ on issues when their goals were _____.

(A) digress . . . ambivalent
(B) concede . . . controversial
(C) dissent . . . viable
(D) demur . . . provocative
(E) collaborate . . . compatible

GO ON TO THE NEXT PAGE →

DIRECTIONS: Each question below consists of a related pair of words or phrases, followed by five lettered pairs of words or phrases. Select the lettered pair that best expresses a relationship similar to that expressed in the original pair.

EXAMPLE:
SMILE : MOUTH ::
(A) wink : eye   (D) tan : skin
(B) teeth : face   (E) food : gums
(C) voice : speech

 ● Ⓑ Ⓒ Ⓓ Ⓔ

10 MINISTER : BIBLE ::
(A) secretary : shoes
(B) Shakespeare : play
(C) comb : cosmetologist
(D) carpenter : hammer
(E) swimmer : dive

11 RAIN : PRECIPITATION ::
(A) copper : metal
(B) ice : glacier
(C) oil : shale
(D) wind : abrasion
(E) heat : evaporation

12 COMPULSORY : REQUIRED ::
(A) committed : promised
(B) normal : aberrant
(C) freedom : democracy
(D) voluntary : mandatory
(E) education : intelligence

13 CRITIC : EVALUATION ::
(A) climax : portrait
(B) sponsor : promotion
(C) reporter : entertainment
(D) poem : representation
(E) artist : mood

14 CRUEL : ATROCIOUS ::
(A) stable : mercurial
(B) athletic : energetic
(C) tired : introverted
(D) interested : consumed
(E) accidental : intrinsic

15 PAULDRON : SHOULDER ::
(A) ligament : knee
(B) sword : scabbard
(C) horse : saddle
(D) skull : brain
(E) shelter : rain

GO ON TO THE NEXT PAGE ➡

DIRECTIONS: Read each passage and answer the questions that follow. Each question will be based on the information stated or implied in the passage or its introduction.

Questions 16–21 are based on the following passage.

The age of Ancient Greece saw many different philosophies come to light. The following passage looks at the ideas and beliefs of Epicurus, Zeno, and Carneades of Cyrene.

The Hellenistic Age produced two major and two minor additions to the history of philosophy. Epicureanism and Stoicism represented the
Line period's dominant philosophical movements.
(5) Skepticism and Cynicism found limited support among those unwilling to accept the Epicureans' and Stoics' confidence in reason. Hellenistic philosophy marked a turning point in the Western intellectual tradition. The classical Greek
(10) philosophers linked the individual's happiness to the community's well being. The philosophers of the Hellenistic period focused on the individual. The business of philosophy shifted from the pursuit of knowledge for its own sake. The goal of
(15) philosophy became the individual's peace of mind and personal happiness.

Epicurus (ca. 342-270 B.C.E.) founded a school in Athens and based his metaphysics on Democritus's atomic theory. Epicurus taught that
(20) the goal of philosophy should be to help the individual find happiness. Unlike Socrates and Plato, he did not make citizenship in a polis the basis of happiness. Epicurus argued that a wise man eschewed public affairs and sought self-
(25) sufficiency. Later critics accused Epicurus and his followers of advocating a life based on pursuing the pleasures of the flesh. To Epicurus, however, the highest pleasure was to be found in contemplation.

Zeno (ca. 335-263 B.C.E.) established a rival
(30) philosophical school under the *Stoa Poikile* (painted porch) of the Athenian *Agora* (marketplace). There are a number of similarities between Stoicism and Epicureanism. Like Epicurus, Zeno emphasized the importance of the
(35) individual. Moreover, both schools were based on a materialistic metaphysics and claimed universal validity for their teachings. There were, however, significant differences between the two philosophical outlooks. Zeno taught that the
(40) cosmos was a unified whole which was based on a universal order (Logos or Fire). Every man carried a spark of this Logos in his reason. At death this spark returned to its origin. The Stoics taught that each person should strive to discover the natural
(45) law governing the universe and live in accordance with it.

The Skeptics attacked the Epicureans and the Stoics. Carneades of Cyrene (ca. 213-129 B.C.E.) argued that all knowledge was relative. The sensory
(50) impressions which we receive from the external world are flawed. Individuals should abandon the quest for knowledge because nothing can be known for certain. The safest course is to doubt everything. Indifference is the only philosophically
(55) defensible position.

Diogenes of Sinope (d. 323 B.C.E.) was the most famous cynic. His goal was to prepare the individual for any disaster. He lived as a beggar and was famous for his outspoken condemnation of
(60) sham and hypocrisy. One story has it that when he met Alexander the Great and the world-conqueror asked him what he wanted, Diogenes replied that Alexander should get out of his light.

16 Education for citizenship was a goal of

(A) Epicurus.   (D) Diogenes.
(B) Socrates.   (E) Zeno.
(C) Carneades.

GO ON TO THE NEXT PAGE

17 The saying, "I am trying to find myself and my happiness" might be employed by a follower of

(A) Diogenes.   (D) Stoics.
(B) Zeno.   (E) Carneades.
(C) Hellenism.

18 The word "polis" in line 22 most nearly means

(A) a group.
(B) in a certain way.
(C) a place of one's own; a place of solitude.
(D) a tradition.
(E) a philosophical outlook.

19 The author focused on the classical Greek philosophers in order to

(A) show similarities with the Jurassic Age.
(B) contrast them with Oriental thinkers.
(C) show their relation to the earlier philosophers of the Hellenistic Age.
(D) contrast them with those of the Hellenistic Age.
(E) show his scorn of the past.

20 The most important element of Stoic thought was

(A) its similarity to Epicureanism.
(B) the universal validity of its teaching.
(C) the idea that each person carried a spark of Logos in his reason.
(D) its establishment under the painted porch of the Athenian marketplace.
(E) its emphasis on the individual.

21 Carneades taught that

(A) all knowledge was relative.
(B) the goal of philosophy should be to help the individual find happiness.
(C) a wise man eschewed public affairs and sought self-sufficiency.
(D) the individual should be prepared for any disaster.
(E) the highest pleasure was to be found in contemplation.

GO ON TO THE NEXT PAGE

Questions 22–30 are based on the following passage.

The following passage examines the social and political issues involved in universal health coverage.

Universal health coverage for all citizens is a political question staunchly supported by proponents and vigorously opposed by detractors.
Line Both groups are emotionally committed to their
(5) idea of what is best for the nation. Today, health care coverage varies from business to business. Employees may or may not be covered by health insurance and/or retirement pension plans provided by employers. Congress has made small
(10) steps toward a national health plan through several laws. For instance, the Health Maintenance Organization Act was passed in 1973. Lobbyists have pressed for leaves of absence without fear of job loss when babies are born, children are ill, or a
(15) parent experiences serious illness. The central issue for business and industry is a personnel management problem and labor costs. Who will perform work duties for up to 26 weeks while the employee is on leave without pay?
(20) Not surprisingly, many female employees support leaves of absence for child-rearing purposes. The National Organization for Women has worked actively to support passage of the federal law. Senator Christopher Dodd feels that
(25) the bill will address problems of working mothers. He cited statistics to prove his point: "half of all mothers with infants less than a year old work outside home" and "85% of all women working outside the home are likely to become pregnant at
(30) some point during their career." Dodd maintained that "we must no longer force parents to choose between their job and caring for a new or sick child." The bill has its critics. The president of the California Merchants and Manufacturers
(35) Association projects discrimination against women in hiring practices if the bill is passed. Roberta Cook of the California Chamber of Commerce said, "We're compassionate. We just don't think the issue should be the employer's responsibility.
(40) *That's* the issue."
Another social issue yet unresolved is drug use and management/labor relations. Employers must consider the problem from several vantage points. Accidents, absenteeism, and reduction of
(45) productive labor are expensive and wasteful. The constitutional right of privacy is often argued when personnel policies for testing and/or searches are proposed. Courts have given qualified approval to some methods that employers may implement.
(50) Employers in the private sector may require drug testing as a precondition for employment. Government personnel directors must be cautious in devising new policies. Based on nothing more than the goal of a drug-free workplace in the public
(55) sector, large-scale drug testing of employees violates their right of privacy.
When comparing social issues in the late nineteenth and the early twentieth centuries with current social issues that affect personnel policies,
(60) the increasing number of complexities of labor/ management relations are apparent. Yet the question can be asked: Were the emotional, physical, and economic damages experienced by workers in the early years less important than the
(65) emotional, physical, and economic damages experienced today? Reuben Dagenhart, plaintiff in a child labor case, was in his 20s, an uneducated man who weighed only about 105 pounds. Today, the "Reubens" do not quit school at a tender age
(70) and work long hours at factories, but modern-day mothers are distraught when in some workplaces they face job loss if they take leave to attend to a sick child or parent. In the late twentieth century the legislative branch continues its struggles with
(75) competing pressures from labor and management, while the judicial branch intercedes from time to time and makes decisions based on what the Constitution requires. National leaders must structure social policies when legal and social
(80) philosophies collide and when economic theories clash in the marketplace of ideas.

22 The passage demonstrates that issues of the marketplace

(A) have repercussions in both legal and moral spheres.
(B) have tended to sway our economy back towards child labor.
(C) have made employers thoroughly insensitive to working mothers.
(D) have no effect on social policies.
(E) have led to unrestricted drug testing.

GO ON TO THE NEXT PAGE ➡

23 One form of possible backlash against Senator Dodd's bill is

(A) the threats from his constituency not to re-elect him.
(B) a deliberate practice of not hiring women.
(C) a boycott from The National Organization for Women.
(D) increased taxation on the employers.
(E) suspension of all leave for child-rearing purposes.

24 The right-to-privacy issue is invoked

(A) with regard to those who fill in for women on leave.
(B) when labor and management discuss personal leave.
(C) when parents miss work on account of a sick child.
(D) when drug tests are administered as part of an employment requirement.
(E) when employee lockers are searched for illegal substances.

25 A critic like Roberta Cook (lines 36 and 37) equates universal health coverage with

(A) putting the burden of responsibility of child-rearing on the employer.
(B) the general loss of workers' rights in recent times.
(C) unconstitutional intrusion by the legislative body of government.
(D) the decline in sympathy between labor and management.
(E) a general upgrading of women's rights in recent history.

26 Reuben Dagenhart (line 66) is cited as an example

(A) of a typical uneducated worker from the 1920s.
(B) of a worker who was exploited and damaged by unfair labor practices.
(C) of the middle manager who feels compassion for his workers.
(D) of the need to separate business practices from national, legal policies.
(E) of a sick child whose parents had to sacrifice either his health or their economic livelihood.

27 According to the article, at the present time

(A) all employees are covered by health and retirement plans.
(B) government personnel directors have unlimited powers to create drug-free environments.
(C) social policies and economic policies are running free of any friction.
(D) accidents, absenteeism, and reduction of productive labor are simply the costs of doing business.
(E) the constitutional right-to-privacy remains a major factor in socioeconomic policy.

28 Senator Dodd cited statistics in order to

(A) garner support for his anti-leave-of-absence bill.
(B) prove that children and mothers suffer under present labor conditions.
(C) discredit mothers of infants with a degree of child neglect.
(D) rally support from management to underwrite welfare costs.
(E) show that women were a potential drain on the workplace.

29 The word "distraught" (line 71) means

(A) disloyal.   (D) angered.
(B) beset by mental   (E) pacified.
    anguish.
(C) unemployed.

30 The Health Maintenance Organization Act of 1973

(A) was a direct blow to labor's call for a right to privacy.
(B) is cited as an example of reduced health benefits.
(C) was a step in moving towards a national health plan.
(D) was the first in a series of steps to make the workplace drug free.
(E) guarantees that a worker on leave will have a job when he returns.

STOP
If time still remains, you may go back and check your work. When the time allotted is up, you may go on to the next section.

TIME: 30 Minutes
25 Questions

DIRECTIONS: Solve each problem, using any available space on the page for scratch work. Then decide which answer choice is the best and fill in the corresponding oval on the answer sheet.

NOTES:

(1)   The use of a calculator is permitted. All numbers used are real numbers.

(2)   Figures that accompany problems in this test are intended to provide information useful in solving the problems. They are drawn as accurately as possible EXCEPT when it is stated in a specific problem that the figure is not drawn to scale. All figures lie in a plane unless otherwise indicated.

REFERENCE INFORMATION:

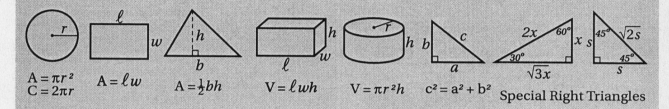

$A = \pi r^2$
$C = 2\pi r$ $A = \ell w$ $A = \frac{1}{2}bh$ $V = \ell wh$ $V = \pi r^2 h$ $c^2 = a^2 + b^2$ Special Right Triangles

The number of degrees of an arc in a circle is 360.
The measure in degrees of a straight angle is 180.
The sum of the measures in degrees of the angles of a triangle is 180.

---

1   Using order of operations, solve:

$3 \times 6 - 12 \div 2.$

(A) –9   (D) 12

(B) 3   (E) 18

(C) 6

2   Change $4\frac{5}{6}$ to an improper fraction.

(A) $\frac{5}{24}$

(B) $\frac{9}{6}$

(C) $\frac{29}{6}$

(D) $\frac{30}{4}$

(E) $\frac{120}{6}$

GO ON TO THE NEXT PAGE →

3   In rhombus *ABCD*, which of the following are true?

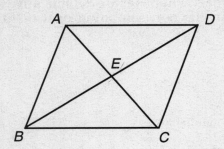

I.   ∠ *BAE* and ∠ *ECD* are congruent.

II.   ∠ *ADE* and ∠ *CDE* are congruent.

III.   ∠ *ABE* and ∠ *ADE* are congruent.

(A) I only.
(B) II only.
(C) I and II only.
(D) I and III only.
⟶(E) I, II, and III.

4   Subtract $4\frac{1}{3} - 1\frac{5}{6}$.

(A) $3\frac{2}{3}$

(B) $2\frac{1}{2}$

(C) $3\frac{1}{2}$

(D) $2\frac{1}{6}$

(E) $5\frac{2}{3}$

5   The rates of a laundromat are \$6.25 for the first 15 pieces and \$0.35 for each additional piece. If the laundry charge is \$8.35, how many pieces were laundered?

(A) 5
(B) 6
(C) 15
(D) 21
(E) 25

6   If *p* and *q* are prime numbers greater than two, which of the following must be true?

I. $pq + 1$ is also a prime number.

II. $pq - 1$ is also a prime number.

III.   *p* and *q* do not have a common factor.

(A) I only.
(B) II only.
(C) III only.
(D) I and II only.
(E) I and III only.

7   Find the sum of $5\frac{3}{4}$, $2\frac{11}{16}$, and $7\frac{1}{8}$.

(A) $14\frac{8}{17}$

(B) $14\frac{15}{16}$

(C) $15\frac{1}{2}$

(D) $15\frac{15}{28}$

(E) $15\frac{9}{16}$

GO ON TO THE NEXT PAGE ⟶

8 A computer is marked up 50 percent and then later marked down 30 percent. If the final price is $3,360, the original price was

(A) $2,240.
(B) $3,200.
(C) $4,200.
(D) $4,800.
(E) $5,600.

10 Two pounds of pears and one pound of peaches cost $1.40. Three pounds of pears and two pounds of peaches cost $2.40. How much is the combined cost of one pound of pears and one pound of peaches?

(A) $2.00
(B) $1.50
(C) $1.60
(D) $1.20
(E) $1.00

9

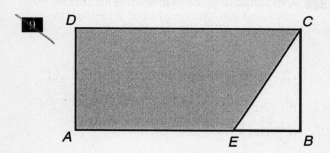

If the length of segment $\overline{EB}$, base of triangle

EBC, is equal to $\frac{1}{4}$ the length of segment $\overline{AB}$

($\overline{AB}$ is the length of rectangle of $ABCD$), and

the area of triangle EBC is 12 square units, find

the area of the shaded region.

(A) 24 square units
(B) 96 square units
(C) 84 square units
(D) 72 square units
(E) 120 square units

11 The solution of the equation $4 - 5\,(2y + 4) = 4$ is

(A) $-\dfrac{2}{5}$.

(B) 8.

(C) 4.

(D) -2.

(E) 2.

12 How many corners does a cube have?

(A) 4
(B) 6
(C) 8
(D) 12
(E) 24

GO ON TO THE NEXT PAGE

13 The number missing in the series 2, 6, 12, 20, *x*, 42, 56 is

(A) 36.
(B) 24.
(C) 30.
(D) 38.
(E) 40.

16 If the cost of 2 pencils and 3 pens is $3.00, and if the cost of a pencil and 5 pens is $4.30, what is the cost of a pen alone?

(A) $0.30
(B) $0.50
(C) $0.80
(D) $1.10
(E) $1.50

14 A truck contains 150 small packages, some weighing 1 kg each and some weighing 2 kg each. How many packages weighing 2 kg each are in the truck if the total weight of all the packages is 264 kg?

(A) 36
(B) 52
(C) 88
(D) 124
(E) 114

17 A rectangular piece of metal has an area of 35m² and a perimeter of 24m. Which of the following are possible dimensions of the piece?

(A) $\dfrac{35}{2}$ m × 2m

(B) 5m × 7m

(C) 35m × 1m

(D) 6m × 6m

(E) 8m × 4m

15 If $c = 18a + 24b$, where *a* and *b* are positive integers, then *c* must be divisible by which of the following?

(A) 4
(B) 6
(C) 9
(D) 12
(E) 72

18 If *A* can do a job in 8 days and *B* can do the same job in 12 days, how long would it take the two men working together to complete the job?

(A) 3 days
(B) 4.8 days
(C) 10 days
(D) 5.8 days
(E) 6 days

GO ON TO THE NEXT PAGE

19 If $x + 2y > 5$ and $x < 3$, then $y > 1$ is true

(A) never.
(B) only if $x = 0$.
(C) only if $x > 0$.
(D) only if $x < 0$.
(E) always.

22 The length of a rectangle is $6L$ and the width is $4W$. What is the perimeter?

(A) $12L + 8W$
(B) $12L^2 + 8W^2$
(C) $6L + 4W$
(D) $20LW$
(E) $24LW$

20 The enrollment in Eastern High School is 1,050. If the attendance for a month was 94%, how many students were absent during the month?

(A) 50
(B) 63
(C) 420
(D) 987
(E) 1,044

23 What is the product of $(\sqrt{3} + 6)$ and $(\sqrt{3} - 2)$?

(A) $9 + 4\sqrt{3}$
(B) -9
(C) $-9 + 4\sqrt{3}$
(D) $-9 + 2\sqrt{3}$
(E) 9

21 If x is an odd integer and y is even, then which of the following must be an even integer?

I. $2x + 3y$

II. xy

III. $x + y - 1$

(A) I only.
(B) II only.
(C) I and II only.
(D) II and III only.
(E) I, II, and III.

24 The sum of four consecutive even integers is 68. What is the value of the smallest one?

(A) 12
(B) 14
(C) 7
(D) 18
(E) 1

GO ON TO THE NEXT PAGE

25   Lynsey is 5 years older than Gretta. The sum of their ages is 95. How old is Lynsey?

(A) 5
(B) 40
(C) 45
(D) 50
(E) 55

STOP
If time still remains, you may go back and check your work.
When the time allotted is up, you may go on to the next section.

TIME: 30 Minutes
35 Questions

For each question in this section, select the best answer from among the given choices and fill in the corresponding oval on the answer sheet.

Each sentence below has one or two blanks, each blank indicating that something has been omitted. Beneath the sentence are five lettered words or sets of words. Choose the word or set of words that BEST fits the meaning of the sentence as a whole.

EXAMPLE:

Although the critics found the book _____, many of the readers found it rather _____.

(A) obnoxious . . . perfect
(B) spectacular . . . interesting
(C) boring . . . intriguing
(D) comical . . . persuasive
(E) popular . . . rare

Ⓐ Ⓑ ● Ⓓ Ⓔ

1 After developing a(n) _____ toward animals, she refused to visit any of her friends who had pets.

(A) derision   (B) compliance
(D) inclination (C) heresy   (E) phobia

2 In the years previous to 1960, when men were perceived as the sole breadwinners of a family, it was _____ for women to aspire to careers outside the home.

(A) inherent   (B) decorous
(C) unconventional   (D) vital   (E) uncouth

3 The _____ activities of the villain in the movie caused the audience to cheer when he was caught by the hero.

(A) intrepid   (B) cursory   (C) lurid
(D) nefarious   (E) jocund

4 American words and phrases have been added to the lexicon of French and Japanese cultures despite the displeasure of politicians and the _____ of purists.

(A) concession (B) neutrality (C) endorsement
(D) resolution (E) denunciation

5 The use of a pen with indelible ink will _____ a student's ability to _____ at a later time.

(A) preclude . . . erase
(B) hinder . . . slander
(C) nullify . . . desecrate
(D) deplete . . . digress
(E) enhance . . . ameliorate

6 Although the explorers often felt _____, they managed to _____ the desert.

(A) defeated . . . achieve
(B) elated . . . survive
(C) exhausted . . . conquer
(D) relentless . . . finish
(E) withdrawn . . . subject

7 Police officers often face _____ situations where they must maintain their _____.

(A) inhospitable . . . agility
(B) impossible . . . gallantry
(C) unequivocable . . . sternness
(D) perilous . . . composure
(E) extraordinary . . . strength

8 The Civil War was the _____ of the inability of the North and South to _____ on an interpretation of the Constitution.

(A) epitome . . . concur
(B) climax . . . agree
(C) drama . . . unite
(D) chaos . . . harmonize
(E) finalization . . . cooperate

9 The _____ of the companies was inevitable since neither could profit without the assets of the other. This showed _____ behavior on the part of the owners.

(A) merger . . . prudent
(B) pivot . . . exemplary
(C) antagonism . . . beneficial
(D) hiatus . . . monotonous
(E) diversity . . . fundamental

10 The gold-studded costume appeared _____ when compared to the _____ of the flannel suit.

(A) chaste . . . gaudiness
(B) laconic . . . opulence
(C) reserved . . . savoir-faire
(D) ornate . . . simplicity
(E) feudal . . . raucousness

GO ON TO THE NEXT PAGE

<u>DIRECTIONS</u>: Each question below consists of a related pair of words or phrases, followed by five lettered pairs of words or phrases. Select the lettered pair that best expresses a relationship similar to that expressed in the original pair.

EXAMPLE:

SMILE : MOUTH ::
(A) wink : eye
(B) teeth : face
(C) voice : speech
(D) tan : skin
(E) food : gums

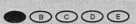

11 HOURGLASS : SAND ::
(A) thermometer : mercury
(B) ruler : inch
(C) scale : number
(D) barometer : tremor
(E) voltmeter : radiation

12 ACCOUNTANT : CALCULATOR ::
(A) actor : stage
(B) mechanic : screwdriver
(C) student : school
(D) senator : page
(E) waitress : restaurant

13 CATERPILLAR : BUTTERFLY ::
(A) oyster : pearl
(B) tadpole : frog
(C) clay : sculpture
(D) raisin : grape
(E) politician : lawyer

14 ARC : CIRCLE ::
(A) moon : earth
(B) hour : day
(C) cabin : mansion
(D) exercise : rest
(E) knowledge : wisdom

15 REFLEX : INVOLUNTARY ::
(A) apparition : real
(B) impulse : sudden
(C) kick : dangerous
(D) detail : general
(E) spasm : lengthy

16 ANXIOUS : NEUROTIC ::
(A) lackadaisical : animated
(B) contemporary : archaic
(C) weak : decrepit
(D) special : temporary
(E) vivacious : ironic

17 NOVICE : NEOPHYTE ::
(A) fugitive : road
(B) virtuoso : expert
(C) pacifist : war
(D) vagrant : street
(E) idealist : principle

18 BANAL : TRITE ::
(A) grave : sad
(B) ephemeral : temporary
(C) murky : clear
(D) long : hard
(E) novel : arduous

19 AMPERE : ELECTRICITY ::
(A) heat : sun
(B) pound : weight
(C) bulb : light
(D) number : salary
(E) inch : ruler

20 CONTRITE : PENITENT ::
(A) reticent : punctual
(B) concise : succinct
(C) dogmatic : levelheaded
(D) sanguine : pessimistic
(E) facsimile : original

21 DOOR : KEY ::
(A) gem : ring
(B) perfume : aroma
(C) enigma : clue
(D) effort : achievement
(E) mold: gelatin

22 REQUEST : EXTORT ::
(A) respond : letter
(B) cheer : smile
(C) mute : speech
(D) defer : judgment
(E) entertain : regale

23 OPPROBRIOUS : HONOR ::
(A) significant : substance
(B) tranquil : agitation
(C) transparent : truth
(D) lecherous : confidence
(E) obtrusive : prominence

GO ON TO THE NEXT PAGE

DIRECTIONS: Read the passage and answer the questions that follow. Each question will be based on the information stated or implied in the passage or its introduction.

Questions 24–35 are based on the following passage.

The following passage discusses the earliest scientific research in sleep and dreams.

Before 1952, most people thought that dreams were rare events, perhaps caused by bodily discomfort or aching conscience, by trauma, sensory
Line stimulation, or the insurgence of an unruly
(5) subconscious. The discovery that all people dream every night came as a surprise to many, although a large number of classical studies had already heralded the finding. Like many developments in science, a long progression of researchers composed
(10) the prelude to the work of this decade although the earlier work attracted less public attention.

The germinal studies, from which much of modern sleep research has burgeoned, began innocuously enough at the University of Chicago
(15) where Dr. Nathaniel Kleitman devoted himself single-mindedly to the study of sleep. Dr. Eugene Aserinsky, then a graduate student working with Kleitman, turned attention toward phenomena that had been spotted before and never thoroughly
(20) studied. Aserinsky, studying the movements of sleeping infants, was arrested by the fact that the slow rolling movements of the eyes would stop periodically, for intervals. He began to watch adults and saw that there were recurrent intervals of body
(25) quiescence when the eyes began making rapid jerky movements beneath the closed lids. At the time it was a curious and startling observation, and it took some doing on the part of a graduate student to demonstrate that this periodic activity did indeed
(30) occur in sleep. When Aserinsky and Kleitman watched sleeping volunteers, they saw that the rapid eye movements (REMs) occurred periodically, at a time when there were sharp increases in respiration and heart rate and the electroencephalogram (EEG)
(35) showed a low-voltage, desynchronized pattern very different from the rolling waves of deep sleep.

Back in the 1930s, shrewd observers indicated that this EEG pattern meant dreaming qualitatively different from dreaming in other stages of sleep but
(40) the time was not then ripe for a surge of corroborating research on this phase of sleep. When Aserinsky and Kleitman awakened volunteers during this REM and EEG pattern, subjects almost always narrated a dream, while awakenings at other periods of sleep

(45) rarely evoked such reports. Dr. William C. Dement, then also a graduate student at Chicago, pursued the finding, affirming the coincidence of dreaming with the REM and low-voltage EEG pattern. Subsequently he noted the same pattern in the sleep of cats, a
(50) finding confirmed by Dr. Michel Jouvet of the Faculty of Medicine in Lyon. At this point two major paths of dream exploration had begun in the animal laboratory of neurophysiology and in the EEG laboratory where human volunteers came to sleep out the night.

(55) Nobody could have predicted how rapidly sleep research would capture the scientific imagination. Where a few men with solitary persistence had concentrated on the overlooked third of life, in 10 years there followed a new generation of scientists,
(60) many of whom elected sleep as their province of research. From the start the arresting differences between the REM intervals and the rest of sleep suggested that REM was a unique physiological and psychological state.

(65) In the early days of dream research, little more than a decade ago, two very remarkable facts were discovered. Today they are taken for granted, but at that time masses of data and many confirmations were required to persuade the scientists that they
(70) really had found what they thought they had found. Everybody dreamt every night, and moreover, they dreamt in regular cycles, each for roughly the same amount of time. Subjectively it is easier to think of dreaming as infrequent, because, in part, memory
(75) for dreams is so brief. Yet the assortment of students and housewives who were paid to sleep in Abbot Hall at the University of Chicago gave richly detailed dream narratives when awakened during REM periods. As Dement and other investigators
(80) repeatedly awakened volunteers it became clear that young adults had a similar pattern of vivid dream episodes. About 90 minutes after falling asleep they would rise into a REM state, usually for a short period, about 10 minutes, then sink down into deep
(85) sleep for about an hour before rising again for a longer dream period. Hundreds and hundreds of people have now been recorded, and the average young adult seems to dream about 20–25 percent of his or her sleeping time, in five or so REM periods, at
(90) roughly hourly intervals. Individuals appear to have somewhat distinctive patterns, and some investigators can look at a person's EEG record of several nights' sleep and predict when he will start dreaming, and for how long.

GO ON TO THE NEXT PAGE →

24 In line 25 the best meaning of the word "quiescence" is

(A) movement.
(B) agitation.
(C) peace.
(D) upheaval.
(E) intervention.

25 Aserinsky and Kleitman noted

(A) that REMs occur when respiration decreased.
(B) that REMs occur when heart rate decreased.
(C) that REMs were accompanied by sharp increases in respiration and a decrease in heart rate.
(D) that REMs were accompanied by sharp increases in respiration and heart rate and a high voltage, desynchronized pattern different from that of deep sleep.
(E) that REMs were accompanied by sharp increases in respiration and heart rate and a low voltage, desynchronized pattern different from that of deep sleep.

26 It is true that

(A) all people dream every night.
(B) the eyes of an infant, unlike those of an adult, remain still during sleep.
(C) rapid eye movement patterns occur generally only in people and not in animals like the cat; this was confirmed by Dement.
(D) dreams are rare events, caused by bodily discomfort, aching conscience, and trauma.
(E) the discovery that people dream every night was not made until after 1956.

27 Two strong evidences of nightly dreaming are

(A) the findings of both neurophysiology laboratories and the veterinary laboratories.
(B) the findings in the EEG laboratories and the neurophysiology laboratories.
(C) the findings in the EEG laboratories and the veterinary laboratories.
(D) the age of the studies and the age of the volunteers.
(E) the fact that the researchers were not merely observers but full professors.

28 An advantage of the study was that the subjects were

(A) forced to participate.
(B) human subjects only and no mammals were involved.
(C) animal subjects only.
(D) willing subjects.
(E) chosen during the 1930s, the depression era when money was in short supply.

29 Aserinsky studied

(A) the movement of waking infants.
(B) the movement of sleeping cats.
(C) the movement of both sleeping infants and sleeping cats.
(D) the movement of both waking infants and waking cats.
(E) the movements of sleeping infants.

30 Aserinsky found that in adults during sleep

(A) body movements were accompanied by rapid eye movements.
(B) periods of body stillness were accompanied by rapid eye movements.
(C) body movements were accompanied by no eye movements.
(D) body movements were accompanied by sporadic eye movements.
(E) body stillness was accompanied by stillness in eye movements.

31 The writer's purpose in this passage is

(A) to contrast sleep research in 1952 with 1992.
(B) to show the lack of thought given to dreams in 1952 and before.
(C) to show the importance of sleep research on animals.
(D) to discuss major findings in dream research before 1952.
(E) to discuss the beginning studies of dream research.

32 In line 12, the word "germinal" most nearly means

(A) definitive.
(B) exhaustive.
(C) early.
(D) contaminated.
(E) refuted.

GO ON TO THE NEXT PAGE →

33 The scientific study of sleep and dreams

(A) came about almost overnight.
(B) was immediately accepted by the scientific community.
(C) was first performed on animals.
(D) took years of research to become accepted.
(E) was initiated by a group of scientists.

34 All of the following are widely held misconceptions about dreams EXCEPT

(A) dreams are infrequent and disjointed.
(B) they are the result of an unruly subconscious.
(C) dreams are richly detailed and coherent.
(D) they are a rare event triggered by bodily discomfort.
(E) they are the result of anxiety and guilt.

35 The initial REM state in young adults usually lasts

(A) 20 to 25 minutes.
(B) about 10 minutes.
(C) about 90 minutes.
(D) one hour.
(E) for an undetermined amount of time.

STOP
If time still remains, you may go back and check your work.
When the time allotted is up, you may go on to the next section.

TIME: 30 Minutes
       25 Questions

Solve each problem, using any available space on the page for scratch work. Then decide which answer choice is the best and fill in the corresponding oval on the answer sheet.

NOTES:

(1) The use of a calculator is permitted. All numbers used are real numbers.

(2) Figures that accompany problems in this test are intended to provide information useful in solving the problems. They are drawn as accurately as possible EXCEPT when it is stated in a specific problem that the figure is not drawn to scale. All figures lie in a plane unless otherwise indicated.

REFERENCE INFORMATION:

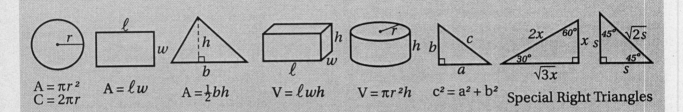

$A = \pi r^2$
$C = 2\pi r$

$A = \ell w$

$A = \frac{1}{2}bh$

$V = \ell wh$

$V = \pi r^2 h$

$c^2 = a^2 + b^2$

Special Right Triangles

The number of degrees of an arc in a circle is 360.
The measure in degrees of a straight angle is 180.
The sum of the measures in degrees of the angles of a triangle is 180.

QUESTIONS 1–15 each consist of two quantities, one in Column A and one in Column B. You are to compare the two quantities on the answer sheet and darken the space

(A) if the quantity in Column A is greater;
(B) if the quantity in Column B is greater;
(C) if the two quantities are equal;
(D) if the relationship cannot be determined from the information given.

NOTES:
1. In certain questions, information concerning one or both of the quantities to be compared is centered above the two columns.
2. In a given question, a symbol that appears in both columns represents the same thing in Column A as it does in Column B.
3. Letters such as *x*, *n*, and *k* stand for real numbers.

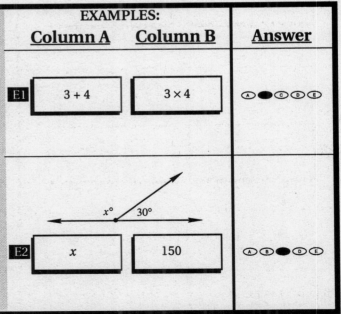

EXAMPLES:

Column A	Column B	Answer
E1 $3 + 4$	3×4	Ⓐ ● Ⓒ Ⓓ Ⓔ
E2 x	150	Ⓐ Ⓑ ● Ⓓ Ⓔ

Column A **Column B**

1 $(1-\sqrt{2})(1-\sqrt{2})$ $(1-\sqrt{2})(1+\sqrt{2})$

The sum of three consecutive even numbers is 42.

2 First number   11

Column A **Column B**

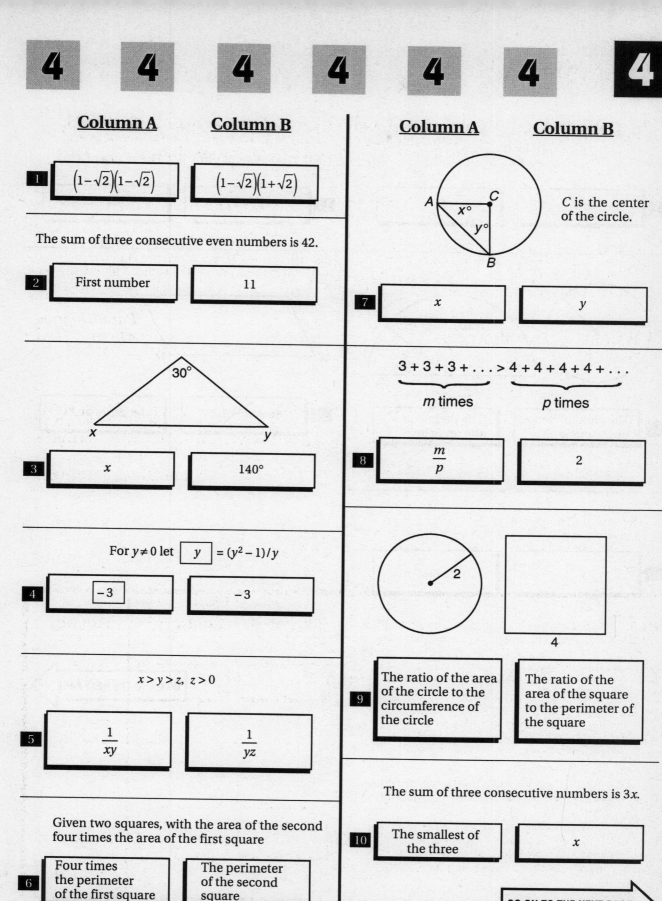

C is the center of the circle.

7 x y

3 x 140°

$$\underbrace{3 + 3 + 3 + \ldots}_{m \text{ times}} > \underbrace{4 + 4 + 4 + 4 + \ldots}_{p \text{ times}}$$

8 $\dfrac{m}{p}$ 2

For $y \neq 0$ let $\boxed{y} = (y^2 - 1)/y$

4 $\boxed{-3}$ -3

9 The ratio of the area of the circle to the circumference of the circle   The ratio of the area of the square to the perimeter of the square

$x > y > z, \ z > 0$

5 $\dfrac{1}{xy}$ $\dfrac{1}{yz}$

Given two squares, with the area of the second four times the area of the first square

6 Four times the perimeter of the first square   The perimeter of the second square

The sum of three consecutive numbers is $3x$.

10 The smallest of the three x

GO ON TO THE NEXT PAGE

Column A	Column B		Column A	Column B

$b < 0$
$a - b = -b$

11 | a | | b |

The values of y in   The values of x in

14 | $y^2 + 12y + 27 = 0$ | | $x^2 - 12x + 27 = 0$ |

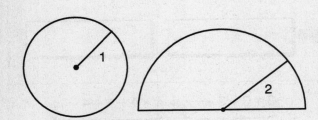

12 The circumference of the circle   The perimeter of the semicircle

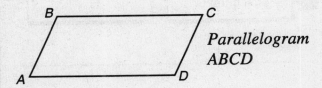

Parallelogram ABCD

15 Measure of $\angle A$ Measure of $\angle C$

6 is $\frac{6}{5}$% of y.

13 | y | | 400 |

GO ON TO THE NEXT PAGE →

DIRECTIONS: Questions 16–25 require you to solve the problem and enter your answer in the ovals in the special grid:

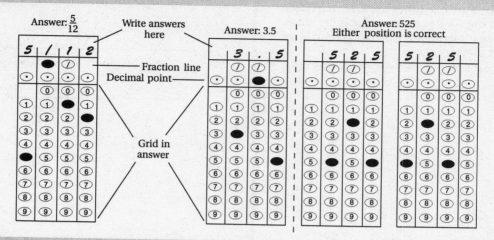

- You may begin filling in your answer in any column, space permitting. Columns not needed should be left blank.

- Answers may be entered in either decimal or fraction form. For example, $\frac{1}{4}$ or .25 are equally acceptable.

- Enter a mixed number such as $4\frac{1}{2}$ as 4.5 or $\frac{9}{2}$. If you entered 41/2, the machine would interpret your answer as $\frac{41}{2}$, not $4\frac{1}{2}$.

- There may be some instances where there is more than one correct answer to a problem. Should this be the case, grid only one answer. Be very careful when filling in ovals. Do not fill

in more than one oval in any column, and make sure to completely darken the ovals.

- It is suggested that you fill in your answer in the boxes above each column. Although you will not be graded incorrectly if you do not write in your answer, it will help you fill in the corresponding ovals.

- If your answer is a decimal, grid the most accurate value possible. For example, if you need to grid a repeating decimal such as 0.6666, enter the answer as .666 or .667. A less accurate value, such as .66 or .67, is not acceptable.

- A negative answer cannot appear for any question.

---

16 The price of a compact disc player was reduced from $200.00 to $147.59. What was the percentage of decrease in the price of the unit?

17 What is the value of y if $\sqrt{81} = 3^y$?

GO ON TO THE NEXT PAGE

18 A child draws three triangles in the sand and labels them triangle *A*, triangle *B*, and triangle *C*. Triangle *A* is three times the area of triangle *B*, triangle *B* is three times the area of triangle *C*, and triangle *B* has an area of 3. If the areas of all three triangles are added together, what would be their sum?

20 In the diagram below, $L_1 \parallel L_2$ and $L_3 \parallel L_4$. If $a + d + b = 8e$, what is the measure of angle *e*?

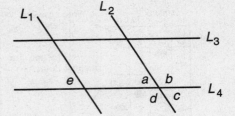

19 Five times the smaller of two whole numbers is less than one-fourth the larger number. If the value of the larger number is 84, what is the *largest* possible value of the smaller?

21 If the sum of the digits of a two-digit positive whole number is 8 and the tens' digit is three times the units' digit, then what is the two-digit number?

GO ON TO THE NEXT PAGE

22 On Sunday there are 15 restaurants open in the city. Each restaurant serves an average (arithmetic mean) of 1,200 customers. On the following day, 7 of the restaurants close for a holiday, but the same number of people use the restaurants. What is the increase in the average number of customers at each restaurant?

23 In the correctly worked multiplication problem below, M, N, and P are nonzero digits.

$$\begin{array}{r} M \\ \times 8 \\ \hline NP \end{array}$$

If the value of N is 3, then what is the value of M?

24 If $m + 2m + 3m = 20 + m$, then what does m equal?

25 The letters below represent consecutive integers on a number line.

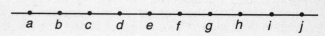

If $2b + f = 13$, what is the value of b?

STOP
If time still remains, you may go back and check your work.
When the time allotted is up, you may go on to the next section.

TIME: 15 Minutes 13 Questions	For each question in this section, select the best answer from among the given choices and fill in the corresponding oval on the answer sheet.

Questions 1–13 are based on the following passages.

The following selections discuss the technological advances and negative implications of both the Industrial Revolution and the Atomic Age.

Passage 1

It is clear to political historians that the Industrial Revolution did not occur overnight. The formation of the mechanical age was a comparatively slow
Line process, punctuated by fits and starts and affected
(5) only certain manufacturers and specific means of production. For the most part it spread region by region throughout Great Britain and later, the whole of Europe and America, until by 1780 its impact could not be ignored. By this time, the changing of
(10) European economies from agrarian-based to industrial was, in the words of one noted expert, as significant as the transformation from Paleolithic hunter-gatherer to Neolithic farmer.

At the forefront of the "Revolution" was the
(15) introduction of mill-driven machinery and the way in which running water was converted into mechanical power. In this way was born the era of precise, tireless machines. The benefits of this type of technology were nothing short of stupendous.
(20) Weavers alone, by the 1820s, increased their output to 20 times that of a hand worker, with power-driven spinning machines making clothing a marketable commodity to the general masses for the first time. Similarly, the introduction of the steam-driven
(25) locomotive allowed the transportation of goods over long distances to improve dramatically, so much so that political shifts of power within the newly industrialized European communities redefined world-wide alliances.
(30)   But the Industrial Revolution, for all its lofty aspirations, far too often engendered neglect and abuse of the individual, the dehumanization of factory workers and the blatant, heartless abuse of children in the labor force being the most notable
(35) examples. The introduction of manifold moving parts, gears, logs, coils, etc. necessitated frequent and often costly repairs. Since these mammoth machines required unusually long "start-up" times,

manufacturers were reluctant to stop production to
(40) fix minor problems in fully functioning machines. As a result, loss of limbs was common and deaths were not infrequent, often with the machines continuing to operate as the brutally mangled "messes" were cleaned-up. In the same way, children, paid just a
(45) fraction of adult wages, were introduced to the factory labor force. Working as long as 16 hours per day with scant breaks, children often met fates similar to their adult counterparts, some succumbing to the dangers of mechanized production, others
(50) from illness brought on by unsanitary working conditions and extreme exhaustion.

Governments basking in the heady glow of revitalized economies ignored the gross atrocities being committed against these laborers, placing the
(55) onus instead upon the employers, who remained impassive. In the end, the workers were forced to fight for more palatable working conditions, proper remunerative compensation, and acceptable safety standards. Though it changed the course of geo-
(60) political relations and vaulted the world into a new age of technology, the dichotomy of the Industrial Revolution prevented it from being a completely benign force.

Passage 2

On July 16, 1945, in a desert in New Mexico, the
(65) first atomic explosion forever altered the face of global politics. Atomic capabilities, the heralds of an entirely new age, came not through a gradual awakening, but with a blinding flash. Like a world of Rip Van Winkles, the global population went to sleep
(70) in the industrial era and awoke on August 6, 1945 firmly ensconced in the atomic age, when the United States dropped a single atomic bomb on the Japanese industrial city of Hiroshima. Four days later, a second bomb, dropped on Japan's Nagasaki,
(75) effectively ended the Second World War. Conservative estimates put the death toll for the detonation of these two bombs at over 110,000 people. To some, the act was seen as a remorseless imperative, to others, a heinous disregard of
(80) humanity. Yet, regardless of one's opinion, Nagasaki and Hiroshima are the only cities to have ever borne the brunt of an atomic attack.

GO ON TO THE NEXT PAGE →

Instead, mankind has endeavored to harness the power of this herculean force. The world, divided at (85) the end of World War II into a bipolar arena headed on the one side by the United States and on the other by the Soviet Union, sought to transform destruction into production and influence. It is quite clear that neither the United States nor the Soviet Union were (90) motivated in these matters by benevolent interest; each nation, engaged in its own realpolitik, saw a window of influence being offered to the country able to provide its neighbors with nuclear power and protection. Thus was the Cold War born.

(95)   With the raising of the Iron Curtain and the formation of the North Atlantic Treaty Organization (NATO) and the Warsaw Pact, the results of each country's drive for hegemony became clear. Alliances and economic interdependencies were formed on (100) the basis of contiguity rather than need, and the results were often strained. Only through rigorous arms control treaties and many failed attempts at detente were both countries able to end overt hostilities. By the latter half of the 1980s, the notion (105) of Mutual Assured Destruction (MAD), upon which the nominally peaceful coexistence of the bipolar world existed, had become anathema, as economic concerns forced the peoples of the Soviet Union and the United States together. What began as a last ditch (110) effort to end World War II ultimately helped prevent the possibility of a third world war. The bombings of Nagasaki and Hiroshima, for all their immediate destructive force, served as a sufficient reminder to the rest of the world of the atom's potential for (115) destruction.

1 In Passage 1, the statement "as significant as the transformation from Paleolithic hunter-gatherer to Neolithic farmer" (lines 11-13) conveys a sense of

(A) how long ago the Industrial Revolution took place.
(B) the types of developments the Industrial Revolution produced.
(C) the profound change the Industrial Revolution had on mankind.
(D) the dietary predilections of the world's population during the Industrial Revolution.
(E) the class struggle that took place during the Industrial Revolution.

2 In lines 15–17 and 24-26, the steam engine and mill-driven machinery are presented as primary examples of

(A) mechanical advances that fueled the Industrial Revolution.
(B) profitable things to own.
(C) daring applications of the use of water.
(D) machines done away with at the beginning of the Industrial Revolution.
(E) failed attempts by companies to develop new products.

3 In line 31, "engendered" most nearly means

(A) prevented.
(B) brought about.
(C) forestalled.
(D) defeated.
(E) ruled out.

4 The author of Passage 2 most likely considers the use of atomic weapons

(A) necessary in most instances.
(B) the best way to achieve peace.
(C) unnecessary following the bombings of Nagasaki and Hiroshima.
(D) the worst atrocity ever committed by mankind.
(E) justifiable only if used against Japan.

5 In lines 68-78, the author most likely describes a specific event in order to

(A) show how it deterred others from using atomic weapons.
(B) explain the principles of nuclear physics.
(C) show the power of an atomic device.
(D) explain the true benefits of atomic capabilities.
(E) place the end of World War II in historical context.

GO ON TO THE NEXT PAGE →

6 In lines 84–88, the author's description of the bipolar arena

(A) shows the direct result of dropping an atomic bomb.
(B) explains the global political situation after 1945.
(C) describes the site of U.S. and U.S.S.R. peace talks.
(D) recognizes the influence of Arctic temperature.
(E) shows a heinous disregard for human life.

7 In lines 46-51, the author most likely describes a particular experience in order to

(A) engage the interest of the reader.
(B) horrify the reader.
(C) explain how important children were to the Industrial Revolution.
(D) impress upon the reader the revolutionary nature of the machines.
(E) make the reader sympathetic to the abuse of children.

8 The word "realpolitik" used in line 91 can also be used to describe

(A) the increased output of weavers using power-driven spinning machines.
(B) the change from hunter-gatherer to farmer.
(C) the birth of the Industrial Revolution and its effects on global economics.
(D) the way in which Great Britain used the Industrial Revolution to become a world power.
(E) the problems faced by the workers of the Industrial Revolution.

9 According to the authors, which of the following is believed to be integral to the development of a revolution?

(A) Gross atrocities committed against the working class
(B) The development of a drastically new idea or technology
(C) The realignment of world-wide alliances
(D) A single country's drive for hegemony
(E) Economic interdependencies formed on the basis of contiguity

10 What additional information would reduce the apparent similarity between these two events?

(A) The Industrial Revolution changed the class structure of Europe.
(B) Many people became rich during the Industrial Revolution.
(C) The Industrial Revolution made Great Britain the most powerful nation in the world.
(D) Atomic energy created thousands of jobs.
(E) Most nations of the world do not have atomic or nuclear weapons capabilities.

11 In line 61 "dichotomy" most nearly means

(A) hugeness.
(B) quickness
(C) changing nature.
(D) contradiction.
(E) success.

12 The author of Passage 1 most likely views the development of the Industrial Revolution as

(A) a comparatively fruitless event in world history.
(B) an heroic advance that ended the problems of the common man.
(C) an important advance that created its own distinctive problems.
(D) a major technological advance that led to the Cold War.
(E) a predominantly agrarian advance.

13 The author of Passage 2 believes the birth of the atomic age

(A) spelled the end of a Soviet dominated political arena.
(B) caused massive political and technological changes.
(C) allowed for man to produce clean and safe power.
(D) prevented world dominance by Japan.
(E) set the stage for World War III.

STOP
If time still remains, you may go back and check your work. When the time allotted is up, you may go on to the next section.

TIME: 15 Minutes
10 Questions

DIRECTIONS: Solve each problem, using any available space on the page for scratch work. Then decide which answer choice is the best and fill in the corresponding oval on the answer sheet.

NOTES:

(1) The use of a calculator is permitted. All numbers used are real numbers.

(2) Figures that accompany problems in this test are intended to provide information useful in solving the problems. They are drawn as accurately as possible EXCEPT when it is stated in a specific problem that the figure is not drawn to scale. All figures lie in a plane unless otherwise indicated.

REFERENCE INFORMATION:

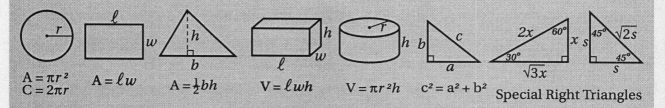

$A = \pi r^2$
$C = 2\pi r$
$A = \ell w$
$A = \frac{1}{2}bh$
$V = \ell wh$
$V = \pi r^2 h$
$c^2 = a^2 + b^2$
Special Right Triangles

The number of degrees of an arc in a circle is 360.
The measure in degrees of a straight angle is 180.
The sum of the measures in degrees of the angles of a triangle is 180.

---

1 In a particular state, the sales tax is $9\frac{1}{2}$%. In that state what will be the total cost of a $110 suit?

(A) $116.35
(B) $117.85
(C) $119.87
(D) $120.25
(E) $120.45

2 If $m \neq 0$, then $(25)^{3m} (125)^{8m} (5)^m$ can be expressed as

(A) 125^{12m}.
(B) 5^{20m}.
(C) 5^{19m}.
(D) 25^{12m}.
(E) 5^{31m}.

GO ON TO THE NEXT PAGE

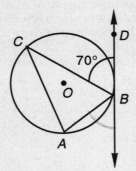

3 The measure of an inscribed angle is equal to one-half the measure of its inscribed arc. In the figure shown, triangle *ABC* is inscribed in circle *O*, and line *BD* is tangent to the circle at point *B*. If the measure of angle *CBD* is 70°, what is the measure of angle *BAC*?

(A) 110°
(B) 70°
(C) 140°
(D) 35°
(E) 40°

4 John, a salesman, traveled 2,000 miles during the month of June. He estimates that it cost him 27¢ per mile to run his automobile. His estimated average daily cost during June was

(A) $5.40.
(B) $9.00.
(C) $10.00.
(D) $17.42.
(E) $18.00.

5 What is the value of *x* in the equation

$$\sqrt{5x-4} - 5 = -1?$$

(A) 2
(B) 5
(C) No value
(D) 4
(E) −4

GO ON TO THE NEXT PAGE

6 $\dfrac{2}{3} + \dfrac{5}{9} =$

(A) $\dfrac{7}{12}$

(B) $\dfrac{11}{9}$

(C) $\dfrac{7}{3}$

(D) $\dfrac{7}{9}$

(E) $\dfrac{11}{3}$

7 If $f(x) = x + 1$, $g(x) = 2x - 3$ and an operation * is defined for all real numbers a and b by the equation $a * b = 2a + b - ab$,

$f(3) * g(4) =$

(A) -9.
(B) -7.
(C) -1.
(D) 0.
(E) 5.

GO ON TO THE NEXT PAGE

8 How many of the scores 10, 20, 30, 35, 55 are larger than their arithmetic mean score?

(A) None
(B) 1
(C) 2
(D) 3
(E) 4

$x = 6$

3

30°

C $y = 5.196$ B

10 Find the area of the triangle in the figure shown above.

(A) $\dfrac{9\sqrt{3}}{2}$

(B) $9\sqrt{3}$

(C) 18

(D) $18\sqrt{3}$

(E) 24

$\sin 30 = \dfrac{3}{x}$

$\tan 30 = \dfrac{3}{y}$

9 Tickets to a high school basketball game cost $4 for adults and $2 for students. One thousand tickets were sold. If the total receipts from the sale of tickets were $3,200, how many student tickets were sold?

(A) 400
(B) 600
(C) 800
(D) 1,000
(E) 1,600

STOP
If time still remains, you may go back and check your work.

SAT PRACTICE TEST
ANSWER KEY

Section 1 - Verbal

1. (D)	19. (D)
2. (C)	20. (E)
3. (D)	21. (A)
4. (C)	22. (A)
5. (E)	23. (B)
6. (B)	24. (D)
7. (B)	25. (A)
8. (C)	26. (B)
9. (E)	27. (E)
10. (D)	28. (B)
11. (A)	29. (B)
12. (A)	30. (C)
13. (B)	
14. (D)	
15. (D)	
16. (B)	
17. (C)	
18. (A)	

Section 2 - Math

1. (D)	19. (E)
2. (C)	20. (B)
3. (E)	21. (E)
4. (B)	22. (A)
5. (D)	23. (C)
6. (C)	24. (B)
7. (E)	25. (D)
8. (B)	
9. (C)	
10. (E)	
11. (D)	
12. (C)	
13. (C)	
14. (E)	
15. (B)	
16. (C)	
17. (B)	
18. (B)	

Section 3 - Verbal

1. (E)	19. (B)
2. (C)	20. (B)
3. (D)	21. (C)
4. (E)	22. (E)
5. (A)	23. (B)
6. (C)	24. (C)
7. (D)	25. (E)
8. (B)	26. (A)
9. (A)	27. (B)
10. (D)	28. (D)
11. (A)	29. (E)
12. (B)	30. (B)
13. (B)	31. (E)
14. (B)	32. (C)
15. (B)	33. (D)
16. (C)	34. (C)
17. (B)	35. (B)
18. (B)	

Section 4 - Math		Section 5 - Verbal	Section 6 - Math
1. (A)	19. 4	1. (C)	1. (E)
2. (A)	20. 40	2. (A)	2. (E)
3. (D)	21. 62	3. (B)	3. (B)
4. (A)	22. 1,050	4. (C)	4. (E)
5. (B)	23. 4	5. (A)	5. (D)
6. (A)	24. 4	6. (B)	6. (B)
7. (C)	25. 3	7. (E)	7. (B)
8. (D)		8. (D)	8. (C)
9. (C)		9. (B)	9. (A)
10. (B)		10. (E)	10. (A)
11. (A)		11. (D)	
12. (B)		12. (C)	
13. (A)		13. (B)	
14. (B)			
15. (C)			
16. 26.2			
17. 2			
18. 13			

Detailed Explanations of Answers

Section 1 - Verbal

1 **(D)** "Reproved" (reprimanded) is the best choice. A frightened mother would reprimand her daughter for disobeying street rules and running in front of a car. The mother would not (A) "implore" (beg) her daughter for doing a dangerous action. This makes no sense. Nor would the mother (B) "extort" (obtain by force) her daughter in this situation. (C) "exhorted" (urge, advise) and (E) "abolished" (to do away with) are not correct in the sentence.

2 **(C)** The implication of this sentence is that drunk drivers are a menace on the road; therefore, if they drive while they are under the influence of alcohol, they put people's lives in "jeopardy" (danger). Choice (C) is the best answer. (A) "Guile" (slyness, deceit), (B) "discord" (disagreement, lack of harmony), and (E) "dissonance" (harsh contradiction) are incorrect choices because they do not fit into the semantic context of the sentence. Choice (D) "distress" (pain, anguish) is a possibility, but is not the best answer. People's lives are in danger from drunk drivers, not in distress, unless they are involved in an accident.

3   **(D)**   "Strident" is the best answer because we are looking for a word to describe a voice that is "exceptionally annoying." A "strident" (harsh–sounding) voice is annoying to hear, and would keep people from going anywhere near someone who speaks that way. (A) "Exorbitant" (excessive) is not correct because it doesn't fit the context of "especially annoying." (B) "Uproarious" (making a great tumult) is a possible answer, but is not the best choice because "uproarious" doesn't fit the context of being a "harsh" sound. (C) "Docile" (easily taught, led or managed) is wrong because the word doesn't fit the meaning of the sentence. (E) "Egocentric" (self-centered) is incorrect because "egocentric" is a word that defines a person, not a voice characteristic.

4   **(C)**   The correct answer is "sarcastic" (ironic, bitter humor designed to wound). We are looking for a word which describes "comments" that "insult" the hostess. "Sarcastic" comments would definitely insult a person, and would cause everyone to avoid Pete because of his ill manners. "Tenacious" (A) is incorrect because "persistently holding to something" does not fit meaningfully into the context of the sentence. (B) "Rancid" is the wrong choice because you couldn't describe a comment as "having a bad odor." (D) "Pessimistic" is also incorrect because, although a comment may "have a gloomy side" or be "hopeless," it would not insult a hostess. (E) "Sagacious" (wise, cunning) would not insult the hostess. In fact, everyone would probably also admire Pete for this trait, and not avoid him.

5   **(E)**   Writers are particularly helped by "financial" independence and personal "leisure," or money and time, in order to focus their efforts on writing. The key phrase here is "in order to focus their efforts on writing." Freedom from the need to work for a living and from other responsibilities gives the writer time. With this, she can focus her efforts on writing. "Talent" (A), "ability" (B), "reputation" (C), and "intelligence" (D) are all helpful also, but a writer without any one of these could still focus her efforts on writing.

6   **(B)**   We are looking for two words which are compatible—a noun and a verb which are related in a meaningful way. (B) is the most logical. If a "charlatan" (imposter) paints a painting, then it should be "repudiated" (rejected) because the painting would have no value. (A) has little meaning, because if a "progeny" (talented child) paints a painting, then why should it be "refurbished" (made new)? (C) is incorrect because a "neophyte" (beginner) may paint a painting, but then it would be unusual for art experts to examine it, and no reason for them to "qualify" it. (D) is obviously incorrect in the context of the sentence, because a "prodigal" is someone who is lavish and wasteful, and probably would not spend time painting or doing anything meaningful. (E) is also incorrect in the context of the sentence because the word "fanatic" (an extremist) would not indicate that the painter was talented.

7   **(B)**   This is a cause–and–effect sentence due to the word "when." We are asked to find two nouns that are related: what will occur when a "natural" something happens. Choice (B) is the best answer. "Pandemonium" (a wild uproar) will sweep the crowd when a "natural catastrophe" (great disaster) occurs. Choice (A) doesn't make any sense because an "infirmary" is a clinic for sick people. Choice (C) is incorrect because "vehemence" (great force) can "sweep the crowd," but "iodides" is a chemical term that doesn't relate to the meaning of the whole sentence. Choice (D) is incorrect because "rectification" means to "make or set right" and is semantically meaningless. For the same reason, choice (E) is wrong because "turbulence" (violence or disturbance) may sweep the crowd, but it has nothing to do with the "atmosphere."

8   **(C)**   The word "rather" implies a contrast of words within the sentence. So we are looking for two words which are the opposite of each other. (C) "demolish . . . enhance" is the only choice that meets this condition. "Demolish" means "to tear down" and "enhance" means "to improve." Choice (A) contains words which are synonyms of each other: "abolish" and "destroy" mean the same thing. Choice (B) is incorrect because "instigate" (to provoke) is not the opposite of "change," which means "to modify." "Hurt" and "harm" are synonymous words, and therefore choice (D) is incorrect. Likewise, "console" and "comfort" are close in meaning, and not antonyms; therefore, choice (E) is incorrect.

---

9 **(E)** Choice (E) is the correct answer because we are looking for two words which, when put into the sentence, will support the phrase "despite the fact." What will follow should be a situation that is not normally expected. Politicians from different political parties wouldn't normally "collaborate" (cooperate) with each other unless their goals were "compatible" (in agreement). Choice (A) "digress" (stray from the subject) and "ambivalent" (undecided) does not make any sense when substituted into the sentence. (B) is only partially correct in that "concede" would fit in, but then "controversial" would not. Politicians wouldn't agree if their goals were controversial. Choice (C) is incorrect because it is rare that people, even politicians, agree to "dissent," or disagree, especially on issues that are "viable" (workable). (D) is a possibility because politicians may agree to "demur," or object, to "provocative" issues, but it is not the best answer. We are looking for a word which is a strong synonym for "agree" and that word is "collaborate."

---

10 **(D)** A MINISTER uses a BIBLE in his or her work as a CARPENTER uses a HAMMER in his or her work. Therefore, choice (D) is the correct answer. (A) is incorrect, because although a SECRETARY wears SHOES to work, they are not part of his or her work. A COSMETOLOGIST also uses a COMB in his or her work (C), but that is in the reverse order from the first pair. SHAKESPEARE did not use a PLAY (B); he wrote them. (E) Although a SWIMMER dives in the course of "work," DIVE is a verb, and BIBLE is a noun.

11 **(A)** RAIN is a form of PRECIPITATION. The correct answer is (A) COPPER : METAL. Copper is a form of metal. The analogy in choice (B) ICE : GLACIER is wrong because a glacier is made of ice, but ice is not an example of a glacier. In relation to choice (C) OIL : SHALE, oil is found in shale but is not an example of shale. Choice (D) WIND : ABRASION has the relationship of cause : effect. Wind is a cause of abrasion. This relationship also exists in choice (E) HEAT : EVAPORATION, as heat is a cause of evaporation.

12 **(A)** COMMITTED and PROMISED are a synonymous relationship. COMPULSORY and REQUIRED also have a synonymous relationship. Therefore, (A) is the correct choice. NORMAL and ABERRANT (B) are antonyms. FREEDOM and DEMOCRACY (C) have no necessary relationship. VOLUNTARY and MANDATORY (D) are antonyms. EDUCATION and INTELLIGENCE (E) are not necessarily related.

13 **(B)** A CRITIC provides an EVALUATION of something. The same relationship exists for (B) SPONSOR : PROMOTION since a sponsor provides a promotion for something. This relationship is not present in the other alternatives. (A) CLIMAX : PORTRAIT has no necessary relationship. (C) A REPORTER may or may not provide ENTERTAINMENT. (D) POEM : REPRESENTATION has no necessary relationship. (E) An ARTIST may or may not provide a MOOD.

14 **(D)** CRUEL is a synonym of lesser degree for ATROCIOUS. The same relationship exists for (D) INTERESTED : CONSUMED since interested is a synonym of lesser degree for infatuated or consumed with something. This relationship is not present in the other alternatives. (A) STABLE is the opposite of MERCURIAL. (B) ATHLETIC :

ENERGETIC, (C) TIRED : INTROVERTED, and (E) ACCIDENTAL : INTRINSIC, have no necessary relationships.

---

15   **(D)**   A PAULDRON is an armor piece that protects the SHOULDER, just as a SKULL is a natural armor that protects the BRAIN. (A) LIGAMENT is part of the KNEE, not a protective covering. While a SCABBARD protects a SWORD (B) and a SADDLE protects a HORSE (C), these choices are presented in the opposite order. A SHELTER protects one *from* the RAIN; it does not protect the RAIN (E).

---

16   **(B)**   Education for citizenship was a goal of Socrates (B). Epicurus (A), on the other hand, emphasized individual happiness. Carneades (C) argued that all knowledge was relative; he was not concerned with society, as was Socrates, and should not be chosen. Diogenes (D) was the most famous cynic; his goal was to prepare the individual for disaster. Zeno (E) taught that the cosmos was a unified whole which was based on a universal order. His primarily concern was not with citizenship.

---

17   **(C)**   The saying, "I am trying to find myself and my happiness" might be employed by a follower of (C) Hellenism. Diogenes (A) was the most famous cynic; his goal was to prepare the individual for disaster. Zeno (B) taught that the cosmos was a unified whole which was based on a universal order. His primary concern was not with citizenship. The Stoics (D) taught that each person should strive to discover the natural law governing the universe and live in accordance with it. (E) Carneades argued that all knowledge was relative.

18   **(A)**   The word "polis" in line 22 most nearly means (A) a group. "In a certain way" (B) has nothing to do with the meaning of "polis." Polis does not refer to "a place of one's own or a place of solitude" (C). "A tradition" (D) is not the best meaning for "polis." Polis is not "a philosophical outlook" (E); therefore, (E) should not be selected.

19   **(D)**   The author focused on the classical Greek philosophers in order to (D) "contrast them with those of the Hellenistic Age." The purpose of the focus on the Hellenistic Age is not to contrast the age with a much earlier time; (A) therefore is not the correct choice. Little emphasis is given to the Oriental thinkers, so choice (B) is not correct. Since the Hellenistic Age followed the Greek Age, the purpose was not to "show their relation to the earlier philosophers of the Hellenistic Period." (C) should not be chosen. The author exhibits no scorn of the past in his writing. (E) is, therefore, not an appropriate answer.

20   **(E)**   The most important element of Stoic thought was "its emphasis on the individual"—not the group as earlier schools of thought had emphasized. The Stoics taught that each person carried a spark of Logos in his reason, but (C) is not the best choice. (D) is also a true statement, but it is not the most important element. It is true that Zeno's school was established under the painted porch of the Athenian marketplace; but (D) should not be selected. Stoic thought was similar to Epicurus' thought, but that was not the most important element of Stoic thought. The writing *claims* universal validity, but since this has not been proven, (B) is not the best choice. Similarity to Epicureanism (A) is also incorrect.

21 **(A)** Carneades taught that all knowledge was relative. (A) is the correct answer. It was Epicurus (B) who taught that "the goal of philosophy should be to help the individual find happiness" and that (C) "a wise man eschewed public affairs and sought self-sufficiency." He also stated that "the highest pleasure was to be found in contemplation" (E). Neither (B) nor (C) nor (E) should be chosen. Diogenes taught that "the individual should be prepared for any disaster"; (D) is not the correct answer.

---

22 **(A)** This passage discusses the interaction between economics and social policy in lines 78–81 which makes (D) incorrect. Lines 66–73 address child labor as a practice of the past. Therefore (B) is incorrect. Lines 33–36 depict employers as sensitive, making (C) wrong. Lines 53–56 show (E) to be incorrect.

---

23 **(B)** The president of the California Merchants and Manufacturer's Association, a critic of the bill, "projects discrimination against women in hiring practices if the bill is passed" (lines 35–36). (B) is the correct answer. Lines 22–24 depict the National Organization for Women's support of the act, not disapproval. Therefore (C) is incorrect. (E) is a strong distractor, but it is not textually mentioned. (A) and (D) are unjustified by the text.

---

24 **(D)** Drug testing issues and right-to-privacy are discussed in lines 50–56, although lockers as such are not discussed (E). While (A), (B), and (C) are answers to issues discussed, the right-to-privacy is not among them.

25 **(A)** Roberta Cook sees child-rearing as a family, not an employer, responsibility; lines 36–40 deny (D) and (E). (B) is a misreading; (C) is a clear distractor.

26 **(B)** While (E) is a strong distractor, lines 66–73 tell us Reuben was a child laborer who quit school. (A) may be partially true, based on lines 66–73. (C) is clearly a distractor; (D) violates the message of the entire passage.

27 **(E)** This is justified by lines 45–49. Choice (B) is negated by lines 52–53. (A) is undermined by lines 5–9. The entire passage contradicts choice (C) (see lines 73–78). (D) is a cynical interpretation devoid of moral consequences and unjustified by the text.

28 **(B)** Senator Dodd defends family values that intrude on the workplace, not the opposite, choices (A) and (E). (C) is absurd, given lines 30–33. Welfare issues (D) are not discussed.

29 **(B)** In context, mental anguish supersedes "angered" (D) as the only strong distractor.

30 **(C)** The aim of establishing, and the problems associated with, universal health coverage is the point of the passage (lines 9–11), although the details of an HMO are omitted and so do not justify choice (E). (B) is a misreading that reverses the aim of an HMO. (A) and (B) are clear distractors.

Section 2 — Math

1   **(D)**   In order of operations, do all multiplication and division from left to right first. Next, do all addition and subtraction from left to right.

$3 \times 6 - 12 \div 2$ Multiply 3 times 6, divide 12 by 2.
$18 - 6$ Subtract 6 from 18.
12

---

2   **(C)**   To change a mixed number to an improper fraction, multiply the whole number (4) by the denominator (6) of the fraction (4 times 6 is 24). Add the numerator (5) to the product (24). Write the sum (29) over the denominator of the fraction, $\frac{29}{6}$.

---

3   **(E)**   All three statements are true. Since a rhombus is a parallelogram, sides *BA* and *CD* are parallel. Using *AC* as a transversal, $\angle BAE$ and $\angle ECD$ are alternate interior angles and are therefore congruent making I true. The diagonals of a rhombus bisect the angles and so $\angle ADE$ and $\angle CDE$ are congruent making II true. In a rhombus, all four sides are congruent so triangle *ABD* is isosceles with congruent sides *AB* and *AD*. The angles opposite those congruent sides are congruent, so $\angle ABE$ and $\angle ADE$ are congruent making III true. Therefore, the answer is choice (E).

4   **(B)**

$$4\frac{1}{3} - 1\frac{5}{6} = \frac{13}{3} - \frac{11}{6}$$

$$= \frac{26}{6} - \frac{11}{6}$$

$$= \frac{15}{6}$$

$$= 2\frac{3}{6}$$

$$= 2\frac{1}{2}$$

---

5   **(D)**   The total cost is $8.35, subtract $6.25 for the cost of the first 15 pieces of laundry.

$$8.35 - 6.25 = \$2.10$$

Divide $2.10 by $0.35 to determine the number of additional pieces of laundry.

$$.35\overline{)2.10}$$

$$35\overline{)\overset{6}{210}}$$

15 pieces of laundry + 6 additional pieces of laundry = 21 pieces of laundry.

---

6   **(C)**   If we want to prove a statement is false, we only have to give one counter example.

Let $p = 3$ and $q = 5$.

$$pq + 1 = 16 \text{ (not prime)}$$

$$pq - 1 = 14 \text{ (not prime)}$$

Therefore, I and II are false. Since p and q are prime, they cannot possibly have a common factor. Thus, III is true.

7   **(E)**   Since the lowest common denominator for $\frac{3}{4}$, $\frac{11}{16}$,

and $\frac{1}{8}$ is 16, we change each fraction into equivalent fractions having a

common denominator of 16.

$$5\frac{3}{4} = 5\frac{12}{16}$$

$$2\frac{11}{16} = 2\frac{11}{16}$$

$$7\frac{1}{8} = 7\frac{2}{16}$$

Adding the whole numbers 5, 2, and 7 yields
$$5 + 2 + 7 = 14.$$
Adding the numerators 12, 11, and 2 yields
$$12 + 11 + 2 = 25.$$

Writing this sum over the common denominator gives $\frac{25}{16}$, which

changes to the proper fraction $1\frac{9}{16}$.

Adding these two terms,

$$14 + 1\frac{9}{16} = 15\frac{9}{16}$$

---

8   **(B)**   If X is the original price, then the 50 percent markup price is $(1.5)X$. Since this price is marked down by 30%, the final price is

$$(.7)\,(1.5)X = 1.05X.$$

Therefore, $1.05X = 3,360$, or,

$$X = \frac{3,360}{1.05} = \$3,200.$$

9   **(C)**   Let (AB) represent the measure (length) of segment AB. Then the length of rectangle $ABCD$ is equal to (AB) and its width is (BC).

The area of the shaded region is equal to the area of rectangle $ABCD$ minus the area of triangle EBC.

Recall that the area of a rectangle is equal to the product of its length and its width. Thus,

$$\text{Area of rectangle } ABCD = (AB)(BC)$$

The area of any triangle is equal to $\frac{1}{2}$ times the measure of its base times the measure of its height (the length of the perpendicular segment drawn from the vertex opposite the base to that base or to the line containing the base). That is, the area of a triangle is equal to $\frac{1}{2}bh$. Thus,

$$\text{area of triangle } EBC = \frac{1}{2}(EB)(BC).$$

But $(EB) = \frac{1}{4}(AB)$, hence,

$$\text{area of triangle } EBC = \frac{1}{2}(\frac{1}{4}(AB))(BC)$$

$$= \frac{1}{8}(AB)(BC)$$

Since the area of triangle EBC is equal to 12 square units, we have

$$\frac{1}{8}(AB)(BC) = 12$$

or $(AB)(BC) = 96.$

But, $(AB)(BC)$ is the area of rectangle $ABCD$. Hence, the area of rectangle $ABCD = 96$ square units.

Thus, the area of the shaded region = $96 - 12 = 84$ square units.

10 **(E)**

X : cost of one pound of pears.

Y : cost of one pound of peaches.

$$2X + Y = 1.4 \qquad (1)$$
$$3X + 2Y = 2.4 \qquad (2)$$

Multiply equation (1) by 2.

$$4X + 2Y = 2.8 \qquad (3)$$
$$3X + 2Y = 2.4 \qquad (2)$$

Subtract equation (3) from equation (2).

$$X = .4$$

Substitute $X = .4$ in equation (1)

$$Y = .6$$

Therefore, $X + Y = 1.00$

---

11 **(D)** On the left-hand side of the equation apply the distributive property to obtain:

$$4 - 10y - 20 = 4.$$

Then, subtract 4 and add 20 to obtain

$$-10y = 20.$$

Then, divide both sides by -10 to get

$$y = -2.$$

---

12 **(C)** Referring to the figure below, it is easy to see that a cube has 8 corners. There are four in the front (points 1, 2, 3, and 4) and four in the back (points 5, 6, 7, and 8).

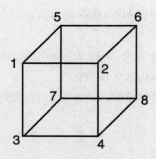

13   **(C)**   The difference between the first two numbers is 4 (6 – 2); the difference between the second and third numbers is 6 (12 – 6) which is two more than the first difference; the difference between the third and fourth numbers is 8 (20 – 12) which is two more than the second difference; the difference between the fourth and fifth numbers is 10 (x – 20), since 10 would be the next number in a series increasing by two at each step. Thus, the value of x is given by $x - 20 = 10$. Solving for x yields $x = 30$. So, the correct answer choice is (C). Similar analysis of each of the other choices will fail to satisfy the missing value of x such that it is a consistent distance in relation to the other numbers in the series.

14   **(E)**   One way to attack this problem is to solve it algebraically. Let x represent the number of packages weighing 2 kg each. Then $(150 - x)$ represents the number of packages weighing 1 kg each.

Therefore, solving for x,

$$2x + (150 - x) = 264$$
$$2x + 150 - x = 264$$
$$x = 264 - 150$$
$$x = 114$$

Thus, there are 114 packages weighing 2 kg each on the truck.

Testing the answer choice yields:

$$2(114) + (150 - 114) = 264$$
$$228 + (36) = 264$$

Thus, (E) is correct.

15   **(B)**

$$c = 18a + 24b$$
$$= 6(3a + 4b)$$

Therefore, c is a multiple of 6 and must be divisible by 6.

16   **(C)**   Let x and y be the cost of a pencil and pen, respectively.

$$2x + 3y = 3 \qquad (1)$$
$$x + 5y = 4.3 \qquad (2)$$

Subtract equation (2) from equation (1). Multiply equation (2) by 2 to cancel like terms.

$$2x + 3y = 3$$
$$\underline{- (2x + 10y = 8.6)}$$
$$-7y = -5.6$$
$$y = 0.8$$

---

17   **(B)**   The shape given is a rectangle. Its area is equal to the length multiplied by the width.

The perimeter is twice the length plus twice the width.

Let $x =$ length, $y =$ width. The relevant equations are

$$xy = 35m^2 \qquad (1)$$
$$2x + 2y = 24m \qquad (2)$$

Rewriting equation (1):

$$y = \frac{35m^2}{x}$$

Substituting for y in equation (2):

$$2x + 2\left(\frac{35m^2}{x}\right) = 24m$$

Multiplying by x:

$$2x^2 + 70m^2 = 24mx$$

Subtracting $24mx$ from both sides:

$$2x^2 + 70m^2 - 24mx = 0$$

Dividing all terms by 2:

$$x^2 + 35m^2 - 12mx = 0$$

This can be factored into

$$(x - 7m)(x - 5m) = 0.$$

From this we get

$$x - 7m = 0 \quad \text{or} \quad x - 5m = 0$$

Two possible lengths: $\quad x = 5m \quad \text{or} \quad x = 7m$

Substituting back into equation (1):

$$(5m)y = 35m^2 \implies \text{Divide by } 5m \implies y = 7m$$
$$(7m)y = 35m^2 \implies \text{Divide by } 7m \implies y = 5m$$

Thus, the dimensions are

$$5m \times 7m \text{ and } 7m \times 5m.$$

$5m \times 7m$ is the only dimension that corresponds to the choices.

---

18   **(B)**   Let $x =$ the number of days it would take the two men working together to complete the job.

Then $\dfrac{x}{8} =$ the part of the job done by A and $\dfrac{x}{12} =$ the part of the job done by B. The relationship used in setting up the equation is

Part of job done by A + Part of job done by $B = 1$ job.

$$\frac{x}{8} + \frac{x}{12} = 1$$

$$\frac{3x}{24} + \frac{2x}{24} = \frac{24}{24}$$

$$3x + 2x = 24$$

$$5x = 24$$

$$x = 4.8$$

---

19   **(E)**   If

$$x + 2y > 5 \text{ and } x < 3,$$

then $\quad 5 < x + 2y < 3 + 2y.$

Thus $\quad 5 - 3 < 2y, \text{ or } y > 1.$

20   **(B)**   Move the decimal point 2 place values to the left and drop the percent sign, then multiply to find the number in attendance.

$$1,050 \times .94 = 987.00$$

Subtract 987 (attended school) from 1,050 (total enrolled) to find the number absent.

$$1,050 - 987 = 63$$

The correct answer is 63.

---

21   **(E)**

I. An odd integer times two will become an even integer. An even integer times any number will remain even. The sum of two even numbers is also an even number.

Therefore, $2x + 3y$ must be even.

II. An even integer times any number will remain even.

Therefore, xy must be even.

III. The sum of an odd integer and an even integer is odd. An odd integer minus one will become even.

Therefore, $x + y - 1$ must be even.

---

22   **(A)**   In order to find the perimeter of the rectangle it is important first to understand the definition, that is, perimeter equals the sum of the figure's sides. Hence for the given rectangle,

$$\text{Perimeter} = 6L + 4W + 6L + 4W \text{ (Add like terms)}$$
$$= 12L + 8W$$

Answer choice (E), $24LW$, is incorrect because it represents the area of the rectangle, which is the product of the length and width. Answer choice (C), $6L + 4W$, is incorrect because it represents only one-half of the perimeter of the rectangle. Answer choice (D), $20LW$, is incorrect because this response is obtained by simply adding the coefficients of L and W which is an incorrect application of algebra. Finally, answer choice (B), $12L^2 + 8W^2$, is incorrect because it is obtained by using the definition of the perimeter of a rectangle incorrectly as follows:

Perimeter = $2L(6L) + 2W(4W)$.

---

23 **(C)** To find the product, first factor:

$$\left(\sqrt{3}+6\right)\left(\sqrt{3}-2\right) = \sqrt{3}\left(\sqrt{3}-2\right)+6\left(\sqrt{3}-2\right)$$
$$= 3 - 2\sqrt{3} + 6\sqrt{3} - 12$$
$$= -9 + 4\sqrt{3}$$

---

24 **(B)** Four consecutive even integers can be represented by $2n$, $2n + 2$, $2n + 4$, and $2n + 6$.

$$(2n) + (2n + 2) + (2n + 4) + (2n + 6) = 68$$
$$8n + 12 = 68$$
$$8n = 56$$
$$2n = 14$$

Therefore, the value of the smallest one is 14.

---

25 **(D)** Set up an algebraic relationship. Let x = Gretta's age, and $(x + 5)$ = Lynsey's age, since Lynsey is 5 years older.

The sum of their ages is 95, so

$$(x) + (x + 5) = 95$$
$$2x + 5 = 95$$
$$2x = 90$$
$$x = 45$$

Since x = Gretta's age which is 45, and Lynsey is 5 years older, Lynsey is 45 + 5, or 50 years old.

Section 3 - Verbal

1   **(E)**   A person who refuses to visit friends who have pets because they're afraid of animals may be said to have a "phobia" (morbid fear) of animals (E). Choice (A) is not appropriate because "derision" (ridicule) would not be a reason for a person not to visit friends who had pets. Choice (B) "compliance" (yielding) is not meaningful in the sentence. People cannot develop a "yielding" towards animals. "Heresy" (opinion contrary to popular belief) is not right, because a person cannot develop a "heresy." Therefore, (C) is an incorrect answer. (D) "Inclination" (likely or apt to) is a possibility, because a person can develop an inclination towards animals, but that would mean she liked animals, and be likely to visit friends who had pets.

2   **(C)**   The context of this sentence is that men were "perceived as the sole breadwinners," or the only members of a family who worked outside the home. Therefore, it was not a common occurrence for a woman to work. The only choice that fits is (C) "unconventional" (not common). "Inherent" (A) means "innate" and applies to a trait or characteristic that is inborn. This word has no relationship within the context of the sentence. Choice (B) "decorous" (characterized by good taste) would mean that it was satisfactory for women to work outside the home, and that is not the implication we are looking for. Choice (D) "vital" (crucial) is not applicable in the sentence, because then we would imply that it was important for women to work outside the home, and that is not the meaning indicated by the first part of the sentence. Choice (E) "uncouth" (crude) is a choice that when inserted into the sentence makes no sense at all.

3 **(D)** There are several clues that should lead you to the appropriate adjective that describes "the activities." "Villain" tells us what kind of person is doing the action (evil), and that "the audience cheered when he was caught." With these conditions in mind, the best answer is (D) "nefarious" (very wicked). (A) "Intrepid" (fearless) might be an appropriate choice, but not when considered in the context of the sentence, where we need an adjective that specifically describes the activities of a villain. (B) "Cursory" (hasty) is not an appropriate choice because the word is not logical within the sentence. (C) "Lurid" (gloomy) is a possible choice, but not the best answer. "Nefarious" fits all the conditions of the sentence in a more appropriate way. (E) "Jocund" (merry) is the opposite of the implied meaning in the sentence.

4 **(E)** The correct answer is "denunciation," because we are looking for a word which supports "displeasure." The key word here is "and" between the phrase "displeasure of politicians" and "purists." This means that whatever attitude the politicians take, so would the purists. (A) is incorrect because "concession" (give in) is the opposite of what you would do if you were displeased. (B) is wrong because "neutrality" means that the purists wouldn't take a stand; however, the sentence tells us that the purists are holding the same attitude as the politicians. (C) "Endorsement" is wrong because it is the opposite in meaning to "denunciation," and we are looking for a word that has a parallel connotation. (D) is wrong because "resolution" (determination) is not logical to the context of the sentence.

5 **(A)** The key word here is "indelible." An indelible pen is one that has permanent ink and can never be erased; therefore, the use of such a pen will "preclude" (make impossible) for him to "erase" at a later time. (A) is the best choice. (B) "Hinder" (interfere) is possible, but whether or not a student uses an indelible pen makes no difference to his ability to "slander" (defame). Choice (C), "nullify" (cancel, invalidate), is possible, but is not essential to "desecrate" (violate a holy place). Choice (D), "deplete" (reduce, empty), is not meaningful in the sentence. "Enhance" (improve), choice (E), and "ameliorate" (to make better) are not semantically logical choices for the sentence.

---

6 **(C)** The key word in this sentence is "although," which indicates an unusual situation. (C) is the correct answer because "exhausted" explorers couldn't normally "conquer" the desert. Although in choice (A), "defeated" and "achieve" are contradictory, you could never say that someone "achieved" the desert. This is not semantically correct. Choice (B) is incorrect because "elated" and "survive" do not relate back to "although." "Relentless" explorers (D) would manage to "finish" the desert, but not with the conditional word "although" in the sentence. It is possible that the explorers might have felt "withdrawn" (E), but the word "subject" has no meaning in the sentence.

---

7 **(D)** The first part of the sentence asks for an adjective that describes the type of situation faced by a police officer. The second part of the sentence requires a word that describes a quality the police officers must maintain in the face of the chosen situation. The best choice is (D). Police officers often face "perilous" (dangerous) situations where they must maintain their "composure" (calmness). Choice (A) is incorrect because although "inhospitable" (not fit for normal living) might be appropriate to the context, "agility" (ability to move quickly) is not a word used with "maintain," nor is it considered a quality of a person's character. Choice (B) "impossible" is a possible choice for the first part, but "gallantry" is not meaningful to the context. Choice (C) "unequivocable" (leaving no doubt, clear) is not an appropriate choice for the first part of the sentence. Police officers often face situations which call for judgments because they are not clear-cut. Choice (E) is a possible answer, but not the best choice. "Perilous" and "composure" fit all the conditions of the sentence in a more appropriate way.

8   **(B)**   "Climax" (a series of ideas or statements so arranged that they increase in force and power from the first to the last) and "agree" are the best word choices. The sentence context tells that the Civil War was the climax of the North and South not being able to agree on an interpretation of the Constitution. (A) "Epitome" (abstract, summary, embodiment) is an inappropriate choice to describe the inability of the North and South to reach an agreement, and, although "concur" is correct, (A) is the wrong choice. (C) "Drama" (dramatic art, literature) is inappropriate to the context of the sentence. (D) "Chaos" (complete disorder, confusion) may describe the actual Civil War, but is not an appropriate description of the North and South reaching an agreement. (E) "Finalization" (put in finished forms) does not fit into the context of the sentence.

---

9   **(A)**   The best choice is (A) "merger . . . prudent." The companies had to "merge" (combine, unite) because they needed each other's profits. This showed "prudent" (foresighted, sensible) behavior. Choice (B) "pivot" (a fixed pin on which something turns) . . . "exemplary" (commendable) is incorrect, because, although "exemplary" is an appropriate choice, "pivot" is semantically incorrect. Choice (C) "antagonism" (hostility) . . . "beneficial" (helpful, advantageous) is also wrong because the words "neither could profit without the assets of the other" imply that the companies needed each other. "Antagonism" is not semantically correct within the context of the sentence. (D) "Hiatus" (break, lapse in continuity) . . . "monotonous" (one-tone, boring) has no meaning when inserted into the sentence. (E) "Diversity" (variety) . . . "fundamental" (basic) are incorrect because they do not fit into the context of the sentence.

---

10   **(D)**   The best choice is (D). "Ornate" (elaborately decorated) is the most effective way of describing a "gold-studded costume," and "simplicity" (lack of complication) is a good way of describing a "flannel suit," especially when compared to a "gold-studded costume." (A) "Chaste" (virtuous, pure) is an incorrect description of something that is "gold-studded," and "gaudiness" (garish, flashy) is not an appropriate choice for describing a "flannel suit." (B) "Laconic" (terse) is an inappropriate way to describe a suit; "laconic" is used to describe people, so (B) is incorrect. (C) "Reserved" (restrained in actions or words) is not the way to compare a "gold-studded costume" to the "savoir-faire" (knowing how to act) of a "flannel suit." (C) makes no sense when substituted into the sentence. (E) "Feudal" (having the characteristics of feudalism) is a meaningless choice in the sentence.

11   **(A)**   An HOURGLASS measures time by using SAND. The same relationship exists for (A) THERMOMETER : MERCURY since a thermometer measures temperature by using mercury. This relationship is not present in the other alternatives. (B) A RULER uses INCHES to measure length. (C) A SCALE is a system of NUMBERS. (D) A BAROMETER measures atmospheric pressure, not the intensity of a TREMOR. (E) VOLTMETER : RADIATION has no necessary relationship.

12   **(B)**   The relationship between the given words can be expressed as an ACCOUNTANT uses a CALCULATOR, or an ACCOUNTANT works with a CALCULATOR. The best choice (B) expresses the same kind of relationship: MECHANIC uses (works with) a SCREWDRIVER. Choice (A) is wrong because although an ACTOR uses a STAGE to work on, the STAGE is not a device used in the work. Choice (C) is incorrect because a STUDENT uses a SCHOOL does not make any sense. Choice (D) is wrong because a PAGE is a young person who works for the SENATOR. Choice (E) is wrong because a WAITRESS works in a RESTAURANT.

13   **(B)**   A CATERPILLAR is the larval form of a BUTTERFLY. The same relationship exists for (B) TADPOLE : FROG. This relationship is not present in the other alternatives. An OYSTER is not a larval form of a PEARL (A). CLAY will not grow to be a SCULPTURE (C). A RAISIN is not the larval form of a GRAPE (D). A POLITICIAN will not grow to be a LAWYER (E).

---

14   **(B)**   An ARC is one part, component, or segment of the CIRCLE. The correct choice is (B), because an HOUR is one part of or segment of a DAY. MOON : EARTH (A) are both examples of celestial bodies. Their relationship is, as in choice (C), one of size. CABINS are small and MANSIONS are large, but both are places to live; again, both are examples of the same entity—homes. EXERCISE and REST (D) are both components of a healthy lifestyle, rather than one being a component of the other. The relationship in choice (E) is one of like terms.

---

15   **(B)**   A REFLEX is an INVOLUNTARY response. The same relationship exists for (B) IMPULSE : SUDDEN since an IMPULSE is a SUDDEN response. This relationship is not present in the other alternatives. (A) APPARITION is not REAL. (C) KICK may or may not be a DANGEROUS response. (D) DETAIL is not GENERAL. (E) SPASM is not a LENGTHY response.

---

16   **(C)**   NEUROTIC is a higher degree of being ANXIOUS. The same relationship exists for (C) WEAK : DECREPIT since decrepit is a higher degree of being weak. This relationship is not present in the other choices. (A) LACKADAISICAL is the opposite of ANIMATED. (B) CONTEMPORARY is the opposite of ARCHAIC. (D) SPECIAL : TEMPORARY has no necessary relationship. (E) VIVACIOUS : IRONIC has no necessary relationship.

---

17   **(B)**   The correct choice is (B) because the relationship between the given words can be expressed as: NOVICE (inexperienced, untrained) is a NEOPHYTE (novice, beginner), or NOVICE is a synonym of NEOPHYTE. Choice (B) expresses the same relationship: VIRTUOSO is an EXPERT. Choice (A) is incorrect because a FUGITIVE is not a ROAD. Choice (C) is wrong because a PACIFIST (someone who looks for calm, peace) is not a synonym for WAR. These words are semantically opposite, and not synonyms. Choice (D) is incorrect because a VAGRANT (a person who wanders from place to place) is not a STREET. Choice (E) is wrong because an IDEALIST is not a PRINCIPLE. An IDEALIST has PRINCIPLES, but the words are not synonyms.

---

18   **(B)**   BANAL and TRITE are synonyms meaning "commonplace." EPHEMERAL and TEMPORARY (B) are also synonyms meaning "short–lived." Choice (A) presents related words, but a GRAVE person is serious, not necessarily SAD. Choice (C) presents antonyms. Choice (E) shows no clear relationship since NOVEL means new while ARDUOUS is difficult.

---

19   **(B)**   ELECTRICITY is measured by the AMPERE. The same relationship exists for (B) since WEIGHT is measured by the POUND. This relationship is not present in the other choices. (A) HEAT : SUN is incorrect. The sun gives off heat. (C) BULB : LIGHT is incorrect. Light is given off by a bulb. (D) NUMBER : SALARY has no necessary relationship. (E) INCH : RULER is incorrect. A ruler measures by the inch, not the other way around.

---

20   **(B)**   CONTRITE and PENITENT are synonyms meaning to be regretful for one's sins. CONCISE and SUCCINCT (B) are also synonyms meaning "brief." Choices (D) and (E) are antonyms. In choice (A), RETICENT (reluctant to speak) and PUNCTUAL have no clear relationship. In choice (C), DOGMATIC means stubborn, so there is no clear relationship there either.

---

21 **(C)** A KEY can be used to unlock a DOOR. This relationship is also evidenced in choice (C) ENIGMA : CLUE. A clue may unlock an Enigma (mystery). The relationship in (A) GEM : RING is that of use. A gem may be used in a ring. The relationship in (B) PERFUME : AROMA is that of entity and characteristic. Aroma is characteristic of perfume. Choice (D) EFFORT : ACHIEVEMENT presents the relationship of prerequisite to event. Effort is a prerequisite to achievement. In the final choice, a MOLD may be used to shape GELATIN (E).

---

22 **(E)** A REQUEST is a mild form of EXTORT. If you REQUEST something, you ask for it. If you EXTORT something, you get it by force. Choice (E) is the best choice because ENTERTAIN is a mild form of REGALE (entertain lavishly). Choice (A) is incorrect, because RESPOND and LETTER are not related in the same manner as REQUEST and EXTORT. (B) is wrong because CHEER is not a form of SMILE. MUTE is not a mild form of SPEECH (C). A MUTE has no form of SPEECH. DEFER and JUDGMENT (D) have no definite relationship.

---

23 **(B)** OPPROBRIOUS describes something that lacks HONOR. The same relationship exists for (B) TRANQUIL : AGITATION since tranquil describes something that lacks agitation. This relationship is not present in the other choices. (A) SIGNIFICANT describes something with SUBSTANCE. (C) TRANSPARENT : TRUTH has no necessary relationship. (D) LECHEROUS : CONFIDENCE has no necessary relationship. (E) OBTRUSIVE describes something that possesses PROMINENCE.

24   **(C)**   The word "quiescence" means still, peaceful. (C) is the best choice. Since movement (A) is not implied, (A) should not be chosen. Agitation (B) is not implied by the word "quiescence"; (B) should be avoided. An upheaval (D) is not implied by a word meaning quiet, calm. (D) should be avoided. "Quiescence" in no way implied intervention; (E) should not be chosen.

---

25   **(E)**   REMs were accompanied by sharp increases in respiration and heart rate and a low-voltage, desynchronized pattern different from that of deep sleep. (E) is the best choice. REMs occurred periodically when there was a sharp increase in respiration and heart rate; the EEG showed a low-voltage, desynchronized pattern different from deep sleep. When REMs occur, respiration increases; (A) could not be chosen. When REMs occur, the heart rate increases; (B) should be omitted. Both an increase in respiration and in heart rate accompany REMs; (C), therefore, should be omitted. A low-voltage (not a high-voltage) desynchronized pattern accompanies the sharp increase in respiration and heart rate with REMs; (D) is not a correct response.

---

26   **(A)**   It is true that all people dream every night (A); this is the correct answer. It should be remembered, however, that not everyone remembers all these dreams. An infant's eyes move in sleep like an adult's; (B) is false. Animals like cats have eye movements just as people do; (C) is false and should not be chosen. Dreams, as already established, are not rare occurrences; (D) is not a correct choice. The discovery that people dream every night was made before 1956; (E) is a poor choice.

---

27   **(B)**   Neurophysiology and EEG laboratory studies gave us much information about dream research. (B) is the best choice. The correct answer is not veterinary laboratories (A) with neurophysiology;

(A) should not be chosen. EEG laboratories and veterinary laboratories should not be selected. (C) is not the correct answer. The age of the studies and the age of the volunteers are not necessarily the strong evidence we need; (D) is incorrect. Observers, and not just full professors, have contributed much to sleep studies; (E) should not be selected.

28 **(D)** Volunteers were used in the study; (D) seems to be the best choice. The subjects were not coerced into participating; (A) is not the best choice. Since mammals were involved, (B) cannot be an accurate choice. Both human and animal subjects were used; (C) is not the best choice. All subjects were not chosen during the 1930s; (E) is not the best choice.

29 **(E)** Aserinsky began his studies by studying sleeping infants. (E) seems to be the best choice. His studies were not focused on waking infants. Dement is noted for his studies on sleeping cats; (B) is not the choice to be selected. Since Aserinsky did not study sleeping cats and infants, choice (C) should not be selected. This article does not deal with waking infants and waking cats, so (D) should not be indicated as the correct choice.

30 **(B)** Aserinsky found that body movements were still when the eyes began making rapid jerky movements beneath the closed lids. (B) is the best choice. Body movements were not accompanied by rapid eye movements, so (A) should not be chosen. References are not made in the reading to body movements and no eye movements. (C) is not the best choice. Sporadic eye movements are not referred to in the passage, so (D) is not the best choice. Body stillness seems to be accompanied by eye movements; (E) should not be the choice.

31   **(E)**   The writer has deliberately given us a beginning study of dream study since 1952. (E) is the best choice. The article does not bring us all the way through 1992, so answer (A) cannot be correct. People did actually think of dreams before 1952, but no scientific studies were done in great detail; (B) is not the best choice. The article does not focus just on animals (people, too, were studied). (C) is not the best choice. The article does not really research dream research before 1952; (D) should not be selected.

---

32   **(C)**   In this context, "germinal" is most nearly defined as "early." The context clue is "from which much of modern sleep research has burgeoned." There is nothing to indicate the author feels the studies were "definitive" (A) or "exhaustive" (B). Although "germinal" suggests "contaminated" (D), it is not correct in this context. "Refuted" (E) is incorrect because nowhere in the passage is it suggested that the studies are invalid.

---

33   **(D)**   It is stated in the passage that it took the work of a selected few in order for studying sleep to be accepted by the scientific community. These select few are discussed by the author and he tells of the large amount of research they had to do in order to prove their beliefs. (A) is incorrect because the passage states the study of sleep caught on slowly and was really only performed by one or two researchers at first. (B) is not correct because it took several researchers to make advancements in order to prove sleep study was important to understand people and dreams. (C) is false, because we are told early research was done on infants and adults. The second paragraph states that dream study was first done by one or two men, not a group (E).

34　　**(C)**　　The correct answer is (C). Research has proven that dreams are richly detailed and coherent. The other choices are all incorrect because they are widely held misconceptions which were refuted by modern science.

35　　**(B)**　　(B) is the correct answer because it is clearly stated that the first period of REM lasts about 10 minutes. (A) is incorrect because this is the percent of sleeping time occupied by dreams in young adults. (C) is not correct because 90 minutes is approximately how long it takes to reach the first REM stage after falling asleep. Choice (D) is also incorrect because the time is 10 minutes not an hour. (E) must therefore be wrong because the time frame has been determined.

Section 4 - Math

1

(A) In Column A expand the product by factoring. Thus, the product of

$$(1 - \sqrt{2})(1 - \sqrt{2}) = 1 - \sqrt{2} - \sqrt{2} + (\sqrt{2})(\sqrt{2})$$
$$= 1 - 2\sqrt{2} + \sqrt{4}$$
$$= 1 - 2\sqrt{2} + 2$$
$$= 3 - 2\sqrt{2}$$

which is positive.

Similarly, in Column B one expands the indicated product to get

$$(1 - \sqrt{2})(1 + \sqrt{2}) = 1 - \sqrt{2} + \sqrt{2} + (\sqrt{2})(\sqrt{2})$$
$$= 1 - \sqrt{4}$$
$$= 1 - 2$$
$$= -1$$

Thus, the quantity in Column A is larger. Any positive number is larger than any negative number.

2

(A) We can define an even number as $2x$, and the following numbers will be $2x + 2$ and $2x + 4$. Therefore,

$$2x + 2x + 2 + 2x + 4 = 42$$
$$6x + 6 = 42$$
$$6x = 36$$
$$x = 6$$

Remember that the first number was $2x$, which is 12 if $x = 6$.

3   **(D)**   Since the sum of the angles in a triangle is 180°,
$$x + y = 180 - 30 = 150.$$
x cannot equal 150 but certainly could be greater than 140. It could also be less than 140, since the problem gives no additional information about y. Consequently, not enough information is given to determine which quantity is greater.

---

4   **(A)**   Using the definition,

$$\boxed{-3} = \frac{(-3)^2 - 1}{-3} = -\frac{8}{3}$$

Note that $-3 = -\frac{9}{3} < \frac{8}{3}$ and so the number in Column A is greater.

---

5   **(B)**   To compare $\frac{1}{yz}$ with $\frac{1}{xy}$ is the same as if we compare $\frac{1}{x}$ with $\frac{1}{z}$ because y appears in both denominators, and we know that $x > z$ (keep in mind that these are fractional values and larger denominators can be lesser in value). Therefore,

$$\frac{1}{x} < \frac{1}{z} \text{ and } \frac{1}{xy} < \frac{1}{zy}.$$

---

6   **(A)**   Let x be the length of the side of the first square and y the length of the side of the second. From the given information, $4x^2 = y^2$ so that $y = 2x$. The perimeter of the first square is $4x$ while the perimeter of the second is $4y = 8x$. Thus the perimeter of the second is twice the perimeter of the first. Therefore, the number represented in Column A is bigger.

7   **(C)**   Since segments *AC* and *BC* are radii of this circle, they are congruent. This means that triangle *ABC* is an isosceles triangle because two of its sides are congruent. In an isosceles triangle, the base angles opposite the congruent sides are congruent. Thus, ∠*A* and ∠*B* are congruent, making *x* and *y* equal quantities. The answer is choice (C).

---

8   **(D)**   We can rewrite the statement as

$$3m > 4p,$$

therefore

$$\frac{m}{p} > \frac{4}{3},$$

but not necessarily bigger than 2.

---

9   **(C)**   For the circle the ratio is

$$\frac{\pi 2^2}{2\pi \times 2} = \frac{\pi 4}{2\pi \times 2} = \frac{\pi 4}{4\pi} = 1.$$

While for the square, the ratio is

$$\frac{4^2}{4 \times 4} = 1.$$

The two ratios are the same.

---

10   **(B)**   Let *x* – 1, *x*, and *x* + 1 be three consecutive numbers, then

$$(x + 1) + x + (x - 1) = 3x,$$

and the smallest of the three is *x* – 1 which is less than *x*.

11   **(A)** $a - b = -b$

if $a = 0$ then b is negative.

Therefore, $a > b$

---

12   **(B)**   The circumference of a circle is $2\pi r$, where r is the radius. Thus the circumference is 2π units in length. The perimeter of the semicircle can be found in the following way. The curved portion is just half the circumference of the full circle, in this case, $\pi r = 2\pi$. To this must be added the length of the diameter, 4. Thus the perimeter of the semicircle is $2\pi + 4$ units in length. This is longer than 2π.

---

13   **(A)**   To eliminate a percent sign, put the number over 100.

$$6 = \frac{6}{5}\%y$$

$$6 = \frac{\frac{6}{5}y}{100}$$

$$6 = \frac{6y}{500}$$

$$6y = 3,000$$

$$y = 500$$

Therefore, $x > 400$

---

14   **(B)**   First factor the left-hand side of each equation as follows:

$$y^2 + 12y + 27 = (y + 9)(y + 3) = 0$$

and $x^2 - 12x + 27 = (x - 9)(x - 3) = 0.$

Notice that the factors are similar except for the signs. However, to compare the values of y in Column A with those of x in Column B, one needs to solve each of the equations as follows:

$$(y + 9)(y + 3) = 0 \qquad\qquad (x - 9)(x - 3) = 0$$
$$y + 9 = 0 \qquad y + 3 = 0 \qquad x - 9 = 0 \qquad x - 3 = 0$$
$$y = -9 \qquad y = -3 \qquad x = 9 \qquad x = 3$$

Hence, the quantity in Column B will always be greater than the quantity in Column A no matter which value of y or x is chosen.

---

15   **(C)**   This diagram shows that $\angle A$ and $\angle C$ are opposite angles of the parallelogram. Opposite angles in a parallelogram have the same measure. Therefore, the answer is choice (C).

---

16   The correctly gridded response is:

To find the percentage decrease, we use the following formula:

$$\frac{\text{amount of change}}{\text{old total}} = \frac{x}{100}$$

The "old total" is where we started from, in this case the original price of the compact disc player: $200.00. The amount of change is the difference between the old total and where we ended up, the new price of the compact disc player. In this case, the amount of change would be

$$200 - 147.59 = 52.41$$

When we solve the equation, *x* will be the percentage change.

$$\frac{52.41}{200} = \frac{x}{100}$$

$$200x = 52.41 \times 100$$

When two fractions are in proportion, we can cross-multiply and the resulting products will be equal.

$200x = 5,241$ Simplify.

$\dfrac{200x}{200} = \dfrac{5,241}{200}$ Divide both sides by the coefficient of the variable.

$x = 26.2$ Simplify.

---

17   The correct response is:

First we must realize that $\sqrt{81} = 9$. Thus, our new equation is $9 = 3^y$. Because

$$3^2 = 3 \times 3 = 9,$$

y must be equal to 2.

18   The correct response is:

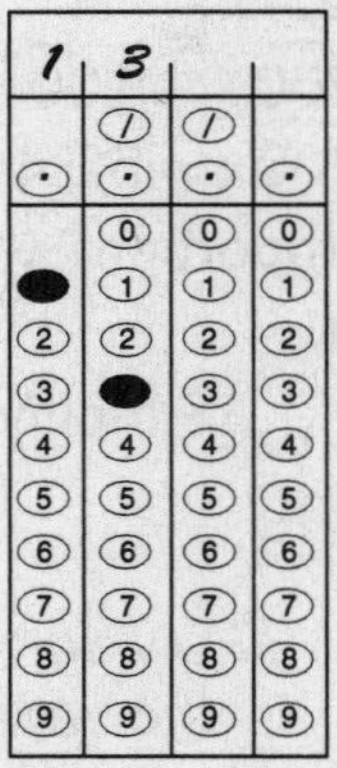

We know that triangle *B* has an area of 3. We also know that triangle *A* has an area three times the area of triangle *B*.

Thus,

$$3 \times \text{area } \triangle B = \text{area } \triangle A.$$

If *A* is three times *B*, to make *A* and *B* equal, we must multiple *B* × 3.

$$3B = A \quad \text{Simplify.}$$
$$3 \times 3 = A \quad \text{Substitute.}$$
$$9 = A \quad \text{Simplify.}$$
$$\text{area } \triangle B = 3 \times \text{area } \triangle C$$

If *B* is three times *C*, to make *C* and *B* equal, we must multiply *C* × 3.

$$B = 3C \quad \text{Simplify.}$$
$$3 = 3C \quad \text{Substitute.}$$

$$\frac{3}{3} = \frac{3C}{3} \quad \text{Divide both sides by the coefficient of the variable.}$$

$$1 = C$$

Thus, *C* = 1, *B* = 3, and *A* = 9 and their sum is 1 + 3 + 9 = 13.

19 The correct response is:

One-fourth of the larger number equals $\frac{1}{4}$ of 84 = 21.

We are told that five times the smaller is less than one-fourth the larger. Thus,

$$5s < 21$$

$$\frac{5s}{5} < \frac{21}{5}$$ Divide both sides by the coefficient of variable.

$$s < 4.2$$ Simplify.

The largest whole number less than 4.2 is 4.

---

20 The correct response is:

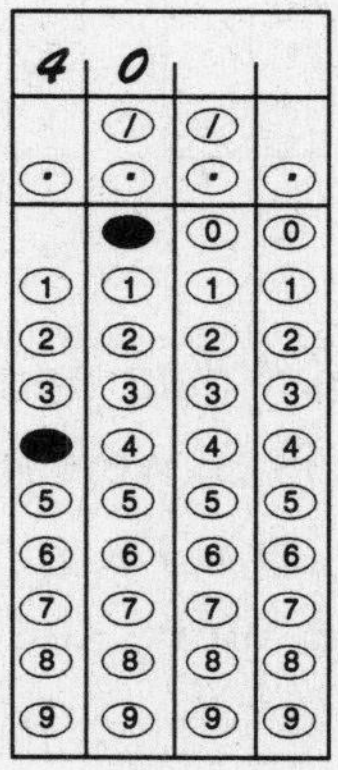

Explanation:

$$\angle c = \angle a$$ Vertical angles are equal.

$$\angle e = \angle a$$ Corresponding angles of ‖ lines are equal.

$$\angle c = \angle e$$ Angles equal to the same angle are equal to each other.

$$a + b + c + d = 360$$ The angles surrounding a point equal 360.

$$a + b + e + d = 360$$ Substitution.

$$8e + e = 360$$ $a + d + b = 8e$ given / substitution.

$$9e = 360$$ Combine like terms.

$$\frac{9e}{9} = \frac{360}{9}$$ Divide both sides by coefficient of variable.

$$e = 40$$ Simplify.

---

21 The correct response is:

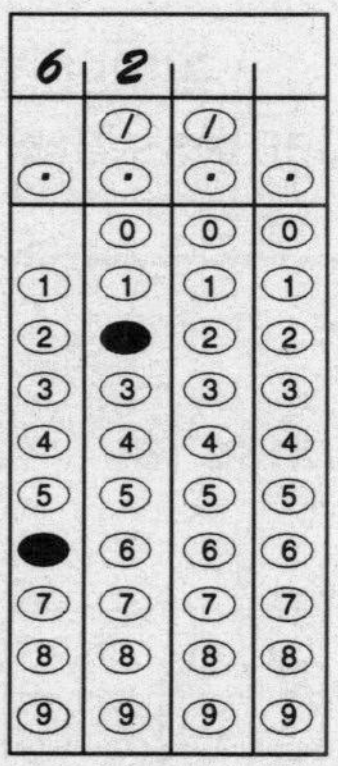

Let U represent the units' digit and T represent the tens' digit.
If the sum of the digits is 8, we can write the equation

$$U + T = 8.$$

And, if the tens' digit is three times the units' digit, we can write the equation

$$3U = T.$$

We now have two equations with two unknowns. Because we know that $T = 3U$, every place in the first equation where we see a T, we can substitute in $3U$. Thus,

$U + T = 8$	Original equation.
$U + 3U = 8$	Substitution.
$4U = 8$	Combine like terms.
$\dfrac{4U}{4} = \dfrac{8}{4}$	Divide both sides by the coefficient of the variable.
$U = 2$	Thus, the units' digit is 2.

If the tens' digit is three times the units' digit, the tens' digit would be

$$3 \times 2 = 6.$$

If the tens' digit is 6 and the units' digit is 2, the number is 62.

---

22   The correct response is:

If 15 restaurants each served an average of 1,200 customers, then the 15 restaurants served a total of 15 × 1,200, or 18,000 customers.
If 7 of 15 restaurants close, 8 restaurants would remain open.

$$15 - 7 = 8$$

If 18,000 customers were served by 8 restaurants, then each served an average of 18,000 ÷ 8, or 2,250 customers. (To find an average we divide the total by the number making up that total.)
If on Sunday each restaurant averaged 1,200 customers, while on

Monday each restaurant averaged 2,250 customers, there would have been an increase of 2,250 − 1,200, or 1,050 customers.

---

23   The correct response is

If the value of N is 3, then NP is either 30, 31, 32, 33, 34, 35, 36, 37, 38, or 39. The only one of these numbers that is a multiple of 8, however, is the number 32.

$$8 \times 3 = 24$$
and $$8 \times 5 = 40$$

The number that must be multiplied by 8 to obtain a product of 32 is 4.

---

24   The correct response is:

$6m = 20 + m$ Combine like terms.

$6m - m = 20 + m - m$ Subtract m from both sides to have all variables on left side of equation and all constants on right.

$5m = 20$ Simplify.

$\dfrac{5m}{5} = \dfrac{20}{5}$ Divide both sides of equation by the coefficient of the variable.

$m = 4$ Simplify.

---

25   The correct response is:

We were told this is a number line, and on any number line numbers become greater as we move to the right. Thus, we know that $f > b$. Additionally, because the letters represent consecutive integers and f is 4 spaces to the right of b, we know that $b + 4 = f$.

In the question, we were told that

$2b + f = 13$ Because we know that $b + 4 = f$, we can substitute.

$2b + (b + 4) = 13$ Substitution.

$3b + 4 = 13$ Combine like terms.

$3b + 4 - 4 = 13 - 4$ Place variables on one side and constants on the other.

$3b = 9$ Simplify.

$\dfrac{3b}{3} = \dfrac{9}{3}$ Divide both sides by the coefficient of the variable.

$b = 3$

Section 5 - Verbal

1   **(C)**   The author uses the simile of man's leap from the earliest stage of mankind to the next to show how the Industrial Revolution profoundly changed the fate of the human race. Choice (A) is incorrect since the statement compares significance, not periods of time. Choice (B) is wrong. There is no mention of the types of developments made during the Industrial Revolution. The comparison between the two ages is used solely as a way to show the development of mankind, not the development of tools. Choice (D) is incorrect. Though the simile does show a shift in hunting to farming, the meaning of the comparison is rooted in man's social and intellectual advances. Therefore, choice (E) is wrong, as it addresses class issues that are never mentioned in the simile.

---

2   **(A)**   Choice (A) correctly identifies the steam engine and mill-driven machinery as mechanical advances which played a big part in the Industrial Revolution's development. While both (B) and (C) may be true statements, the article is not primarily concerned with profitability or the daring uses of water. (D) and (E) are wrong. The machines were created, not abandoned, during the Industrial Revolution and were very successful.

---

3   **(B)**   The Industrial Revolution in fact "brought about" the neglect and abuse of individuals. This abuse was a direct result of the advances during that era. Therefore choices (A) and (D) are incorrect. Those in power during the Industrial Revolution made little or no effort to avoid or negate the abuse of workers. In fact, in many instances gross abuses were ignored. Thus choice (C) is incorrect. The Industrial Revolution, while it boosted economies and the power of nations, did not stave off or rule out neglect and abuse of workers. Choice (C) is incorrect. Though an impersonal force, the Industrial Revolution in many ways treated men like the precise, tireless machines they operated.

4　　**(C)**　　The author sites a number of statistics explaining the devastating effects the atomic bombs had on Japan, yet he notes that the bombs "served as sufficient reminder(s) to the rest of the world of the atom's potential for destruction." He implies that the fear of comparable destruction prevents its use. Choices (A) and (B) are wrong. The author believes the opposite of both these choices and provides evidence of Soviet and American efforts to avoid the use of atomic and nuclear weapons at all cost. Choices (D) and (E) are also incorrect since the author provides no concrete evidence to support those statements.

5　　**(A)**　　Choice (A) best describes the purpose of the description and explains the purpose of the passage. The author builds a case that justifies the use of the atom bomb, but then explains the reasons why it was never used again. By focusing on the destruction, the author impresses upon the reader the event's power as a deterrent. (B) is incorrect since the author never discusses the theoretic/scientific aspect of atomic weapons. (C) and (E) are incorrect. Even though the description might show the power of an atomic device and show how World War II ended, neither is the reason the description was included. (D) is obviously wrong since the statement deals with destruction, not benefits.

6　　**(B)**　　Choice (B) discusses the way in which world politics was divided between two factions following the end of World War II, headed on one side by the United States and on the other by the former Soviet Union. This two-sided breakdown of nations led to the Cold War. (A) is incorrect. The author does not directly link the bombing of Japan to the bipolar global arena; rather he shows how the two combined to influence history. (C) is wrong. Though the U.S. and the U.S.S.R. peace talks are mentioned, the author's description does not address that issue. (D) and (E) are both incorrect since neither relates to the way in which the bipolar arena impacted upon world politics.

7   **(E)**   Choice (E) is correct since the author's purpose, to show the inhumane treatment of children, is best explained by recounting actual abuses. The graphic nature of the description impresses the seriousness of the situation upon the reader. (A) is incorrect. Though the passage may engage the reader's interest, its purpose is to inform rather than entertain. (B) is incorrect. Although the lives led by child workers were horrible, the author's ultimate goal is to inform, not horrify. (C) is wrong. Children were an important part of the Industrial Revolution's labor force, but the incident shows their vulnerability, not their importance. (D) is incorrect. Though the passage itself explains the advantages of the machines, this particular section focuses on the dangers faced by children working them.

8   **(D)**   Great Britain, concerned only with expanding its base of power, used the Industrial Revolution to become the dominant global force in the same way that both the U.S. and the U.S.S.R. used the threat of nuclear weapons. Since realpolitik is concerned with national developments and goals, choices (A) and (E) are incorrect. Though the increase of power-driven machines did increase output, and the author of Passage 1 did address the problems faced by industrial workers, realpolitik does not apply. Choice (B) is wrong, because the change from hunter to gatherer precludes all such advanced political systems. (C) is also incorrect since the Industrial Revolution's effects on global economics does not in and of itself describe any specific political tactic.

9 **(B)** Choice (B) is correct since the development of both the Industrial Revolution's massive factories and the atomic bomb provided new intellectual and technological advances that outstripped all other technologies of their time. Only through the introduction of these types of radically new advances could a revolution occur. Choices (A) and (C) are wrong. Though gross atrocities and realignment of worldwide alliances are sometimes a cause or effect of a revolution, the author does not cite either as being integral to a revolution. Likewise, (D) is incorrect since a country's need for control is not in and of itself necessary for a revolution to occur. (E) is wrong. Economic interdependencies are not mentioned in the second passage as having any influence on the development of the atomic age.

10 **(E)** By stating that very few nations have access to nuclear or atomic weapons, the similarities between the two passages are reduced. Where the Industrial Revolution spread its technology throughout the world, atomic weapons have been strictly guarded. With less widespread development, atomic weapons did not alter day-to-day living to the degree the Industrial Revolution did. Neither (A) nor (B) is correct since the shift in class structure and the accumulation of wealth do little to change the two passages' theme of trade-off inherent in the development of new technologies. Choices (C) and (D) while true, do not lessen the similarities between the two passages. Just as the atomic age created new jobs, so too did the Industrial Revolution. Great Britain's rise to power is similar to the rise of both the U.S. and the U.S.S.R. during the dawn of the atomic age.

11 **(D)** Choice (D) is correct since dichotomy is defined as "a division into two usually contradictory parts" and the benefits of increased production were contradicted by the damage done to the labor force and children. Choices (A) and (B) are wrong. Neither the Industrial Revolution's size nor the quickness with which it developed affected its contradictory nature. (C) is incorrect since the changing nature of the Industrial Revolution would not prevent it from being a benign force. **(E)** is also incorrect. The fact that the Industrial Revolution was a success cannot change the nature of the benefits and drawbacks it created.

12　　**(C)**　　The author shows how the Industrial Revolution both benefited and damaged European life. Choices **(A)** and **(B)** both go well beyond the author's scope. **(A)** underplays the Industrial Revolution's importance while **(B)** completely ignores the many drawbacks of the "machine age." **(D)** is wrong. The Industrial Revolution occurred almost 100 years before the Cold War, though the birth of the atomic age was a factor in the development of the Cold War. **(E)** is incorrect since the Industrial Revolution moved European economies away from an agrarian base toward an industrial one.

13　　**(B)**　　The atomic age did cause massive political and social change in the form of a bipolar world order and the harnessing of nuclear power. **(A)** is wrong. Atomic technologies played little or no role in the downfall of the Soviet Union. Though **(C)** may be a true statement, the author never overtly states that it is true. **(D)** is incorrect. The author does not state that without the atomic bomb Japan would have achieved world dominance. **(E)** is incorrect. The author provides an argument stating that the notion of Mutual Assured Destruction (MAD) prevented a third world war.

Section 6 - Math

1   **(E)**   Since
$$.095 \times 110 = 10.45$$
and since
$$110 + 10.45 = 120.45,$$
the total cost is $120.45.

---

2   **(E)**   We use the laws of exponents to solve this problem. $(25)^{3m}$ can be expressed as $(5^2)^{3m}$, which can also be written as 5^{6m}.
   $(125)^{8m}$ can, by similar argument, be expressed as 5^{24m}. When we multiply a number of the same base raised to different powers, we simply keep the same base and add the exponents. Thus:
$$(25)^{3m} (125)^{8m} (5)^m = 5^{6m} \, 5^{24m} \, 5^m = 5^{31m}.$$

---

3   **(B)**   Let $m\angle A =$ the measure of angle A, and arc $m(ABC) =$ the measure of arc ABC. Since angle DBC is formed by a tangent to circle O, $\overline{BD}$, and a chord, $\overline{CB}$, intersecting at the point of tangency, B, it follows that,

$$m\angle BDC = \frac{1}{2} \text{ arc } m(BEC)$$

$$70 = \frac{1}{2} \text{ arc } m(BEC)$$

arc $m(BED) = (70)(2)$
arc $m(BEC) = 140$

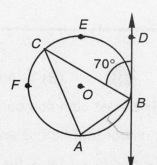

Since $\angle BAC$ is an inscribe angle in the arc *BAC*, and since arc *BEC* is intercepted by angle *BAC*, it follows that

$$m \angle BAC = \frac{1}{2} \text{ arc } m(BEC)$$

$$= \frac{1}{2}(140)$$

$$= 70°$$

4   **(E)**   John's cost for the month of June is $2,000 (.27) = $540. Since June has 30 days, John's average daily cost is

$$\frac{540}{30} = \$18.00.$$

5   **(D)**   First add 5 to both sides of the equation and then square both sides as follows:

$$\sqrt{5x-4} - 5 + 5 = -1 + 5$$

$$(\sqrt{5x-4})^2 = 4^2$$

$$5x - 4 = 16$$

$$5x = 16 + 4$$

$$5x = 20$$

$$x = 4$$

6   **(B)**   A common denominator is needed to add fractions. The least common denominator in this problem is 9 since the smallest number that both 3 and 9 will divide into is 9. If the denominator of $\frac{2}{3}$ is multiplied by 3 then the numerator must also be multiplied by 3.

Thus,

$$\frac{2 \times 3}{3 \times 3} = \frac{6}{9}.$$

Adding the numerators and using the common denominator,

$$\frac{6}{9} + \frac{5}{9} = \frac{6+5}{9} = \frac{11}{9}$$

---

7   **(B)**   Substitute for x:

$$f(3) = (3) + 1$$
$$= 4$$
$$g(4) = 2(4) - 3$$
$$= 5$$
$$f(3) \times g(4) = 4 \times 5$$
$$= 2(4) + 5 - (4)(5)$$
$$= -7$$

---

8   **(C)**   The arithmetic mean of the scores is

$$\frac{10 + 20 + 30 + 35 + 55}{5} = \frac{150}{5} = 30.$$

Since only two scores, namely, 35 and 55 are larger than 30, the answer is 2, (C).

---

9   **(A)**   If X student tickets were sold, then $1,000 - X$ adults tickets were sold. The total receipts would be

$$2(X) + 4(1,000 - X) = 4,000 - 2X.$$

Therefore,

$$4,000 - 2X = 3,200, \text{ or } X = 400.$$

10   **(A)**   The formula for the area of a triangle is

$$\frac{1}{2} \times \text{base} \times \text{height}$$

or $\frac{1}{2}(b)(h).$

Segment *BC* is the base of the triangle with segment *AC* the corresponding height. To find the measurement of segment *BC*, notice that $\angle A + \angle B + \angle C$ must equal 180° and $\angle B + \angle C = 90 + 30 = 120$. So $\angle A$ measures 60° and this triangle is a 30-60-90 triangle. The leg opposite the 60° angle measures $\sqrt{3}$ times the length of the leg opposite the 30° angle. Therefore,

$$BC = \left(\sqrt{3}\right)(AC) = \left(\sqrt{3}\right)(3) = 3\sqrt{3}$$

The area, then, is

$$\frac{1}{2}(BC)(AC) = \frac{1}{2}\left(3\sqrt{3}\right)(3) = \frac{9\sqrt{3}}{2}.$$

Building Your Vocabulary for the SAT

Your success on the SAT Verbal Test begins with one fundamental insight: **these questions have been written and designed to test your vocabulary**. No matter what section you are working in, you will be expected to demonstrate that you have a good command of vocabulary words. Because of this, you should devote as much time as possible to strengthening your vocabulary.

You may be feeling a bit intimidated right now because you may think your vocabulary skills aren't that great. But don't get discouraged. First, remember one of the most important strategies to beating the SAT: Don't be intimidated! Second, there are plenty of ways to build up your vocabulary skills before taking the SAT. The simplest and best way of improving your vocabulary is to READ! It doesn't matter what you read — books, magazines, newspapers — as long as you read!

Bust it!

While you're reading, however, you have to pay attention. You should be asking yourself some questions while reading. These questions include:

- What is the main idea?
- What is the author's purpose?
- How does the author make his or her argument?
- What tone does the author use?

If you keep asking yourself these questions, you'll be surprised how much more you understand while reading. And understanding more will lead to a stronger vocabulary.

Unfortunately, you may not remember all of the words you read. That's why we've provided you with an extremely valuable tool to build your vocabulary: The SAT Vocabulary Builder. The Builder includes a list of the most frequently appearing vocabulary words on the SAT verbal sections. In addition, the SAT Vocabulary Builder has lists of the most important prefixes, roots, and suffixes that you'll need to know to help you recognize more words on the SAT.

The SAT Vocabulary Builder

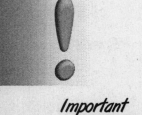

Important Information!

Learning words requires a lot of time and concentration. It's easy to become overwhelmed by looking at the vast number of words that make up the English language. Instead of giving you a list of thousands and thousands of words, we've picked 300 that are guaranteed to help you on the SAT.

We've given you the 300 words that appear most often on the SAT. Study and know these 300 words and you WILL get a better score.

In addition to learning words, recognizing the **most important prefixes, roots, and suffixes** will give you the skills to understand words that you don't even know. Even though we've provided you with the 300 words that appear the most on the SAT, you will encounter words that you don't know. Luckily, most English words are based on Greek or Latin words. Studying the meanings of Greek and Latin words will help you "break down" unfamiliar English words so you can understand them. These Greek and Latin words have survived in modern English language as parts of words such as prefixes, roots, and suffixes. The SAT Vocabulary Builder teaches you to recognize these Greek and Latin meanings of prefixes, roots, and suffixes that are used in English to understand the meaning of an unfamiliar words. So learning these prefixes, roots, and suffixes is like having a key to open the lock that guards the SAT's answers!

How to Use the SAT Vocabulary Builder

The SAT Vocabulary Builder presents 12 groups of words and then lists of prefixes, roots, and suffixes. The best way for you to use the Builder is to study it one section at a time. Turn to the first group of words and then identify the ones that you don't know or that are defined in unusual ways. Write these words down on index cards with the word on one side and definition on the other. Study these cards and then test yourself by completing the drills that follow each section. Check your answers and review any words that you missed. Then go on to the next group of words.

Look!

Important Strategy

Once you've gone through the 12 groups of words, turn to the list of prefixes. Review the list and identify the prefixes that are not familiar to you. Write these prefixes down on the front of an index card and their meanings on the back of the card. Study the cards and test yourself by answering the drill questions that follow the list. Check your answers and review any prefixes that you missed. Move on to the roots list and repeat these steps. Then study the suffixes list.

The SAT Vocabulary Builder will enable you to attack the SAT Verbal Test with confidence that you never knew you could possess. Like we stated at the beginning of this chapter, you will be expected to demonstrate that you have a good command of vocabulary words to do well on the SAT. The SAT Vocabulary Builder will give you that command of vocabulary. So let's get started!

The SAT Vocabulary Builder

The most frequently tested words on the SAT

Group 1

abstract – *adj.* – not easy to understand; theoretical

acclaim – *n.* – loud approval; applause

acquiesce – *v.* – agree or consent to an opinion

adamant – *adj.* – not yielding; firm

adversary – *n.* – an enemy; foe

advocate – 1. – *v.* – to plead in favor of;
– 2. – *n.* – supporter; defender

aesthetic – *adj.* – showing good taste; artistic

alleviate – *v.* – to lessen or make easier

aloof – *adj.* – distant in interest; reserved; cool

altercation – *n.* – controversy; dispute

altruistic – *adj.* – unselfish

amass – *v.* – to collect together; accumulate

ambiguous – *adj.* – not clear; uncertain; vague

ambivalent – *adj.* – undecided

ameliorate – *v.* – to make better; to improve

amiable – *adj.* – friendly

amorphous – *adj.* – having no determinate form

anarchist – *n.* – one who believes that a formal government is unnecessary

antagonism – *n.* – hostility; opposition

apathy – *n.* – lack of emotion or interest

appease – *v.* – to make quiet; to calm

apprehensive – *adj.* – fearful; aware; conscious

arbitrary – *adj.* – based on one's preference or   judgment

arrogant – *adj.* – acting superior to others; conceited

articulate – 1. – *v.* – to speak distinctly;
— 2. – *adj.* – eloquent; fluent;
— 3. – *adj.* – capable of speech;
— 4. – *v.* – to hinge; to connect;
— 5. – *v.* – to convey; to express effectively

Drill: Group 1

DIRECTIONS: Match each word in the left column with the word in the right column that is most **OPPOSITE** in meaning.

Word	**Match**
1. _____ articulate	A. hostile
2. _____ apathy	B. concrete
3. _____ amiable	C. selfish
4. _____ altruistic	D. reasoned
5. _____ ambivalent	E. ally
6. _____ abstract	F. disperse
7. _____ acquiesce	G. enthusiasm
8. _____ arbitrary	H. certain
9. _____ amass	I. resist
10. _____ adversary	J. incoherent

DIRECTIONS: Match each word in the left column with the word in the right column that is most **SIMILAR** in meaning.

Word	**Match**
11. _____ adamant	a. afraid
12. _____ aesthetic	b. disagreement
13. _____ apprehensive	c. tasteful
14. _____ antagonism	d. insistent
15. _____ altercation	e. hostility

Group 2

assess – *v.* – to estimate the value of

astute – *adj.* – cunning; sly; crafty

atrophy – *v.* – to waste away through lack of nutrition

audacious – *adj.* – fearless; bold

augment – *v.* – to increase or add to; to make larger

austere – *v.* – harsh; severe; strict

authentic – *adj.* – real; genuine; trustworthy

authoritarian – *n.* – acting as a dictator; demanding obedience

banal – *adj.* – common; petty; ordinary

belittle – *v.* – to make small; to think lightly of

benefactor – *n.* – one who helps others; a donor

benevolent – *adj.* – kind; generous

benign – *adj.* – mild; harmless

biased – *adj.* – prejudiced; influenced; not neutral

blasphemous – *adj.* – irreligious; away from acceptable standards

blithe – *adj.* – happy; cheery; merry

brevity – *n.* – briefness; shortness

candid – *adj.* – honest; truthful; sincere

capricious – *adj.* – changeable; fickle

caustic – *adj.* – burning; sarcastic; harsh

censor – *v.* – to examine and delete objectionable material

censure – *v.* – to criticize or disapprove of

charlatan – *n.* – an imposter; fake

coalesce – *v.* – to combine; come together

collaborate – *v .* – to work together; cooperate

Drill: Group 2

DIRECTIONS: Match each word in the left column with the word in the right column that is most OPPOSITE in meaning.

Word		Match
1. _____ augment		A. permit
2. _____ biased		B. religious
3. _____ banal		C. praise
4. _____ benevolent		D. diminish
5. _____ censor		E. dishonest
6. _____ authentic		F. malicious
7. _____ candid		G. neutral
8. _____ belittle		H. mournful
9. _____ blasphemous		I. unusual
10. _____ blithe		J. fake

DIRECTIONS: Match each word in the left column with the word in the right column that is most SIMILAR in meaning.

Word		Match
11. _____ collaborate		a. harmless
12. _____ benign		b. cunning
13. _____ astute		c. changeable
14. _____ censure		d. cooperate
15. _____ capricious		e. criticize

Group 3

compatible – *adj.* – in agreement with; harmonious

complacent – *adj.* – content; self-satisfied; smug

compliant – *adj.* – yielding; obedient

comprehensive – *adj.* – all-inclusive; complete; thorough

compromise – *v.* – to settle by mutual adjustment

concede – 1. – *v.* – to acknowledge; admit;
       – 2. – *v.* – to surrender; to abandon one's position

concise – *adj.* – in few words; brief; condensed

condescend – *v.* – to come down from one's position or dignity

condone – *v.* – to overlook; to forgive

conspicuous – *adj.* – easy to see; noticeable

consternation – *n.* – amazement or terror that causes confusion

consummation – *n.* – the completion; finish

contemporary – *adj.* – living or happening at the same time;
                 modern

contempt – *n.* – scorn; disrespect

contrite – *adj.* – regretful; sorrowful

conventional – *adj.* – traditional; common; routine

cower – *v.* – crouch down in fear or shame

defamation – *n.* – to harm a name or reputation; to slander

deference – *adj.* – yielding to the opinion of another

deliberate – 1. – *v.* – to consider carefully; weigh in the mind;
       – 2. – *adj.* – intentional

denounce – *v.* – to speak out against; condemn

depict – *v.* – to portray in words; present a visual image

deplete – *v.* – to reduce; to empty

depravity – *n.* – moral corruption; badness

deride – *v.* – to ridicule; laugh at with scorn

Drill: Group 3

DIRECTIONS: Match each word in the left column with the word in the right column that is most OPPOSITE in meaning.

Word		Match	
1. _____	deplete	A.	unintentional
2. _____	contemporary	B.	disapprove
3. _____	concise	C.	invisible
4. _____	deliberate	D.	respect
5. _____	depravity	E.	fill
6. _____	condone	F.	support
7. _____	conspicuous	G.	beginning
8. _____	consummation	H.	ancient
9. _____	denounce	I.	virtue
10. _____	contempt	J.	verbose

DIRECTIONS: Match each word in the left column with the word in the right column that is most SIMILAR in meaning.

Word		Match	
11. _____	compatible	a.	portray
12. _____	depict	b.	content
13. _____	conventional	c.	harmonious
14. _____	comprehensive	d.	thorough
15. _____	complacent	e.	common

Group 4

desecrate – *v.* – to violate a holy place or sanctuary

detached – *adj.* – separated; not interested; standing alone

deter – *v.* – to prevent; to discourage; hinder

didactic – 1. – *adj.* – instructive;
— 2. – *adj.* – dogmatic; preachy

digress – *v.* – stray from the subject; wander from topic

diligence – *n.* – hard work

discerning – *adj.* – distinguishing one thing from another

discord – *n.* – disagreement; lack of harmony

discriminating – 1. – *v.* – distinguishing one thing from another;
— 2. – *v.* – demonstrating bias;
— 3. – *adj.* – able to distinguish

disdain – 1. – *n.* – intense dislike;
— 2. – *v.* – look down upon; scorn

disparage – *v.* – to belittle; undervalue

disparity – *n.* – difference in form, character, or degree

dispassionate – *adj.* – lack of feeling; impartial

disperse – *v.* – to scatter; separate

disseminate – *v.* – to circulate; scatter

dissent – *v.* – to disagree; differ in opinion

dissonance – *n.* – harsh contradiction

diverse – *adj.* – different; dissimilar

document – 1. – *n.* – official paper containing information;
— 2. – *v.* – to support; substantiate; verify

dogmatic – *adj.* – stubborn; biased; opinionated

dubious – *adj.* – doubtful; uncertain; skeptical; suspicious

eccentric – *adj.* – odd; peculiar; strange

efface – *v.* – wipe out; erase

effervescence – 1. – *n.* – liveliness; spirit; enthusiasm;
— 2. – *n.* – bubbliness

egocentric – *adj.* – self-centered

Drill: Group 4

DIRECTIONS: Match each word in the left column with the word in the right column that is most OPPOSITE in meaning.

Word	Match
1. _____ detached	A. agree
2. _____ deter	B. certain
3. _____ dissent	C. lethargy
4. _____ discord	D. connected
5. _____ efface	E. assist
6. _____ dubious	F. respect
7. _____ diligence	G. compliment
8. _____ disdain	H. sanctify
9. _____ desecrate	I. harmony
10. _____ disparage	J. restore

DIRECTIONS: Match each word in the left column with the word in the right column that is most SIMILAR in meaning.

Word	Match
11. _____ effervescence	a. stubborn
12. _____ dogmatic	b. distribute
13. _____ disseminate	c. substantiate
14. _____ document	d. liveliness
15. _____ eccentric	e. odd

Group 5

elaboration – *n.* – act of clarifying; adding details

eloquence – *n.* – the ability to speak well

elusive – *adj.* – hard to catch; difficult to understand

emulate – *v.* – to imitate; copy; mimic

endorse – *v.* – support; to approve of; recommend

engender – *v.* – to create; bring about

enhance – *v.* – to improve; compliment; make more attractive

enigma – *n.* – mystery; secret; perplexity

ephemeral – *adj.* – temporary; brief; short-lived

equivocal – *adj.* – doubtful; uncertain

erratic – *adj.* – unpredictable; strange

erroneous – *adj.* – untrue; inaccurate; not correct

esoteric – *adj.* – incomprehensible; obscure

euphony – *n.* – pleasant sound

execute – 1. – *v.* – put to death; kill;
   – 2. – *v.* – to carry out; fulfill

exemplary – *adj.* – serving as an example; outstanding

exhaustive – *adj.* – thorough; complete

expedient – *adj.* – helpful; practical; worthwhile

expedite – *v.* – speed up

explicit – *adj.* – specific; definite

extol – *v.* – praise; commend

extraneous – *adj.* – irrelevant; not related; not essential

facilitate – *v.* – make easier; simplify

fallacious – *adj.* – misleading

fanatic – *n.* – enthusiast; extremist

Drill: Group 5

Word		Match	
1. _____	extraneous	A.	incomplete
2. _____	ephemeral	B.	delay
3. _____	exhaustive	C.	dependable
4. _____	expedite	D.	comprehensible
5. _____	erroneous	E.	dissonance
6. _____	erratic	F.	eternal
7. _____	explicit	G.	condemn
8. _____	euphony	H.	relevant
9. _____	elusive	I.	indefinite
10. _____	extol	J.	accurate

Word		Match	
11. _____	endorse	a.	enable
12. _____	expedient	b.	recommend
13. _____	facilitate	c.	create
14. _____	fallacious	d.	worthwhile
15. _____	engender	e.	deceptive

Group 6

fastidious – *adj.* – fussy; hard to please

fervent – *adj.* – passionate; intense

fickle – *adj.* – changeable; unpredictable

fortuitous – *adj.* – accidental; happening by chance; lucky

frivolity – *adj.* – giddiness; lack of seriousness

fundamental – *adj.* – basic; necessary

furtive – *adj.* – secretive; sly

futile – *adj.* – worthless; unprofitable

glutton – *n.* – overeater

grandiose – *adj.* – extravagant; flamboyant

gravity – *n.* – seriousness

guile – *n.* – slyness; deceit

gullible – *adj.* – easily fooled

hackneyed – *adj.* – commonplace; trite

hamper – *v.* – interfere with; hinder

haphazard – *adj.* – disorganized; random

hedonistic – *adj.* – pleasure seeking

heed – *v.* – obey; yield to

heresy – *n.* – opinion contrary to popular belief

hindrance – *n.* – blockage; obstacle

humility – *n.* – lack of pride; modesty

hypocritical – *adj.* – two-faced; deceptive

hypothetical – *adj.* – assumed; uncertain

illuminate – *v.* – make understandable

illusory – *adj.* – unreal; false; deceptive

Drill: Group 6

Word	Match
1. _____ heresy	A. predictable
2. _____ fickle	B. dispassionate
3. _____ illusory	C. simple
4. _____ frivolity	D. extraneous
5. _____ grandiose	E. real
6. _____ fervent	F. beneficial
7. _____ fundamental	G. orthodoxy
8. _____ furtive	H. organized
9. _____ futile	I. candid
10. _____ haphazard	J. seriousness

Word	Match
11. _____ glutton	a. hinder
12. _____ heed	b. obstacle
13. _____ hamper	c. trite
14. _____ hackneyed	d. overeater
15. _____ hindrance	e. obey

Group 7

immune – *adj.* – protected; unthreatened by

immutable – *adj.* – unchangeable; permanent

impartial – *adj.* – unbiased; fair

impetuous – 1. – *adj.* – rash; impulsive;
            – 2. – *adj.* – forcible; violent

implication – *n.* – suggestion; inference

inadvertent – *adj.* – not on purpose; unintentional

incessant – *adj.* – constant; continual

incidental – *adj.* – extraneous; unexpected

inclined – 1. – *adj.* – apt to; likely to;
         – 2. – *adj.* – angled

incoherent – *adj.* – illogical; rambling

incompatible – *adj.* – disagreeing; disharmonious

incredulous – *adj.* – unwilling to believe; skeptical

indifferent – *adj.* – unconcerned

indolent – *adj.* – lazy; inactive

indulgent – *adj.* – lenient; patient

inevitable – *adj.* – sure to happen; unavoidable

infamous – *adj.* – having a bad reputation; notorious

infer – *v.* – form an opinion; conclude

initiate – 1. – *v.* – begin; admit into a group;
        – 2. – *n.* – a person who is in the process of being
                 admitted into a group

innate – *adj.* – natural; inborn

innocuous – *adj.* – harmless; innocent

innovate – *v.* – introduce a change; depart from the old

insipid – *adj.* – uninteresting; bland

instigate – *v.* – start; provoke

intangible – *adj.* – incapable of being touched; immaterial

Drill: Group 7

Word		Match	
1. _____	immutable	A.	intentional
2. _____	impartial	B.	articulate
3. _____	inadvertent	C.	gullible
4. _____	incoherent	D.	material
5. _____	incompatible	E.	biased
6. _____	innate	F.	changeable
7. _____	incredulous	G.	avoidable
8. _____	inevitable	H.	harmonious
9. _____	intangible	I.	learned
10. _____	indolent	J.	energetic

Word		Match	
11. _____	impetuous	a.	lenient
12. _____	incidental	b.	impulsive
13. _____	infer	c.	provoke
14. _____	instigate	d.	conclude
15. _____	indulgent	e.	extraneous

Group 8

ironic – *adj.* – contradictory; inconsistent; sarcastic

irrational – *adj.* – not logical

jeopardy – *n.* – danger

kindle – *v.* – ignite; arouse

languid – *adj.* – weak; fatigued

laud – *v.* – praise

lax – *adj.* – careless; irresponsible

lethargic – *adj.* – lazy; passive

levity – *n.* – silliness; lack of seriousness

lucid – 1. – *adj.* – shining;
      – 2. – *adj.* – easily understood

magnanimous – *adj.* – forgiving; unselfish

malicious – *adj.* – spiteful; vindictive

marred – *adj.* – damaged

meander – *v.* – wind on a course; go aimlessly

melancholy – *n.* – depression; gloom

meticulous – *adj.* – exacting; precise

minute – *adj.* – extremely small; tiny

miser – *n.* – penny pincher; stingy person

mitigate – *v.* – alleviate; lessen; soothe

morose – *adj.* – moody; despondent

negligence – *n.* – carelessness

neutral – *adj.* – impartial; unbiased

nostalgic – *adj.* – longing for the past; filled with bittersweet
                memories

novel – *adj.* – new

Drill: Group 8

DIRECTIONS: Match each word in the left column with the word in the right column that is most **OPPOSITE** in meaning.

Word	Match
1. _____ irrational	A. extinguish
2. _____ kindle	B. jovial
3. _____ meticulous	C. selfish
4. _____ malicious	D. logical
5. _____ morose	E. seriousness
6. _____ magnanimous	F. ridicule
7. _____ levity	G. kindly
8. _____ minute	H. sloppy
9. _____ laud	I. huge
10. _____ novel	J. stale

DIRECTIONS: Match each word in the left column with the word in the right column that is most **SIMILAR** in meaning.

Word	Match
11. _____ ironic	a. lessen
12. _____ marred	b. damaged
13. _____ mitigate	c. sarcastic
14. _____ jeopardy	d. carelessness
15. _____ negligence	e. danger

Group 9

nullify – *v.* – cancel; invalidate

objective – 1. – *adj.* – open-minded; impartial;
    – 2. – *n.* – goal

obscure – *adj.* – not easily understood; dark

obsolete – *adj.* – out of date; passé

ominous – *adj.* – threatening

optimist – *n.* – person who hopes for the best; sees the good side

orthodox – *adj.* – traditional; accepted

pagan – 1. – *n.* – polytheist;
    – 2. – *adj.* – polytheistic

partisan – 1. – *n.* – supporter; follower;
    – 2. – *adj.* – biased; one-sided

perceptive – *adj.* – full of insight; aware

peripheral – *adj.* – marginal; outer

pernicious – *adj.* – dangerous; harmful

pessimism – *n.* – seeing only the gloomy side; hopelessness

phenomenon – 1. – *n.* – miracle;
    – 2. – *n.* – occurrence

philanthropy – *n.* – charity; unselfishness

pious – *adj.* – religious; devout; dedicated

placate – *v.* – pacify

plausible – *adj.* – probable; feasible

pragmatic – *adj.* – matter-of-fact; practical

preclude – *v.* – inhibit; make impossible

predecessor – *n.* – one who has come before another

prodigal – *adj.* – wasteful; lavish

prodigious – *adj.* – exceptional; tremendous

profound – *adj.* – deep; knowledgeable; thorough

profusion – *n.* – great amount; abundance

Drill: Group 9

DIRECTIONS: Match each word in the left column with the word in the right column that is most **OPPOSITE** in meaning.

Word	Match
1. _____ objective	A. scanty
2. _____ obsolete	B. assist
3. _____ placate	C. mundane
4. _____ profusion	D. biased
5. _____ peripheral	E. improbable
6. _____ plausible	F. minute
7. _____ preclude	G. anger
8. _____ prodigious	H. pessimism
9. _____ profound	I. modern
10. _____ optimism	J. central

DIRECTIONS: Match each word in the left column with the word in the right column that is most **SIMILAR** in meaning.

Word	Match
11. _____ nullify	a. invalidate
12. _____ ominous	b. follower
13. _____ partisan	c. lavish
14. _____ pernicious	d. threatening
15. _____ prodigal	e. harmful

Group 10

prosaic – *adj.* – tiresome; ordinary

provincial – *adj.* – regional; unsophisticated

provocative – 1. – *adj.* – tempting;
– 2. – *adj.* – irritating

prudent – *adj.* – wise; careful; prepared

qualified – *adj.* – experienced; indefinite

rectify – *v.* – correct

redundant – *adj.* – repetitious; unnecessary

refute – *v.* – challenge; disprove

relegate – *v.* – banish; put to a lower position

relevant – *adj.* – of concern; significant

remorse – *n.* – guilt; sorrow

reprehensible – *adj.* – wicked; disgraceful

repudiate – *v.* – reject; cancel

rescind – *v.* – retract; discard

resignation – 1. – *n.* – quitting;
– 2. – *n.* – submission

resolution – *n.* – proposal; promise; determination

respite – *n.* – recess; rest period

reticent – *adj.* – silent; reserved; shy

reverent – *adj.* – respectful

rhetorical – *adj.* – having to do with verbal communication

rigor – *n.* – severity

sagacious – *adj.* – wise; cunning

sanguine – 1. – *adj.* – optimistic; cheerful;
– 2. – *adj.* – red

saturate – *v.* – soak thoroughly; drench

scanty – *adj.* – inadequate; sparse

Drill: Group 10

Group 10

DIRECTIONS: Match each word in the left column with the word in the right column that is most OPPOSITE in meaning.

Word		Match
1. _____	provincial	A. inexperienced
2. _____	reticent	B. joy
3. _____	prudent	C. pessimistic
4. _____	qualified	D. unrelated
5. _____	relegate	E. careless
6. _____	remorse	F. affirm
7. _____	repudiate	G. extraordinary
8. _____	sanguine	H. sophisticated
9. _____	relevant	I. forward
10. _____	prosaic	J. promote

DIRECTIONS: Match each word in the left column with the word in the right column that is most SIMILAR in meaning.

Word		Match
11. _____	provocative	a. drench
12. _____	rigor	b. tempting
13. _____	saturate	c. retract
14. _____	rescind	d. severity
15. _____	reprehensible	e. disgraceful

Group 11

scrupulous – *adj.* – honorable; exact

scrutinize – *v.* – examine closely; study

servile – *adj.* – slavish; groveling

skeptic – *n.* – doubter

slander – *v.* – defame; maliciously misrepresent

solemnity – *n.* – seriousness

solicit – *v.* – ask; seek

stagnant – *adj.* – motionless; uncirculating

stanza – *n.* – group of lines in a poem having a definite pattern

static – *adj.* – inactive; changeless

stoic – *adj.* – detached; unruffled; calm

subtlety – 1. – *n.* – understatement;
– 2. – *n.* – propensity for understatement;
– 3. – *n.* – sophistication;
– 4. – *n.* – cunning

superficial – *adj.* – on the surface; narrowminded; lacking depth

superfluous – *adj.* – unnecessary; extra

surpass – *v.* – go beyond; outdo

sycophant – *adj.* – flatterer

symmetry – *n.* – correspondence of parts; harmony

taciturn – *adj.* – reserved; quiet; secretive

tedious – *adj.* – time-consuming; burdensome; uninteresting

temper – *v.* – soften; pacify; compose

tentative – *adj.* – not confirmed; indefinite

thrifty – *adj.* – economical; pennywise

tranquility – *n.* – peace; stillness; harmony

trepidation – *n.* – apprehension; uneasiness

trivial – *adj.* – unimportant; small; worthless

Drill: Group 11

DIRECTIONS: Match each word in the left column with the word in the right column that is most **OPPOSITE** in meaning.

Word	**Match**
1. _____ scrutinize	A. frivolity
2. _____ skeptic	B. enjoyable
3. _____ solemnity	C. prodigal
4. _____ static	D. chaos
5. _____ tedious	E. give
6. _____ tentative	F. skim
7. _____ thrifty	G. turbulent
8. _____ tranquility	H. active
9. _____ solicit	I. believer
10. _____ stagnant	J. confirmed

DIRECTIONS: Match each word in the left column with the word in the right column that is most **SIMILAR** in meaning.

Word	**Match**
11. _____ symmetry	a. understated
12. _____ superfluous	b. unnecessary
13. _____ sycophant	c. balance
14. _____ subtle	d. fear
15. _____ trepidation	e. flatterer

Group 12

tumid – *adj.* – swollen; inflated

undermine – *v.* – weaken; ruin

uniform – *adj.* – consistent; unvaried; unchanging

universal – *adj.* – concerning everyone; existing everywhere

unobtrusive – *adj.* – inconspicuous; reserved

unprecedented – *adj.* – unheard of; exceptional

unpretentious – *adj.* – simple; plain; modest

vacillation – *n.* – fluctuation

valid – *adj.* – acceptable; legal

vehement – *adj.* – intense; excited; enthusiastic

venerate – *v.* – revere

verbose – *adj.* – wordy; talkative

viable – 1. – *adj.* – capable of maintaining life;
– 2. – *adj.* – possible; attainable

vigor – *n.* – energy; forcefulness

vilify – *v* . – slander

virtuoso – *n.* – highly skilled artist

virulent – *adj.* – deadly; harmful; malicious

vital – *adj.* – important; spirited

volatile – *adj.* – changeable; undependable

vulnerable – *adj.* – open to attack; unprotected

wane – *v.* – grow gradually smaller

whimsical – *adj.* – fanciful; amusing

wither – *v.* – wilt; shrivel; humiliate; cut down

zealot – *n.* – believer; enthusiast; fan

zenith – *n.* – point directly overhead in the sky

Drill: Group 12

Word	Match
1. _____ uniform	A. amateur
2. _____ virtuoso	B. trivial
3. _____ vital	C. visible
4. _____ wane	D. placid
5. _____ unobtrusive	E. unacceptable
6. _____ vigor	F. support
7. _____ volatile	G. constancy
8. _____ vacillation	H. lethargy
9. _____ undermine	I. wax
10. _____ valid	J. varied

Word	Match
11. _____ wither	a. intense
12. _____ whimsical	b. deadly
13. _____ viable	c. amusing
14. _____ vehement	d. possible
15. _____ virulent	e. shrivel

Prefixes

Prefixes	Meaning	Examples
ab–, a–, abs–	away, without, from	**absent** – away, not present **apathy** – without interest **abstain** – keep from doing, refrain
ad–	to, toward	**adjacent** – next to **address** – to direct towards
ante–	before	**antecedent** – going before in time **anterior** – occurring before
anti–	against	**antidote** – remedy to act against an evil **antibiotic** – substance that fights against 　　　　bacteria
be–	over, thoroughly	**bemoan** – to mourn over **belabor** – to exert much labor upon
bi–	two	**bisect** – to divide **biennial** – happening every two years
cata–, cat–, cath–	down	**catacombs** – underground passageways **catalogue** – descriptive list **catheter** – tubular medical device
circum–	around	**circumscribe** – to draw a circle around **circumspect** – watchful on all sides
com–	with	**combine** – to join together **communication** – to have dealings with
contra–	against	**contrary** – opposed **contrast** – to stand in opposition
de–	down, from	**decline** – to bend downward **decontrol** – to release from government 　　　　control

Prefixes	Meaning	Examples
di–	two	**dichotomy** – cutting in two **diarchy** – system of government with two authorities
dis–, di–	apart, away	**discern** – to distinguish as separate **dismiss** – to send away **digress** – to turn aside
epi–, ep–, eph–	upon, among	**epidemic** – happening among many people **epicycle** – circle whose center moves round in the circumference of a greater circle **epaulet** – decoration worn to ornament or protect the shoulder **ephedra** – any of a large genus of desert shrubs
ex–, e–	from, out	**exceed** – go beyond the limit **emit** – to send forth
extra–	outside, beyond	**extraordinary** – beyond or out of the common method **extrasensory** – beyond the senses
hyper–	beyond, over	**hyperactive** – over the normal activity level **hypercritic** – one who is critical beyond measure
hypo–	beneath, lower	**hypodermic** – parts beneath the skin **hypocrisy** – to be under a pretense of goodness
in–, il–, im–, ir–	not	**inactive** – not active **illogical** – not logical **imperfect** – not perfect **irreversible** – not reversible
in–, il–, im–, ir–	in, on, into	**instill** – to put in slowly **illation** – action of bringing in **impose** – to lay on **irrupt** – to break in

Prefixes	**Meaning**	**Examples**
inter –	among, between	**intercom** – to exchange conversations between people **interlude** – performance given between parts in a play
intra –	within	**intravenous** – within a vein **intramural** – within the walls, as of a town or university
meta –	beyond, over, along with	**metamorphosis** – change over in form or nature **metatarsus** – part of foot beyond the flat of the foot
mis –	badly, wrongly	**misconstrue** – to interpret wrongly **misappropriate** – to use wrongly
mono –	one	**monogamy** – to be married to one person at a time **monotone** – a single, unvaried tone
multi –	many	**multiple** – of many parts **multitude** – a great number
non –	no, not	**nonsense** – lack of sense **nonentity** – not existing
ob –	against	**obscene** – offensive to modesty **obstruct** – to hinder the passage of
para –, par –	beside	**parallel** – continuously at equal distance apart **parenthesis** – sentence or phrase inserted within a passage
per –	through	**persevere** – to maintain an effort **permeate** – to pass through

Prefixes	Meaning	Examples
poly–	many	**polygon** – a plane figure with many sides or angles **polytheism** – belief in the existence of many gods
post–	after	**posterior** – coming after **postpone** – to put off until a future time
pre–	before	**premature** – ready before the proper time **premonition** – a previous warning
pro–	in favor of, forward	**prolific** – bringing forth offspring **project** – throw or cast forward
re–	back, against	**reimburse** – to pay back **retract** – to draw back
semi–	half	**semicircle** – half a circle **semiannual** – half-yearly
sub–	under	**subdue** – to bring under one's power **submarine** – to travel under the surface of the sea
super–	above	**supersonic** – above the speed of sound **superior** – higher in place or position
tele–, tel–	across	**telecast** – transmit across a distance **telepathy** – communication between mind and mind at a distance
trans–	across	**transpose** – to change the position of two things **transmit** – to send from one person to another
ultra–	beyond	**ultraviolet** – beyond the limit of visibility **ultramarine** – beyond the sea

Prefixes	Meaning	Examples
un–	not	**undeclared** – not declared **unbelievable** – not believable
uni–	one	**unity** – state of oneness **unison** – sounding together
with–	away, against	**withhold** – to hold back **withdraw** – to take away

Drill: Prefixes

DIRECTIONS: Provide a definition for each prefix.

1. pro– _____
2. com– _____
3. epi– _____
4. ob– _____
5. ad– _____

DIRECTIONS: Identify the prefix in each word.

6. efface _____
7. hypothetical _____
8. permeate _____
9. contrast _____
10. inevitable _____

Roots

Root	Meaning	Examples
act, ag	do, act, drive	**activate** – to make active **agile** – having quick motion
alt	high	**altitude** – height **alto** – highest male singing voice
alter, altr	other, change	**alternative** – choice between two things **altruism** – living for the good of others
am, ami	love, friend	**amiable** – worthy of affection **amity** – friendship
anim	mind, spirit	**animated** – spirited **animosity** – violent hatred
annu, enni	year	**annual** – every year **centennial** – every hundred years
aqua	water	**aquarium** – tank for water animals and plants **aquamarine** – semiprecious stone of sea-green color
arch	first, ruler	**archenemy** – chief enemy **archetype** – original pattern from which things are copied
aud, audit	hear	**audible** – capable of being heard **audience** – assembly of hearers **audition** – the power or act of hearing
auto	self	**automatic** – self-acting **autobiography** –the story of a person's life written or told by that person
bell	war	**belligerent** – a party taking part in a war **bellicose** – war-like

Root	Meaning	Examples
ben, bene	good	**benign** – kindly disposition **beneficial** – advantageous
bio	life	**biotic** – relating to life **biology** – the science of life
brev	short	**abbreviate** – make shorter **brevity** – shortness
cad, cas	fall	**cadence** – fall in voice **casualty** – loss caused by death
cap, capit	head	**captain** – the head or chief **decapitate** – to cut off the head
cede, ceed, cess	to go, to yield	**recede** – to move or fall back **proceed** – to move onward **recessive** – tending to go back
cent	hundred	**century** – hundred years **centipede** – insect with a hundred legs
chron	time	**chronology** – science dealing with historical dates **chronicle** – register of events in order of time
cide, cis	to kill, to cut	**homicide** – the act of killing **incision** – a cut
claim, clam	to shout	**acclaim** – receive with applause **proclamation** – announce publicly
cogn	to know	**recognize** – to know again **cognition** – awareness
corp	body	**incorporate** – combine into one body **corpse** – dead body

Root	Meaning	Examples
cred	to trust, to believe	**incredible** – unbelievable **credulous** – too prone to believe
cur, curr, curs	to run	**current** – flowing body of air or water **excursion** – short trip
dem	people	**democracy** – government formed for the people **epidemic** – affecting all people
dic, dict	to say	**dictate** – to read aloud for another to transcribe **verdict** – decision of a jury
doc, doct	to teach	**docile** – easily instructed **indoctrinate** – to instruct
domin	to rule	**dominate** – to rule **dominion** – territory of rule
duc, duct	to lead	**conduct** – act of guiding **induce** – to overcome by persuasion
eu	well, good	**eulogy** – speech or writing in praise **euphony** – pleasantness or smoothness of sound
fac, fact, fect, fic	to do, to make	**facilitate** – to make easier **factory** – location of production **confect** – to put together **fiction** – something invented or imagined
fer	to bear, to carry	**transfer** – to move from one place to another **refer** – to direct to
fin	end, limit	**infinity** – unlimited **finite** – limited in quantity

Root	Meaning	Examples
flex, flect	to bend	**flexible** – easily bent **reflect** – to throw back
fort	luck	**fortunate** – lucky **fortuitous** – happening by chance
fort	strong	**fortify** – strengthen **fortress** – stronghold
frag, fract	break	**fragile** – easily broken **fracture** – break
fug	flee	**fugitive** – fleeing **refugee** – one who flees to a place of safety
gen	class, race	**engender** – to breed **generic** – of a general nature in regard to all members
grad, gress	to go, to step	**regress** – to go back **graduate** – to divide into regular steps
graph	writing	**telegraph** – message sent by telegraph **autograph** – person's own handwriting or signature
ject	to throw	**projectile** – capable of being thrown **reject** – to throw away
leg	law	**legitimate** – lawful **legal** – defined by law
leg, lig, lect	to choose, gather, read	**illegible** – incapable of being read **ligature** – something that binds **election** – the act of choosing
liber	free	**liberal** – favoring freedom of ideals **liberty** – freedom from restraint

Root	Meaning	Examples
log	study, speech	**archaeology** – study of human antiquities **prologue** – address spoken before a performance
luc, lum	light	**translucent** – slightly transparent **illuminate** – to light up
magn	large, great	**magnify** – to make larger **magnificent** – great
mal, male	bad, wrong	**malfunction** – to operate incorrectly **malevolent** – evil
mar	sea	**marine** – pertaining to the sea **submarine** – below the surface of the sea
mater, matr	mother	**maternal** – motherly **matriarch** – government exercised by a mother
mit, miss	to send	**transmit** – to send from one person or place to another **mission** – the act of sending
morph	shape	**metamorphosis** – a changing in shape **anthropomorphic** – having a human shape
mut	change	**mutable** – subject to change **mutate** – to change or alter
nat	born	**innate** – inborn **native** – a person born in a place
neg	deny	**negative** – expressing denial **renege** – to deny
nom	name	**nominate** – to put forward a name **nomenclature** – process of naming

Root	Meaning	Examples
nov	new	**novel** – new **renovate** – to make as good as new
omni	all	**omnipotent** – all powerful **omnipresent** – all present
oper	to work	**operate** – to work on something **cooperate** – to work with others
pass, path	to feel	**passionate** – moved by strong emotion **pathetic** – affecting the tender emotions
pater, patr	father	**paternal** – fatherly **patriarch** – government exercised by a father
ped, pod	foot	**pedestrian** – one who travels on foot **podiatrist** – foot doctor
pel, puls	to drive, to push	**impel** – to drive forward **compulsion** – irresistible force
phil	love	**philharmonic** – loving harmony or music **philanthropist** – one who loves and seeks to do good for others
port	carry	**export** – to carry out of the country **portable** – able to be carried
psych	mind	**psychology** – study of the mind **psychiatrist** – specialist in mental disorders
quer, ques, quir, quis	to ask	**querist** – one who inquires **question** – that which is asked **inquiry** – to ask about **inquisitive** – inclined to ask questions
rid, ris	to laugh	**ridiculous** – laughable **derision** – to mock

Root	Meaning	Examples
rupt	to break	**interrupt** – to break in upon **erupt** – to break through
sci	to know	**science** – systematic knowledge of physical or natural phenomena **conscious** – having inward knowledge
scrib, script	to write	**transcribe** – to write over again **script** – text of words
sent, sens	to feel, to think	**sentimental** – feel great emotion **sensitive** – easily affected by changes
sequ, secut	to follow	**sequence** – connected series **consecutive** – following one another in unbroken order
solv, solu, solut	to loosen	**dissolve** – to break up **absolute** – without restraint
spect	to look at	**spectator** – one who watches **inspect** – to look at closely
spir	to breathe	**inspire** – to breathe in **respiration** – process of breathing
string, strict	to bind	**stringent** – binding strongly **restrict** – to restrain within bounds
stru, struct	to build	**strut** – a structural piece designed to resist pressure **construct** – to build
tang, ting, tact, tig	to touch	**tangent** – touching, but not intersecting **contact** – touching **contiguous** – to touch along a boundary
ten, tent, tain	to hold	**tenure** – holding of office **contain** – to hold

Root	Meaning	Examples
term	to end	**terminate** – to end **terminal** – having an end
terr	earth	**terrain** – tract of land **terrestrial** – existing on earth
therm	heat	**thermal** – pertaining to heat **thermometer** – instrument for measuring temperature
tort, tors	to twist	**contortionist** – one who twists violently **torsion** – act of turning or twisting
tract	to pull, to draw	**attract** – draw toward **distract** – to draw away
vac	empty	**vacant** – empty **evacuate** – to empty out
ven, vent	to come	**intervene** – to come between **prevent** – to stop from coming
ver	true	**verify** – to prove to be true **veracious** – truthful
verb	word	**verbose** – use of excess words **verbatim** – word for word
vid, vis	to see	**video** – picture phase of television **vision** – act of seeing external objects
vinc, vict, vang	to conquer	**invincible** – unconquerable **victory** – defeat of enemy **vanguard** – troops moving at the head of an army
vit, viv	life	**vital** – necessary to life **vivacious** – lively

Root	Meaning	Examples
voc	to call	**vocation** – a summons to a course of action **vocal** – uttered by voice
vol	to wish, to will	**involuntary** – outside the control of will **volition** – the act of willing or choosing

Drill: Roots

DIRECTIONS: Provide a definition for each root.

1. cede   _____
2. fact   _____
3. path   _____
4. ject   _____
5. ver   _____

DIRECTIONS: Identify the root in each word.

6. acclaim   _____
7. verbatim   _____
8. benefactor   _____
9. relegate   _____
10. tension   _____

Suffixes

Suffixes	Meaning	Examples
–able, –ble	capable of	**believable** – capable of believing **legible** – capable of being read
–acious, –icious, –ous	full of	**vivacious** – full of life **delicious** – full of pleasurable smell or taste **wondrous** – full of wonder
–ant, –ent	full of	**expectant** – full of expectation **eloquent** – full of eloquence
–ary	connected with	**disciplinary** – relating to a field of study **honorary** – for the sake of honor
–ate	to make	**ventilate** – to make public **consecrate** – to dedicate
–fy	to make	**magnify** – to make larger **testify** – to make witness
–ile	pertaining to, capable of	**docile** – capable of being managed easily **infantile** – pertaining to infancy
–ism	belief, ideal	**conservationism** – ideal of keeping safe **sensationalism** – matter, language designed to excite
–ist	doer	**artist** – one who creates art **pianist** – one who plays the piano
–ose	full of	**verbose** – full of words **grandiose** – striking, imposing
–osis	condition	**neurosis** – nervous condition **psychosis** – psychological condition
–tude	state	**magnitude** – state of greatness **multitude** – state of quantity

Drill: Suffixes

DIRECTIONS: Provide a definition for each suffix.

1. –ant, –ent _____

2. –tude _____

3. –ile _____

4. –fy _____

5. –ary _____

DIRECTIONS: Identify the suffix in each word.

6. audacious _____

7. expedient _____

8. gullible _____

9. grandiose _____

10. antagonism _____

VERBAL DRILLS ANSWER KEY

Drill: Group 1	Drill: Group 2	Drill: Group 3	Drill: Group 4
1. (J)	1. (D)	1. (E)	1. (D)
2. (G)	2. (G)	2. (H)	2. (E)
3. (A)	3. (I)	3. (J)	3. (A)
4. (C)	4. (F)	4. (A)	4. (I)
5. (H)	5. (A)	5. (I)	5. (J)
6. (B)	6. (J)	6. (B)	6. (B)
7. (I)	7. (E)	7. (C)	7. (C)
8. (D)	8. (C)	8. (G)	8. (F)
9. (F)	9. (B)	9. (F)	9. (H)
10. (E)	10. (H)	10. (D)	10. (G)
11. (d)	11. (d)	11. (c)	11. (d)
12. (c)	12. (a)	12. (a)	12. (a)
13. (a)	13. (b)	13. (e)	13. (b)
14. (e)	14. (e)	14. (d)	14. (c)
15. (b)	15. (c)	15. (b)	15. (e)

Drill: Group 5	Drill: Group 6	Drill: Group 7	Drill: Group 8
1. (H)	1. (G)	1. (F)	1. (D)
2. (F)	2. (A)	2. (E)	2. (A)
3. (A)	3. (E)	3. (A)	3. (H)
4. (B)	4. (J)	4. (B)	4. (G)
5. (J)	5. (C)	5. (H)	5. (B)
6. (C)	6. (B)	6. (I)	6. (C)
7. (I)	7. (D)	7. (C)	7. (E)
8. (E)	8. (I)	8. (G)	8. (I)
9. (D)	9. (F)	9. (D)	9. (F)
10. (G)	10. (H)	10. (J)	10. (J)
11. (b)	11. (d)	11. (b)	11. (c)
12. (d)	12. (e)	12. (e)	12. (b)
13. (a)	13. (a)	13. (d)	13. (a)
14. (e)	14. (c)	14. (c)	14. (e)
15. (c)	15. (b)	15. (a)	15. (d)

Drill: Group 9	Drill: Group 10	Drill: Group 11	Drill: Group 12
1. (D)	1. (H)	1. (F)	1. (J)
2. (I)	2. (I)	2. (I)	2. (A)
3. (G)	3. (E)	3. (A)	3. (B)
4. (A)	4. (A)	4. (H)	4. (I)
5. (J)	5. (J)	5. (B)	5. (C)
6. (E)	6. (B)	6. (J)	6. (H)
7. (B)	7. (F)	7. (C)	7. (D)
8. (F)	8. (C)	8. (D)	8. (G)
9. (C)	9. (D)	9. (E)	9. (F)
10. (H)	10. (G)	10. (G)	10. (E)
11. (a)	11. (b)	11. (c)	11. (e)
12. (d)	12. (d)	12. (b)	12. (c)
13. (b)	13. (a)	13. (e)	13. (d)
14. (e)	14. (c)	14. (a)	14. (a)
15. (c)	15. (e)	15. (d)	15. (b)

Drill: Prefixes	Drill: Roots	Drill: Suffixes
1. forward	1. to go, to yield	1. full of
2. with	2. to do, to make	2. state
3. upon, among	3. to feel	3. pertaining to, capable of
4. against	4. to throw	4. to make
5. to, toward	5. true	5. connected with
6. e–	6. claim	6. –acious
7. hypo–	7. verb	7. –ent
8. per–	8. ben(e)	8. –ible
9. contra–	9. leg	9. –ose
10. in–	10. ten	10. –ism

Chapter 5

Attacking Sentence Completion Questions

Bust it!

Regardless of what part of the SAT Verbal Test you are working on, all the problem-solving techniques you'll use can be divided into two main categories: skills and strategies. Using these skills and strategies, in addition to the important strategies to bust the SAT that you learned in the beginning of this book, will enable you to successfully attack the Sentence Completion questions and attain a higher score on your SAT Verbal Test.

In this chapter, we will present the skills and strategies that will help you successfully answer Sentence Completion questions. These skills and strategies include:

Bust it!

- **Learning the two types of Sentence Completion questions**

- **Learning the skill of recognizing context clues**

- **Knowing the strategy of using the levels of difficulty in the Sentence Completion sections**

- **Learning the skill of applying deductive reasoning**

- **Learning the strategy involved in using the logical structure of Sentence Completion questions**

Your success on the SAT Verbal Test begins with one fundamental insight: these questions have been written and designed to test your vocabulary. See Chapter 4 on building your vocabulary for the SAT. No matter what section you are working in, you will be expected to demonstrate that you have a good command of vocabulary words. Because of this, you should devote as much time as possible to strengthening your vocabulary, especially by studying the prefixes and roots of Greek- and Latin-derived words.

Now let's get started....

About the Directions

The directions for Sentence Completion questions are relatively straightforward.

<u>DIRECTIONS</u>: Each sentence below has one or two blanks, each blank indicating that something has been omitted. Beneath the sentence are five lettered words or sets of words. Choose the word or set of words that BEST fits the meaning of the sentence as a whole.

Example:

Although the critics found the book _____, many of the readers found it rather _____.

(A) obnoxious . . . perfect
(B) spectacular . . . interesting
(C) boring . . . intriguing
(D) comical . . . persuasive
(E) popular . . . rare

About the Questions

You will encounter two main types of questions in the Sentence Completion section of the SAT. In addition, the questions will appear in varying difficulties which we will call Level I **(easy)**, Level II **(average)**, and Level III **(difficult)**. The following explains the structure of the questions.

Important Information!

Question Type 1: ONE-WORD COMPLETIONS

One-Word Completions will require you to fill in one blank. The one-word completion can appear as a Level I (easy), II (average), or III (difficult) question depending on the difficulty of the vocabulary included.

Question Type 2: TWO-WORD COMPLETIONS

Two-Word Completions will require you to fill in two blanks. As with the one-word completion, this type may be a Level I, II, or III question. **This will depend not only on the difficulty of the vocabulary, but also on the relationship between the words and between the words and the sentence.**

The remainder of this review will provide explicit details on what you will encounter when dealing with Sentence Completion questions, in addition to strategies for correctly completing these sentences.

Important Information!

Points to Remember

Important Strategy

✔   Like other verbal sections of the test, Sentence Completions can be divided into three basic levels of difficulty, and, as a general rule, SAT verbal exercises increase in difficulty as they progress through a section.

✔   Level I exercises allow you to rely on your instincts and common sense. You should not be obsessed with analysis or second-guessing in Level I problems.

✔   In Level II questions, the SAT often presents words that appear easy at first glance but that may have secondary meanings. Be wary of blindly following your gut reactions and common sense.

✔   Most SAT verbal questions contain **"magnet words,"** answer choices that look good but are designed to draw the student away from the correct answer. Magnet words can effectively mislead you in Level III questions. Always watch for them. Remember that Level III questions are intentionally designed to work against your common sense and natural inclinations.

✔   Deductive reasoning is a tool that will be of constant assistance to you as you work through SAT verbal questions. To deduce means to derive a truth (or answer) through a reasoning process.

On Target!

✔   Sentence Completion questions are puzzles, and they are put together with a certain amount of predictability. One such predictable characteristic is the structure of an SAT word exercise. Since there are always five possible answers from which to choose, you must learn to see which answers are easy to eliminate first. Use the process of elimination.

✔   Most SAT verbal questions are designed around a "three-two" structure. This means that there are three easier answers to eliminate before you have to make the final decision between the remaining two.

✔   Use word roots, prefixes, and suffixes to find the meanings of words you do not know.

Answering Sentence Completion Questions

Follow these steps as you attempt to answer each question.

STEP 1 Identifying context clues is one of the most successful ways for you to locate correct answers in Sentence Completions. Practicing constantly in this area will help you strengthen one of your main strategies in this type of verbal problem.

Bust it!

The Sentence Completion question below is an example of a **Level I** (easy) question.

Pamela played her championship chess game _____ , avoiding all traps and making no mistakes.

(A)   hurriedly   (D)   imaginatively

(B)   flawlessly   (E)   aggressively

(C)   prodigally

The **phrase** "avoiding all traps and making no mistakes" is your **context clue**. Notice that the phrase both follows *and* modifies the word in question. Since you know that Sentence Completions are exercises seeking to test your vocabulary knowledge, attack these problems accordingly. For example, ask yourself what word means "avoiding all traps and making no mistakes." In so doing, you discover the answer "flawlessly" (B), which means perfectly or without mistakes. If Pamela played "hurriedly" (A), she might well make mistakes. Difficult words are seldom the answer in easier questions; therefore, "prodigally" (C) stands out as a suspicious word. This could be a magnet word. However, before you eliminate it, ask yourself whether you know its meaning. If so, does it surpass "flawlessly" (B) in defining the context clue, "making no mistakes"? It does not. "Imaginatively" (D) is a tempting answer, since one might associate a perfect game of chess as one played imaginatively; however, there is no connection between the imagination and the absence of mistakes. "Aggressively" (E) playing a game may, in fact, cause you to make mistakes.

Here is an example of a **Level II** (average) Sentence Completion. Try to determine the context clue.

> **Although most people believe the boomerang is the product of a _____ design, that belief is deceptive; in fact, the boomerang is a _____ example of the laws of aerodynamics.**
>
> **(A)   foreign . . . modern**
> **(B)   symbolic . . . complex**
> **(C)   practical . . . scientific**
> **(D)   primitive . . . sophisticated**
> **(E)   faulty . . . invalid**

Bust it!

The most important **context clue** in this sentence is the opening word "although," which indicates that some kind of antonym relationship is present in the sentence. It tells us there is a reversal in meaning. Therefore, be on the lookout for words which will form an opposite relationship. The phrase "that belief is deceptive" makes certain the idea that there will be an opposite meaning between the missing words. "Primitive . . . sophisticated" (D) is the best answer, since the two are exact opposites. "Primitive" means crude and elementary, whereas "sophisticated" means refined and advanced. "Foreign . . . modern" (A) and "symbolic . . . complex" (B) have no real opposite relationship. Also, "complex" is a magnet word that sounds right in the context of scientific laws, but "symbolic" is not its counterpart. "Practical . . . scientific" (C) and "faulty . . . invalid" (E) are rejectable because they are generally synonymous pairs.

The following is an example of a **Level III** question:

The weekly program on public radio is the most _____ means of educating the public about pollution.

(A) proficient   (D) capable
(B) effusive   (E) competent
(C) effectual

Bust it!

The **context clue** in this sentence is "means of educating the public about pollution." "Effectual" (C) is the correct answer. "Effectual" means having the power to produce the exact effect or result. "Proficient" (A) is not correct as it implies competency above the average—radio programs are not described in this manner. "Effusive" (B) does not fit the sense of the sentence. Both "capable" (D) and "competent" (E) are incorrect because they refer to people, not things.

STEP 2 | Since the verbal SAT is fundamentally a vocabulary test, it must resort to principles and techniques necessary for testing your vocabulary. Therefore, certain dynamics like antonyms (word opposites) and synonyms (word similarities) become very useful in setting up a question or word problem.

This idea can be taken one step further:

Another type of technique that utilizes the tension of opposites and the concurrence of similarities is *word values*. Word values begin with the recognition that most pivotal words in a SAT Sentence Completion can be assigned a positive or negative value. Marking a "+" or "–" next to choices may help you eliminate inappropriate choices. In turn, you will be able to more quickly identify possible correct answers.

Dealing with Positive Value Words

Positive value words are usually easy to recognize. They usually convey a meaning which can be equated with gain, advantage, liveliness, intelligence, virtue, positive emotions, conditions, or actions.

Look!

Important Strategy

The ability to recognize positive and negative word values, however, will not bring you very far if you do not understand how to apply it to your advantage in Sentence Completions. Below you will find examples of how to do this, first with a study of positive value Sentence Completions, then with a study of negative value Sentence Completions.

The following is an example of a **Level I** (easy) question:

An expert skateboarder, Tom is truly _____ ; he smoothly blends timing with balance.

(A) coordinated   (D) supportive
(B) erudite   (E) casual
(C) a novice

As you know, the context clue is the clause after the word in question, which acts as a modifier. Naturally, anyone who "smoothly blends" is creating a *positive* situation. Look for the positive answer.

An expert skateboarder, Tom is truly _+_ ; *he smoothly blends timing with balance.*

+(A)   coordinated   +(D)   supportive

+(B)   erudite   −(E)   casual

−(C)   a novice

Bust it!

"Coordinated" (A), a positive value word that means ordering two or more things, fits the sentence perfectly. "Erudite" (B) is positive, but it is too difficult to be a Level I answer. A "novice" (C) in this context is negative. "Supportive" (D) and "casual" (E) don't fulfill the definition of the context clue, and "casual" is negative, implying a lack of attention. Notice that eliminating negatives *immediately reduces the number of options from which you have to choose.* This raises the odds of selecting the correct answer. (One of the analytic skills you should develop for the SAT is being able to see the hidden vocabulary question in any exercise.)

A **Level II** (average) question may appear as follows:

Despite their supposedly primitive lifestyle, Australian aborigines developed the boomerang, a _____ and _____ hunting tool that maximizes gain with minimum effort.

(A)   ponderous . . . expensive

(B)   clean . . . dynamic

(C)   dangerous . . . formidable

(D)   sophisticated . . . efficient

(E)   useful . . . attractive

In this case, the context clues begin and end the sentence (in italics below).

Despite their supposedly primitive lifestyle, Australian aborigines developed the boomerang, a   +   and   +   hunting *tool that maximizes gain with minimum effort.*

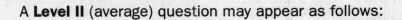

- (A) ponderous . . . expensive
+ (B) clean . . . dynamic
- (C) dangerous . . . formidable
+ (D) sophisticated . . . efficient
+ (E) useful . . . attractive

The first context clue (*despite*) helps you determine that this exercise entails an antonym relationship with the word "primitive", which means simple or crude. The second context clue offers a definition of the missing words. Since the meaning of primitive in this context is a negative word value, you can be fairly confident that the answer will be a pair of positive word values. "Sophisticated . . . efficient" (D) is positive *and* it satisfies the definition of the latter context clue. This is the best answer. "Ponderous . . . expensive" (A) is not correct. "Clean . . . dynamic" (B) is positive, but does not meet the definition of the latter context clue. "Dangerous . . . formidable" (C) is negative. "Useful . . . attractive" (E) is positive, but it does not work with the latter context clue.

Bust it!

Here is a **Level III** (difficult) example.

When a physician describes an illness to a colleague, he must speak an _____ language, using professional terms and concepts understood mostly by members of his profession.

(A) extrinsic
(B) inordinate
(C) ambulatory
(D) esoteric
(E) abbreviated

Looking at this question, we can see an important context clue. This appears in italics below.

When a physician describes an illness to a colleague, he must speak an __+__ language, *using professional terms and concepts understood mostly by members of his profession.*

+ (A) extrinsic   + (D) esoteric
− (B) inordinate   − (E) abbreviated
+ (C) ambulatory

Bust it!

This clue gives us a definition of the missing word. Begin by eliminating the two obvious negatives, "inordinate" (B) and "abbreviated" (E). This leaves us with three positives. Since this is a Level III exercise, at first you may be intimidated by the level of vocabulary. Note that "esoteric" (D) is the best answer, since it is an adjective that means *inside* or *part of a group.* "Ambulatory" (C) is positive, but it is a trap. It seems like an easy association with the world of medicine. In Level III there are *no* easy word associations. "Extrinsic" (A) is positive, but it means *outside of,* which would not satisfy the logic of the sentence.

Dealing with Negative Value Words

Here are examples of how to work with negative value Sentence Completion problems. The first example is **Level I** (easy).

Important Strategy

Although Steve loves to socialize, his fellow students find him _____ and strive to _____ his company.

(A)   generous . . . enjoy
(B)   boring . . . evade
(C)   altruistic . . . accept
(D)   sinister . . . delay
(E)   weak . . . limit

The context clue (in italics) tells us that a reversal is being set up between what Steve thinks and what his fellow students think.

Although Steve loves to socialize, his fellow students find him __⁻__ and strive to __⁻__ his company.

+ **(A)** generous . . . enjoy
− **(B)** boring . . . evade
+ **(C)** altruistic . . . accept
− **(D)** sinister . . . delay
− **(E)** weak . . . limit

Bust it!

"Boring . . . evade" (B) is the best answer. The words appearing in Level 1 questions are not overly difficult, and they satisfy the logic of the sentence. "Generous . . . enjoy" (A) is positive. "Altruistic . . . accept" (C) is not only positive but contains a very difficult word (altruistic), and it would be unlikely that this would be a Level I answer. The same is true of "sinister . . . delay" (D), even though it is negative. "Weak . . . limit" (E) does not make sense in the context of the sentence.

This next example is **Level II** (average).

Because they reject _____ , conscientious objectors are given jobs in community work as a substitute for participation in the armed services.

(A) labor   **(D)** dictatorships
(B) belligerence   **(E)** poverty
(C) peace

Essentially, this example is a synonym exercise. The description of conscientious objectors (in italics on the next page) acts as a strong context clue. Conscientious objectors avoid ("reject") militancy.

Because they reject ___–___ , conscientious objectors *are given jobs in community work as a substitute for participation in the armed services.*

+ (A) labor   –(D) dictatorships
– (B) belligerence   –(E) poverty
+ (C) peace

Bust it!

Since we are looking for a negative word value (something to do with militancy), "labor" (A) is incorrect since it is positive. "Belligerence" (B) fits perfectly, as this is a negative value word having to do with war. Not only is "peace" (C) a positive value word, it is hardly something to be rejected by conscientious objectors. "Dictatorships" (D), although a negative word value, has no logical place in the context of this sentence. The same is true of "poverty" (E).

Here is a **Level III** (difficult) example:

Dictators understand well how to centralize power, and that is why they combine a(n) _____ political process with military _____.

(A)   foreign . . . victory
(B)   electoral . . . escalation
(C)   agrarian . . . strategies
(D)   domestic . . . decreases
(E)   totalitarian . . . coercion

"Totalitarian . . . coercion" (E) is the best answer. These are difficult words, and both have to do with techniques useful in the centralizing of power by a dictator. "Totalitarian" means centralized, and "coercion" means force.

Dictators understand well how to *centralize power,* and that is why they combine a(n) ___⁻___ political process with military ___⁻___.

Bust it!

+ (A)   foreign . . . victory
+ (B)   electoral . . . escalation
+ (C)   agrarian . . . strategies
+ (D)   domestic . . . decreases
− (E)   totalitarian . . . coercion

"Foreign . . . victory" (A) are not only easy words, they do not appear to be strictly negative. Remember that easy word answers should be suspect in Level III questions. "Agrarian . . . strategies" (C) is positive. "Domestic . . . decreases" (D) is a positive combination. Since you are searching for two negatives, this answer is incorrect. There will be more about this in the next section.

Dealing with Mixed Value Words

In examples with two-word answers so far, you have searched for answers composed with identical word values, such as negative/negative and positive/positive. However, every SAT Sentence Completion section will have exercises in which two-word answers are found in combinations. Below you will find examples of how to work with these. Here is a **Level I** (easy) example:

Despite a healthy and growing environmental _____ in America, there are many people who prefer to remain _____ .

(A)   awareness . . . ignorant
(B)   movement . . . enlightened
(C)   bankruptcy . . . wealthy
(D)   crisis . . . unencumbered
(E)   industry . . . satisfied

The context clue *despite* sets up the predictable antonym warning. In this case, the sentence seems to call for a positive and then a negative value word answer.

Despite a healthy and growing environmental 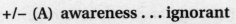 __+__ in America, there are many people who prefer to remain __−__ .

+/− (A)   awareness . . . ignorant
+/+ (B)   movement . . . enlightened
−/+ (C)   bankruptcy . . . wealthy
−/+ (D)   crisis . . . unencumbered
+/+ (E)   industry . . . satisfied

Bust it!

"Awareness . . . ignorant" (A) is the best answer. These are logical antonyms, and they fit the meaning of the sentence. Notice that the order of the missing words is positive, *then* negative. This should help you eliminate (C) and (D) immediately, as they are a reversal of the correct order. Furthermore, "industry . . . satisfied" (E) and "movement . . . enlightened" (B) are both identical values, and so are eliminated. Practice these techniques until you confidently can recognize word values *and* the order in which they appear in a sentence.

Here is a **Level II** (average) example:

Prone to creating characters of _____ quality, novelist Ed Abbey cannot be accused of writing _____ stories.

(A)   measly . . . drab
(B)   romantic . . . imaginative
(C)   mythic . . . mundane
(D)   sinister . . . complete
(E)   two-dimensional . . . flat

The best answer is "mythic . . . mundane" (C). "Measly . . . drab" (A) does not make sense when you consider the context clue *cannot*, which suggests the possibility of antonyms. The same is true for "sinister . . . complete" (D), "romantic . . . imaginative" (B), and "two-dimensional . . . flat" (E).

Prone to creating characters of __+__ quality, novelist Ed Abbey *cannot* be accused of writing __−__ stories.

–/– (A) measly . . . drab
+/+ (B) romantic . . . imaginative
+/– (C) mythic . . . mundane
–/+ (D) sinister . . . complete
–/– (E) two-dimensional . . . flat

Bust it!

Notice that the value combinations help you determine where to search for the correct answer. You can easily eliminate three of the five answer choices and have to make your choice from only two.

Here is a **Level III** (difficult) example:

Reminding his students that planning ahead would protect them from _____, Mr. McKenna proved to be a principal who understood the virtues of _____.

(A)   exigency . . . foresight
(B)   grades . . . examinations
(C)   poverty . . . promotion

    (D)   deprivation ... abstinence
    (E)   turbulence ... amelioration

The best answer is "exigency ... foresight" (A). The first context clue tells us that we are looking for a negative value word. The second context clue tells us the missing word is most likely positive. Furthermore, "exigency ... foresight" is a well-suited antonym combination. "Exigencies" are emergencies, and "foresight" helps to lessen their severity, if not their occurrence.

Bust it!

Reminding his students that planning ahead would *protect them* from 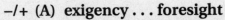**, Mr. McKenna proved to be a principal who understood the *virtues* of** **+** **.**

–/+ (A) exigency ... foresight
0/0 (B) grades ... examinations
–/+ (C) poverty ... promotion
–/– (D) deprivation ... abstinence
–/+ (E) turbulence ... amelioration

"Grades ... examinations" (B) are a trap, since they imply school matters. Furthermore, they are neutrals. There will be more on neutrals in the next section. "Poverty ... promotion" (C) is an easy word answer and should be immediately suspect, especially if there are no difficult words in the sentence completion itself. Also, this answer does not satisfy the logic of the sentence. "Turbulence ... amelioration" (E) is a negative/positive combination, but it does not make sense in this sentence. Even if you are forced to guess between this answer and "exigency ... foresight" (A), you have narrowed the field to two. These are excellent odds for success.

Dealing with Neutral Value Words

There is another category of word values that will help you determine the correct answer in a Sentence Completion problem. These are **neutral word values**. Neutral words are words that convey neither loss nor gain, advantage nor disadvantage, etc. Consider our previous example:

Important Strategy

> Reminding his students that planning ahead would *protect them* from ___−___ , Mr. McKenna proved to be a principal who understood the *virtues* of ___+___ .
>
> −/+ (A) **exigency . . . foresight**
> 0/0 (B) **grades . . . examinations**
> −/+ (C) **poverty . . . promotion**
> −/− (D) **deprivation . . . abstinence**
> −/+ (E) **turbulence . . . amelioration**

Bust it!

Notice that "grades . . . examinations" (B) is rated as neutral. In fact, in this case, both words are considered of neutral value. This is because neither word conveys a usable value. Grades in and of themselves are not valued until a number is assigned. Examinations are not significant until a passing or failing value is implied or applied.

Neutral word values are significant because they are *never* the correct answer. Therefore, when you identify a neutral word or combination of words, you may eliminate that choice from your selection. **You may eliminate a double-word answer even if only one of the words is obviously neutral.**

Neutral words are rare, and you should be careful to measure their value before you make a choice. Here is another example from an exercise seen previously (Note: The answer choices have been altered.):

Bust it!

Dictators understand well how *to centralize power,* and that is why they combine a(n) _‾_ political process with military _‾_.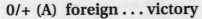

0/+ (A) foreign . . . victory
0/+ (B) electoral . . . escalation
0/+ (C) agrarian . . . strategies
0/0 (D) current . . . jobs
–/– (E) totalitarian . . . coercion

Here, "current . . . jobs" (D) is an obvious neutral word combination, conveying no positive or negative values. You may eliminate this choice immediately. There is no fixed list of words that may be considered neutral. Rather, you should determine *from the context* of a word problem whether you believe a word or word combination is of a neutral value. This ability will come with practice and a larger vocabulary. As before, the correct answer remains "totalitarian . . . coercion" (E).

STEP 3 | Another way to determine the correct answer is by using etymology. Etymology is the study of the anatomy of words. The most important components of etymology on the SAT are prefixes and roots. SAT vocabulary is derived almost exclusively from the etymology of Greek and Latin word origins, and that is where you should concentrate your study.

In this section, you will learn how to apply your knowledge of prefixes and roots to Sentence Completion problems.

Etymological skills will work well in conjunction with other techniques you have learned, including positive/negative word values. Furthermore, the technique of "scrolling" will help you understand how to expand your knowledge of etymology.

Scrolling is a process whereby you "scroll" through a list of known related words, roots, or prefixes to help you discover the meaning of a word. As an example, consider the common SAT word "apathy." The prefix of apathy is *a*. This means "without." To scroll this prefix, think of any other words that may begin with this prefix, such as *a*moral, *a*typical, or *a*symmetrical. In each case, the meaning of the word is preceded by the meaning "without."

Important Information!

At this point, you know that "apathy" means without something. Now try to scroll the root, *path*, which comes from the Greek word "pathos." Words like pathetic, sympathy, antipathy, and empathy may come to mind. These words all have to do with feeling or sensing. In fact, that is what "pathos" means: feeling. So apathy means without feeling.

With this process you can often determine the fundamental meaning of a word or part of a word, and this may give you enough evidence with which to choose a correct answer. Consider the following familiar Level I (easy) example:

An expert skateboarder, Tom is truly ⟨+⟩ ; he smoothly blends timing with balance.

+ (A) coordinated   + (D) supportive
+ (B) erudite   – (E) casual
– (C) a novice

Bust it!

As you should remember, the correct answer is "coordinated" (A). The prefix of this word is *co–*, meaning together, and the root is *order*. Something that is "ordered together" fits the context clue perfectly. Combining that with the knowledge that you are looking for a positive value word certifies "coordinated" (A) as the correct answer.

Here is a **Level II** (average) example:

Because they reject __−__ , conscientious objectors *are given jobs in community work as a substitute for participation in the armed services.*

+ (A) labor   – (D) dictatorships
– (B) belligerence   – (E) poverty
+ (C) peace

From working with this example previously, you know that the correct answer is "belligerence" (B). The root of this word is *bellum*, Latin for war. Belligerence is an inclination toward war. Other words that may be scrolled from this are bellicose, belligerent, and antebellum, all of which have to do with war. Study your roots and prefixes carefully. A casual knowledge is not good enough. Another root, *bellis*, might be confused with *bellum*. *Bellis* means beauty. Is it logical that a conscientious objector would reject beauty? Know when to use which root and prefix. This ability will come with study and practice.

Here is a **Level III** (difficult) example:

When a physician describes an illness to a colleague, he must speak an __+__ language, *using professional terms and concepts understood mostly by members of his profession.*

+ (A) extrinsic   + (D) esoteric
– (B) inordinate   – (E) abbreviated
+ (C) ambulatory

Bust it!

Recalling this example, you will remember that the context clue defines the missing word as one meaning language that involves a special group of people, i.e., "inside information." The correct answer is "esoteric" (D). *Eso–* is a prefix that means "inside." The prefix of "extrinsic" (A) is *ex–,* which means "out", the opposite of the meaning you seek. "Inordinate" (B) means "not ordered." In this case, the prefix *in–* means "not." This is Level III, so beware of easy assumptions! The root of "ambulatory" (C) is *ambulare,* which means "to walk." "Abbreviated" (E) breaks down to *ab,* meaning *"to;"* and *brevis,* Latin for brief or short.

Bust it!

In many Level III words you may not be able to scroll or break down a word completely. However, often, as in the example above, a partial knowledge of the etymology may be enough to find the correct answer.

Now, take what you have learned and apply it to the questions appearing in the following drill. If you are unsure of an answer, refer back to the review material for help.

Drill: Sentence Completion

DIRECTIONS: Each sentence below has one or two blanks, each blank indicating that something has been omitted. Beneath the sentence are five lettered words or sets of words. Choose the word or set of words that BEST fits the meaning of the sentence as a whole.

Example:
Although the critics found the book _____, many of the readers found it rather _____.

(A) obnoxious . . . perfect
(B) spectacular . . . interesting
(C) boring . . . intriguing
(D) comical . . . persuasive
(E) popular . . . rare

(A) (B) ● (D) (E)

1 The problems of the homeless were so desperate that he felt a need to help _____ them.

(A) increase   (D) collaborate
(B) ameliorate   (E) justify
(C) authenticate

2 The activities of the business manager were so obviously unethical that the board had no choice but to _____ him.

(A) censure   (D) censor
(B) commend   (E) reiterate
(C) consecrate

3 _____ people often are taken in by _____ salespeople.

(A) Suave . . . futile
(B) Benevolent . . . inept
(C) Gullible . . . larcenous
(D) Erratic . . . passive
(E) Pious . . . obstinate

4 The speaker _____ the work of environmentalists as ineffective.

(A) dissented   (D) conceded
(B) savored   (E) tantalized
(C) disparaged

5 Her exceptionally well-written first novel was happily reviewed by the critics with _____ .

(A) ennui   (D) acclaim
(B) pessimism   (E) chagrin
(C) remorse

6 That commentator never has anything good to say; every remark is _____.

(A) inept   (D) bombastic
(B) frivolous   (E) caustic
(C) aberrant

7 The principal's plan to gain students' and parents' cooperation by forming small work groups has worked well; it is both creative and _____ .

(A) sagacious   (D) erroneous
(B) ignoble   (E) conventional
(C) dissonant

8 Our boss is so arrogant that we're surprised when he _____ to speak to us in the cafeteria.

(A) forbears   (D) delays
(B) declines   (E) deigns
(C) abhors

9 Scientists and environmentalists are very concerned about the _____ of the ozone layer.

(A) depletion   (D) defamation
(B) dissonance   (E) enhancement
(C) conglomeration

10 Resolving racist attitudes seems to happen most successfully in communities where different ethnic groups _____ around issues of justice.

(A) educe   (D) coalesce
(B) collapse   (E) diverge
(C) dissolve

11 One obstacle to solving the mass transit problem is a _____ of funds to build and repair systems.

(A) euphony   (D) dearth
(B) profusion   (E) vindication
(C) periphery

12 Terrorists, who are usually _____ , seldom can be dealt with _____ .

(A) rabid . . . timorously
(B) unruly . . . fairly
(C) zealots . . . rationally
(D) blasphemous . . . tersely
(E) hedonistic . . . honestly

13 The candidate argued that it was _____ to _____ democracy and yet not vote.

(A) malicious . . . denounce
(B) lucrative . . . allocate
(C) commendable . . . delineate
(D) inarticulate . . . defend
(E) hypocritical . . . advocate

14 Of all the boring speeches I have ever heard, last night's address had to be the most _____ yet!

(A) arrogant   (D) fervent
(B) insipid   (E) indolent
(C) effervescent

15 Malcolm X was a _____ of Martin Luther King, Jr., yet he had a _____ different view of integration.

(A) disciple . . . reciprocally
(B) codependent . . . uniquely
(C) contemporary . . . radically
(D) fanatic . . . futilely
(E) biographer . . . unrealistically

16 In order to pass the hearing test, you have to be able to _____ high pitch tones from low pitch tones.

(A) surmise   (D) document
(B) define   (E) vindicate
(C) discriminate

17 The committee _____ carefully before making the final report; nevertheless, a minority report _____ its conclusions.

(A) deliberated . . . refuted
(B) analyzed . . . abased
(C) discerned . . . emulated
(D) gloated . . . implemented
(E) argued . . . accepted

18 In general, _____ behavior will bring rewards.

(A) languid   (D) disruptive
(B) rhetorical   (E) exemplary
(C) questionable

19 Colonial Americans, who had little extra money or leisure time, built simple and _____ homes.

(A) baroque   (D) prodigious
(B) unpretentious   (E) disreputable
(C) grandiose

20 Communist countries today are trying to _____ the ineffective economic policies of the past.

(A) ignore   (D) condone
(B) rectify   (E) provoke
(C) reiterate

21 Albert Einstein is the _____ of a genius.

(A) rebuttal   (D) mentor
(B) digression   (E) epitome
(C) antithesis

22 He was tempted to cheat but did not want to _____ his morals.

(A) obscure   (D) concede
(B) refute   (E) succumb
(C) compromise

23 Religious services have spiritual significance for those who are _____ .

(A) fastidious   (D) pious
(B) pessimistic   (E) phlegmatic
(C) pragmatic

24 Her _____ remarks seemed innocent enough, but in reality they were _____ .

(A) caustic . . . fallacious
(B) acrid . . . insipid
(C) magnanimous . . . affable
(D) innocuous . . . malicious
(E) ebullient . . . frivolous

25 The legend of Beowulf is a famous Norse _____ .

(A) saga   (D) utopia
(B) reverie   (E) satire
(C) soliloquy

26 An effective way to prevent the spread of infectious disease is to _____ the sick person.

(A) alleviate   (D) salvage
(B) efface   (E) absolve
(C) quarantine

27 In international business and politics, English is virtually a _____ language.

(A) mundane   (D) palpable
(B) finite   (E) universal
(C) dead

28 Spring break is a welcome _____ from _____ school work.

(A) dichotomy . . . garbled
(B) quandary . . . lax
(C) respite . . . arduous
(D) liaison . . . difficult
(E) zenith . . . phenomenal

29 If you can't find an original form, just prepare a reasonable _____ .

(A) paradigm   (D) aberration
(B) facsimile   (E) equivocation
(C) facade

30 Their generous donation provided the _____ needed to raise the entire goal.

(A) catalyst   (D) ideology
(B) alacrity   (E) plethora
(C) duress

31 The protestors got a better response to their requests when they _____ their anger.

(A) invoked   (D) tempered
(B) appeased   (E) censured
(C) condoned

32 Carelessly dumping chemicals has created many _____ waste sites.

(A) choleric   (D) toxic
(B) utopian   (E) vaunted
(C) torpid

33 The investment counselor had a _____ reputation for purchasing companies and then stripping them of all the assets.

(A) potent   (D) notorious
(B) commendable   (E) pervasive
(C) subtle

34 Staying active is important for people of all ages, so that neither the brain nor the muscles _____ .

(A) expand   (D) vacillate
(B) atrophy   (E) condescend
(C) endure

35 When a student consistently does not turn in homework, the teacher often _____ that the student is _____ .

(A) implies . . . zealous
(B) concludes . . . ambitious
(C) assumes . . . depraved
(D) assures . . . taciturn
(E) infers . . . indolent

36 Looking through the photo album brought warm feelings of _____ .

(A) remorse   (D) ambiguity
(B) nostalgia   (E) deference
(C) complacence

37 There is a marked _____ between the salaries of skilled and unskilled workers.

(A) disparity
(B) increase
(C) cohesion
(D) calamity
(E) amorphousness

38 Although the chairperson seemed to be neutral in her support of the plan, they suspected she had _____ motives.

(A) satirical
(B) palpable
(C) occult
(D) guileless
(E) ulterior

39 They were elated to learn that the salary increases were _____ to the beginning of the year.

(A) reciprocal
(B) recessive
(C) retroactive
(D) germane
(E) subsidiary

40 Scientists debate whether it is possible to even _____ exactly how life begins.

(A) fathom
(B) juxtapose
(C) gloat
(D) rebut
(E) suppress

Sentence Completion Drill
ANSWER KEY

1. (B)	21. (E)
2. (A)	22. (C)
3. (C)	23. (D)
4. (C)	24. (D)
5. (D)	25. (A)
6. (E)	26. (C)
7. (A)	27. (E)
8. (E)	28. (C)
9. (A)	29. (B)
10. (D)	30. (A)
11. (D)	31. (D)
12. (C)	32. (D)
13. (E)	33. (D)
14. (B)	34. (B)
15. (C)	35. (E)
16. (C)	36. (B)
17. (A)	37. (A)
18. (E)	38. (E)
19. (B)	39. (C)
20. (B)	40. (A)

Attacking Analogy Questions

Bust it!

Before we begin, you should understand exactly what an analogy is. **An analogy is a comparison between items that are different, but that also have some similarities**. We know that may sound confusing, but if we give you an example you'll see what we mean.

Look at this analogy:

GALAXY : UNIVERSE :: STATE : COUNTRY

At first you may think that what you just read was gibberish. That may be because you need to **learn how to *read* an analogy**. The above analogy can be read as "Galaxy is to Universe as

State is to Country." The way to *translate* an analogy is to substitute "is to" for all single colons and "as" for all double colons. Pretty simple, right?

"But," you might ask, "what do these words have in common?" Well, as we said, analogies are comparisons between items that are different but are also similar in some way. Because of these similarities, terms in an analogy may share a common bond or relationship that is the key to understanding the analogy.

Let's look at our example again:

GALAXY : UNIVERSE :: STATE : COUNTRY

Ask yourself, what do the terms have in common? You may note that a galaxy is much smaller than the universe and that states are smaller than their country. This is one way to understand the analogy. You may also conclude that there are many galaxies in the universe as there are many states in a country. This is an equally acceptable way to *read* this analogy.

Important Strategy

For each Analogy question on the SAT, you must compare a sample pair of words with five other pairs, and then pick the pair that best matches the relationship between the words in the sample pair. That's all there is to it!

Now that you understand what an analogy is, how to *read* one, and how to answer an Analogy question, you're ready to start preparing to attack them on the SAT. This chapter will teach you to excel on Analogy questions through:

- Learning the eight different types of analogy patterns

- Identifying the meanings of the words in the analogy.

- Identifying the pattern of the analogy.

- Eliminating any answer choice that does not match the sample analogy's pattern.

- Comparing the differences of answer choices with the sample analogy to eliminate wrong choices.

On Target!

As with every other section of the SAT, you can use the test's structure to beat itself. It is very important to know that the analogies at the beginning of each section are usually simple and later analogies are more difficult. Don't feel discouraged if you cannot complete the first or second analogy on the test. Remember, one of the important strategies to beating the SAT is to skip questions that you are spending too much time on. This means you should work on each item in the order in which it is presented. If you are stumped by an item, mark it and leave it; then go on to the next one. At the very end of the section, return to any items you could not complete earlier. Often, you will find that you can complete analogies that stopped you earlier. This is because success breeds confidence, which breeds further success. If you have successfully solved several questions, you can sometimes reach back and find solutions that eluded you before.

Look!

Important Strategy

Look!

*Important
Strategy*

This review for analogies assumes that you have an adequate vocabulary; it therefore does not employ any special word-building exercises. However, that does not mean that you can ignore vocabulary. Reading, of course, develops vocabulary. You are urged to build your vocabulary to improve on the verbal skills you will need to successfully attack the Analogy questions of the SAT. Studying and completing the drills in Chapter 4 of this book is an excellent way to build your vocabulary.

About the Directions

*Important
Information!*

As with all sections of the SAT, it is important that you know the directions before the day of the test. That way you won't waste valuable time while taking the actual test.

The directions for Analogy questions will appear similar to the following:

DIRECTIONS: Each question below consists of a related pair of words or phrases, followed by five lettered pairs of words or phrases. Select the lettered pair that best expresses a relationship similar to that expressed in the original pair.

Example:

SMILE : MOUTH ::
(A) wink : eye
(B) teeth : face
(C) voice : speech
(D) tan : skin
(E) food : gums

About the Questions

The following is an overview of the different types of analogy questions you will encounter on the SAT, along with strategies for solving them quickly and accurately.

Question Type 1: PART-TO-WHOLE

One frequent pattern is a part of an item or concept to the whole idea or concept. Examples are:

SONG : REPERTORY   **CHAPTER : BOOK**

If we assume that a singer has a repertory of songs, we see that a "song" is a part of a whole "repertory." A "chapter" is also a part of a whole "book." So, the pattern is Part-to-Whole, and the answer choice to look for will have the same pattern.

This pattern can also be reversed, as indicated below:

Look !

Important Strategy

BANK : VAULT   **ZOO : CAGE**

Now the pattern is Whole-to-Part. For example, if we assume that a "bank" is the whole building or organization, then a "vault" is a smaller part of it. Also, "zoo" is a whole organization, a "cage" is a part of this whole.

Question Type 2: CAUSE-AND-EFFECT

Another frequent pattern is the relationship of the Cause to its Effect. Look at these examples:

BACTERIA : DISEASE   SUN : HEAT

In the first example, "bacteria" are the cause of the result "disease." In the second example, "sun" is the cause of the result "heat." In each case so far, you will look for a pattern with nouns.

The reverse pattern is Result–to–Cause. Examples are:

FOOD : AGRICULTURE   LAUGHTER : JOKE

Here, "food" is the result of "agriculture," which causes it to be produced. And "laughter" is the result that follows (or *should* follow) a "joke."

Important Strategy

Question Type 3: USER-TO-TOOL

These are examples of a third pattern, the relationship of the User-to-Tool:

DENTIST : DRILL   GARDENER : RAKE

A "dentist" uses a "drill" as a tool, and a "gardener" uses a "rake" as a tool.

The reversal of this pattern is Tool-to-User. For example:

COMPUTER : PROGRAMMER   HAMMER : CARPENTER

Important Strategy

The "computer" is the tool, and the "programmer" is the user. The "hammer" is the tool, and the "carpenter" is the user.

A variation of this pattern might be the Instrument-to-Application, or Tool-to-Application, and its reversal. For example:

Important Strategy

COMPUTER : WRITING   **TROWEL : GARDENING**

Examples of the reverse are:

OVEN : BAKING   **PIANO : CONCERT**

In these examples, too, the words are nouns.

Question Type 4: GROUP-TO-MEMBER

A fourth common pattern is the Group-to-Member. Examples are:

PRIDE : LION   **SENATE : SENATOR**

A "pride" is the group to which a "lion" belongs. The "Senate" is the group to which a senator belongs.

The reversal then is Member-to-Group. For example:

Important Strategy

WOLF : PACK   **WITCH : COVEN**

The "wolf" is a member of a group called a "pack." And a "witch" is a member of a group called a "coven."

There are other variations of this basic pattern, such as Members-to-Group and the reverse.

Question Type 5: TRAIT-TO-EXAMPLE

Another pattern is a Trait or Characteristic to an Example of this Trait or Characteristic. For example:

DISHONESTY : LIE　　　　BRILLIANCE : DIAMOND

Note that "dishonesty" is a character trait, and one example of this trait is a "lie." Also, "brilliance" is a physical trait and "diamond" is an example. Reversals of this pattern are common as well.

A variation of this pattern is a **Greater Degree of a Characteristic to the Characteristic itself**. For example:

INGENIOUS : INTELLIGENT　　　BRAZEN : EXTROVERTED

In these examples, "ingenious" is a greater degree of the trait "intelligent," and "brazen" is a greater degree of the trait "extroverted." Note, too, that all four words here are adjectives.

One variation of the pattern is **Lesser Degree of a Trait to the Trait** itself. Another variation might be a **Trait to an Opposite Trait**, as here:

Look!

Important Strategy

VALOR : COWARDICE　　　COURAGEOUS : PUSILLANIMOUS

The words in the first example are nouns; in the second example they are adjectives.

At times, you may not know the exact meanings of all the words. In that case, you will have to make some educated guesses. For example, you probably know words that bear resemblance to "valor" and "cowardice," such as "valiant" and "coward." So, "valor" must be a trait resembling courage, whereas "cowardice" is the opposite trait. And don't give up on the second example because of "pusillanimous." You already know what "courageous" means. If you did not know what "pusillanimous" meant, you will know what it means from now on: it means "cowardly," or the trait opposite to "courageous." However, on a test, you will know that you are looking for an adjective either opposite in meaning to "courageous" or having the same meaning. That narrows your options considerably. If you should see the answer choice "brave : fearful," you can be reasonably sure that it is the correct answer choice.

Bust it!

Question Type 6: OBJECT-TO-MATERIAL

The pattern of Object-to-Material creates an analogy between an object and the material from which it is made. This type of question is quite common, as is its reversal. For example:

SKIRT : GABARDINE   or   COTTON : SHIRT

The "skirt" is the object made of the material "gabardine," and "cotton" is the material of which the object "shirt" is made.

Important Strategy

Question Type 7: WORD-TO-DEFINITION, SYNONYM, OR ANTONYM

These patterns are heavily dependent on their dictionary meanings. Examples include:

Important Strategy

✔ **Word-to-Definition**

SEGREGATE : SEPARATE

✔ **Word-to-Synonym**

VACUOUS : EMPTY

✔ **Word-to-Antonym**

DESOLATE : JOYOUS

In the first example, the word "segregate" means "separate'—it is both a definition and a synonym. Next, a synonym and definition for the word "vacuous" is "empty." Finally, a word opposite in meaning to "desolate" is the word "joyous."

Question Type 8: SYMBOL-TO-INSTITUTION

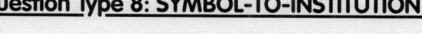

Important Strategy

These are examples of the pattern Symbol-to-Institution:

FLAG : GOVERNMENT   **CROWN : MONARCHY**

In the first case, "flag" is a symbol of the institution "government"; "crown" is the symbol of "monarchy."

These are the most commonly occurring patterns. However, many other types may appear including Plural-to-Singular, Creator-to-Creation, Male-to-Female, or Broad-Category-to-Narrow-Category (for example, FISH : SALMON).

Points to Remember

✔   If you do not know the meanings, try to recall in what context you have heard the words used. This might provide some clues. However, keep in mind that you are looking for a match with the same relationship as the capitalized sample pair. You are not looking for a pair that matches in meaning.

✔   Check that the parts of speech used in both pairs of the analogy are consistent.

INAUGURATE : PRESIDENT :: CORONATION : KING

would not be correct because "inaugurate" is a verb and "coronation" is a noun. The two words are not the same part of speech.

On Target!

✔   Sometimes, two answer choices exhibit the same pattern and have the same grammatical form. This means they are the same parts of speech, and they are the same in number—that is, both are singular or both are plural. In this case, you can eliminate them both, because they cannot both be right. One of the other choices must be right—one that refines the pattern.

✔   Often, the correct answer choice is of the same class, type, or species as the pair in the example. But this isn't ALWAYS true.

For example, in the analogy

PUPPY : DOG :: SAPLING : TREE,

the first pair of words refers to an animal, whereas the second pair refers to a plant. However, the link between the words in both pairs is the same: the "immature subject" to the "mature subject."

✔ *Sometimes, two answer choices have a pattern that is the same as the sample except that one choice shows the pattern in reverse. For example, assume that the sample exhibits the pattern Part-to-Whole. One choice shows this pattern, and another shows Whole-to-Part. In that case, one of these two choices is probably right. The one that is right, of course, is presented in the same order as in the sample.*

Answering Analogy Questions

The recommended strategy for completing an analogy is to examine the two sample words; then, from the meanings of these words, trace the pattern or relationship between them. It is also helpful to identify the grammatical form of the words. Once you can identify the pattern and form, you can forget the meanings and search the five answer choices for the same pattern.

You will not be looking for a match of dictionary meanings, although you will certainly need to use the dictionary meanings as clues. The match you want is the choice whose members resemble one another in the same way the words of the sample pair are related. For example, if the relationship between the same pair is "part-to-whole," you will look for the answer choice showing "part-to-whole." If the link between the same pair is "cause-to-effect," then the matching choice must also be "cause-to-effect."

There are four basic steps to answering any analogy question:

STEP 1	Identify the meanings of both words in the sample.

STEP 2	From the meanings, identify the pattern of the sample. Also identify the part of speech and the number (singular or plural) of each word.

Look!

Important Strategy

Look!

Important Strategy

STEP 3

Ignoring the meanings of the words in the sample, now look over the answer choices. Use the meanings of the words in each choice ONLY to identify its pattern. Eliminate any choices that do not match the pattern in every way, including the order of presentation and grammatical form.

STEP 4

If one answer choice remains, it is the exact match. If two choices remain, examine them to see what is different about them. Compare these differences with the sample. Eliminate the answer choice that does not match the sample perfectly.

For example, suppose the original pair is

AUTOMOBILE : BRAKE;

an "automobile" is a whole and the "brake" is a part. The answer choices are:

(A) doer : thinker   (D) carburetor : choke

(B) man : conscience   (E) society : detergent

(C) horse : ride

Bust it!

We can eliminate (A), since the two words have opposite meanings, and also (C), since "horse" is the doer and "ride" is what is done. We can also eliminate (E), since "society" is a whole, or producer, and "detergent" is a soap—what is produced by society.

Two choices remain: (B) and (D). In (D), a "carburetor" is the part of an automobile that supplies the fuel, and "choke" is a part that restricts the amount of fuel flowing to the engine. Since these are two separate parts, we can eliminate (D). What is left is (B), the perfect match, since "conscience" is a part of the whole "man." Besides, a conscience restrains a man just as the brake restrains an automobile.

Always look for answer choices to eliminate. However, occasionally you can save a lot of time if you just happen to note the perfect match from the start. In that case, though, you should review the other choices, just to be sure your hunch was correct. For example:

Important Strategy

CLOCK : SECOND ::

  (A) ruler : millimeter   **(D) product : shelf life**

  (B) sundial : shadow   **(E) quart : capacity**

  (C) arc: ellipse

Right from the start, choice (A) looks right. The pattern seems to be an instrument and one of its measures, and choice (A) fits nicely. A cursory look at the other options shows that no other choice would be even tempting to select.

Not all the analogies are so simple. In the previous example, suppose the original pair and all choices except for choice (B) remained the same. Then assume that choice (B) is replaced by "scale : pounds." The pattern again is an instrument and one of its measures. Now we must choose between two options:

Bust it!

  (A) ruler : millimeter   **(B) scale : pounds**

What is different about them? A ruler is calibrated in centimeters first and then millimeters. A scale is calibrated in pounds and then ounces. There's the difference: a millimeter is the smaller measure, but a pound is the larger measure. How is a clock calibrated? By minutes and then seconds. Obviously, the matching choice should show the smaller measure—choice (A).

Let's try an example in which you may need to refine the pattern you first identify. For example, suppose the original pair is

SHELL : WALNUT.

The five choices are:

(A) **coating : candy**   (D) **loaf : bread**

(B) **peel : banana**   (E) **root : tree**

(C) **icing : cake**

Our first assumption seems obvious here: Part-to-Whole. Looking more closely, we see this pattern won't work because it fits all the options except (D), loaf : bread. So, we need a more specific pattern. One possibility is "Covering-to-What-is-Covered." A "shell" covers a "walnut." Now we can eliminate (E), since the root doesn't cover the tree, and also (C), since icing doesn't cover the bottom of the cake. That leaves options (A) coating : candy and (B) peel : banana. So, what is different about a coating for a candy and the peel of a banana? The difference is that coating on candy is edible, but the peel on a banana is not. Since the shell of a walnut is not edible, we can eliminate (A). This means that choice (B) is the exact match.

Completing the following drill questions will help you learn to apply the information you have just studied. When you complete the drill, make sure to check your answer. Refer back to the review material if you are unsure of an answer. Keep in mind that speed is important. Try to correctly answer each question in a minute or less.

Bust it!

Drill: Analogies

DIRECTIONS: Each question below consists of a related pair of words or phrases, followed by five lettered pairs of words or phrases. Select the lettered pair that best expresses a relationship similar to that expressed in the original pair.

EXAMPLE:
SMILE : MOUTH ::
(A) wink : eye
(B) teeth : face
(C) voice : speech
(D) tan : skin
(E) food : gums

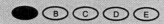

1. BLUEPRINT : BUILDING ::
    (A) letter : alphabet
    (B) chapter : segment
    (C) score : music
    (D) clothes : closet
    (E) preface : novel

2. FINGER : KNUCKLE ::
    (A) eye : eyelid
    (B) ankle : knee
    (C) arm : elbow
    (D) hand : palm
    (E) jaw : tooth

3. RIDDLE : ENIGMA ::
    (A) string : labyrinth
    (B) ancient : sphinx
    (C) matador : bull
    (D) maze : labyrinth
    (E) alternative : dilemma

4. ENVY : GREEN ::
    (A) depressed : yellow
    (B) red : henna
    (C) rage : red
    (D) cadaverous : ashen
    (E) fright : chalk

5. OX : PLOW ::
    (A) teacher : prodigy
    (B) Shetland : pony
    (C) hen : egg
    (D) horse : carriage
    (E) mule : automobile

6. MOTORIST : ROAD SIGN ::
    (A) telegraph operator : Morse code
    (B) English : pronunciation
    (C) vocabulary : alphabet
    (D) bicyclist : roadblock
    (E) reader : pronunciation

7. WALL : MASON ::
    (A) cement : bricklayer
    (B) magic : magician
    (C) friendship : stranger
    (D) picture : painter
    (E) cure : doctor

8. TERSE : TURGID ::
    (A) cow : pig
    (B) tremendous : prodigious
    (C) state : nation
    (D) slim : obese
    (E) mountain : sea

9. BOOK : COVER ::
    (A) window : door
    (B) write : compose
    (C) ink : crayon
    (D) spelling : grammar
    (E) body : skin

10. SUNSET : SUNRISE ::
    (A) coming : going
    (B) spring : autumn
    (C) ten : five
    (D) despair : hope
    (E) evening : morning

11. TALON : HAWK ::
    (A) fang : snake
    (B) horn : bull
    (C) claw : tiger
    (D) tail : monkey
    (E) shell : tortoise

12. REHEARSAL : PLAY ::
    (A) draft : essay
    (B) manual : process
    (C) applause : performance
    (D) recital : concert
    (E) journal : news

13 PRESS : NATION ::
(A) village : reputation
(B) truth : story
(C) gossip : hamlet
(D) chapter : book
(E) rumor : newspaper

14 LOOM : DISASTER ::
(A) impend : catastrophe
(B) howl : storm
(C) hurt : penalty
(D) question : puzzle
(E) imminent : eminent

15 BULB : TULIP ::
(A) pistil : stamen
(B) root : grass
(C) tree : leaf
(D) rose : thorn
(E) acorn : oak

16 PROBLEM : SOLUTION ::
(A) crossword puzzle : design
(B) suitcase : handle
(C) frame: window
(D) password : entry
(E) door : key

17 VACILLATE : CHANGE ::
(A) vacate : rent
(B) index : chart
(C) trend : graph
(D) fluctuate : move
(E) endure : stamina

18 BEACH : LIFEGUARD ::
(A) fish : fisherman
(B) forest : ranger
(C) doctor : hospital
(D) mountain : climber
(E) restaurant : supplier

19 ECOLOGIST : ENVIRONMENT ::
(A) psychologist : plants
(B) botanist : animals
(C) geologist : earth
(D) ventriloquist : dummy
(E) cartographer : people

20 IMPROMPTU : MEMORIZED ::
(A) spontaneous : calculated
(B) read : recited
(C) glib : forced
(D) unrehearsed : extemporaneous
(E) tacit : verbose

21 HALCYON : MARTIAL ::
(A) moon : Mars
(B) military song : militant fighting
(C) peaceful : warlike
(D) soothed : worried
(E) belligerent :

22 TEAM : COACH ::
(A) corporal : squad
(B) army : general
(C) team : member
(D) club : advisor
(E) club : president

23 HYPOCHONDRIAC : HEALTH ::
(A) addict : drugs
(B) miser : money
(C) glutton : food
(D) narcotic : sickness
(E) weakness : strength

24 GOLD : ORE ::
(A) dear : cheap
(B) iron : steel
(C) pearls : oysters
(D) coal : miner
(E) intelligence : astuteness

25 EXUBERANT : DOWNCAST ::
(A) exultant : lavish
(B) parsimonious : abundant
(C) congregation : dispersal
(D) eager : overzealous
(E) effusive : melancholy

26 MAY : MONTH ::
(A) year : decade
(B) Thursday : day
(C) second : minute
(D) day : hour
(E) Friday : week

27 PASSED : ELATION ::
(A) poem : intellectual
(B) failed : dejection
(C) rejected : angry
(D) success : emotion
E) approved : disapproval

28 LARIAT : COWBOY ::
(A) medicine : patient
(B) scalpel : surgeon
(C) manuscript : author
(D) lawyer : client
(E) spice : gourmet

29 SALUTATORIAN : VALEDICTORIAN ::
    (A) crisis : climax
    (B) beginning : end
    (C) runner-up : best
    (D) prologue : play
    (E) incipient : terminal

30 GOURMET : CAVIAR ::
    (A) plebeian : patrician
    (B) clairvoyant : seance
    (C) connoisseur : masterpiece
    (D) critic : edition
    (E) million : wine

31 STAR : GALAXY ::
    (A) kennel : dog
    (B) atom : molecule
    (C) sea : fish
    (D) regiment : soldier
    (E) shelf : hook

32 MOVEMENT : SYMPHONY ::
    (A) act : play
    (B) notes : staff
    (C) melody : harmony
    (D) key : piano
    (E) harmony : counterpoint

33 LAUGH : JOKE ::
    (A) moral : story
    (B) pain : headache
    (C) film : negative
    (D) painting : sketch
    (E) caboose : train

34 RELIGION : RITUAL ::
    (A) society : etiquette
    (B) protocol : diplomacy
    (C) wisdom : education
    (D) science : truth
    (E) rules : game

35 EARTH : AXIS ::
    (A) wheel : hub
    (B) earth : sun
    (C) state : nation
    (D) orbit : firmament
    (E) mountain : sea

36 PHILOLOGIST : LANGUAGE ::
    (A) ornithologist : birds
    (B) botanist : animals
    (C) biologist : cells
    (D) etymologist : insects
    (E) pediatrician : feet

37 AGNOSTIC : ATHEIST ::
    (A) orthodox : heterodox
    (B) heretic : pagan
    (C) unbeliever : iconoclast
    (D) doubt : definition
    (E) vague : defiant

38 SPECTACLES : VISION ::
    (A) statement : contention
    (B) airplane : locomotion
    (C) canoe : paddle
    (D) hay : horse
    (E) hero : worship

39 WATER : SPONGE ::
    (A) desert : dry
    (B) pen : pencil
    (C) ink : blotter
    (D) margin : hole
    (E) wet : drink

40 PRESCIENCE : ORACLE ::
    (A) blunderbuss : soldier
    (B) unimpressiveness : gnome
    (C) priest : deity
    (D) omniscience : seer
    (E) highness : prince

Analogies Drill
ANSWER KEY

1. (C)	21. (C)
2. (C)	22. (D)
3. (D)	23. (B)
4. (C)	24. (C)
5. (D)	25. (E)
6. (E)	26. (B)
7. (D)	27. (B)
8. (D)	28. (B)
9. (E)	29. (C)
10. (E)	30. (C)
11. (C)	31. (B)
12. (A)	32. (A)
13. (C)	33. (B)
14. (A)	34. (A)
15. (E)	35. (A)
16. (E)	36. (A)
17. (D)	37. (D)
18. (B)	38. (B)
19. (C)	39. (C)
20. (A)	40. (D)

Attacking Critical Reading Questions

The Critical Reading sections of the SAT are indeed very critical. **They make up 50 percent of the entire Verbal Test content and 75 percent of its given time**. That's a pretty big part of the Verbal Test. In all, you'll encounter 40 Critical Reading questions. So it is extremely *critical* that you successfully attack these questions.

"Why," you must wonder, "would this much importance be attached to reading?" The reason is simple: Your ability to read at a strong pace while grasping a solid understanding of the material is a key factor in your potential college success. And, as you know, predicting your abilities at the college level is what the SAT is designed to do.

But let's look at the title of this chapter again: Attacking Critical Reading Questions. **The word *critical* has another meaning, for the SAT will ask you to be a reading critic**. You'll not only need to

Important Information!

summarize the material you've read, but also analyze it, make judgments about it, and make educated guesses about what the writer implies and infers. Even your ability to understand vocabulary in context will come under scrutiny. "Can I," you ask yourself, "meet the challenge?" Yes you can. And in this chapter we'll teach you the skills and strategies needed to meet that challenge!

In a nutshell, you'll learn how to:

On Target!

- **Identify the four different types of reading passages.**

- **Use the test format to increase the number of questions you can answer in the allotted time.**

- **Read the question stems first to eliminate any obviously wrong choices.**

- **Quickly identify the main point of the passage.**

- **Work with the order of questions to let you answer the most questions in the allotted time.**

Critical Reading Passages and Questions

Within the SAT Verbal Test you'll be given five Critical Reading passages. One passage will be 400-550 words long, one 550-700 words long, one 700-850 words long, and two reading selections 700-850 words long. The last two passages are referred to as a double passage. The double passage will contain two separate works of writing which you will be asked to compare or contrast.

Important Information!

The chart below shows the type of passages in the critical reading sections.

TYPES OF PASSAGES

- **Humanities** (philosophy, the fine arts)

- **Social Sciences** (psychology, archaeology, anthropology, economics, political science, sociology, history)

- **Natural Sciences** (biology, geology, astronomy, chemistry, physics)

- **Narration** (fiction, nonfiction)

Following each passage are 5-13 questions, depending on the length of the passage. There are four types of questions:

TYPES OF QUESTIONS

- **Synthesis/Analysis**

- **Evaluation**

- **Vocabulary-in-Context**

- **Interpretation**

Important Information!

Through this review, you'll learn not only how to identify these types of questions, but how to successfully attack each one. Familiarity with the test format, combined with solid reading strategies, will prove invaluable in answering the questions quickly and accurately

About the Directions

Make sure to study and learn the directions to save yourself time during the actual test. The directions will read similar to the following.

DIRECTIONS: Read each passage and answer the questions that follow. Each question will be based on the information stated or implied in the passage or its introduction.

A variation of these directions will be presented as follows for the double passage.

DIRECTIONS: Read the passages and answer the questions that follow. Each question will be based on the information stated or implied in the selections or their introductions, and may be based on the relationship between the passages.

Important Information!

About the Passages

You may encounter any of a number of passage types in the Critical Reading section. These passages may consist of straight text, dialogue and text, or narration. A passage may appear by itself or as part of a pair in a double passage. A brief introduction will be provided for each passage to set the scene for the text being presented.

To familiarize yourself with the types of passages you will encounter, review the examples which follow. Remember that one passage in the section will be 400-550 words, one will be 550-700

Important Information!

words, one will be 700-850 words, and that the two passages in the double passage will consist of 700-850 words combined. The content of the passages will include the humanities, social sciences, natural sciences, and also narrative text.

A **humanities passage** may discuss such topics as philosophy, the fine arts, and language. The following is an example of such a passage. It falls into the 550 to 700 word range.

Throughout his pursuit of knowledge and •enlightenment, the philosopher Socrates made many enemies among the Greek citizens. The following passage is an account of the trial resulting from their accusations.

The great philosopher Socrates was put on trial in Athens in 400 B.C. on charges of corrupting the youth and of impiety. As recorded in Plato's
Line dialogue *The Apology*, Socrates began his defense
(5) by saying he was going to "speak plainly and honestly," unlike the eloquent sophists the Athenian jury was accustomed to hearing. His appeal to unadorned language offended the jurors, who were expecting to be entertained.
(10) Socrates identified the two sets of accusers that he had to face: the past and the present. The former had filled the jurors' heads with lies about him when they were young, and were considered by Socrates to be the most dangerous. The accusers
(15) from the past could not be cross-examined, and they had already influenced the jurors when they were both naive and impressionable. This offended the jury because it called into question their ability to be objective and render a fair judgment.
(20) The philosopher addressed the charges himself, and dismissed them as mere covers for the deeper attack on his philosophical activity. That activity, which involved questioning others until they revealed contradictions in their beliefs, had given
(25) rise to Socrates' motto, "The unexamined life is not worth living," and the "Socratic Method," which is still employed in many law schools today. This critical questioning of leading Athenians had made Socrates very unpopular with those in power and,
(30) he insisted, was what led to his trial. This challenge to the legitimacy of the legal system itself further alienated his judges.

Socrates tried to explain that his philosophical life came about by accident. He had been content
(35) to be a humble stone mason until the day that a friend informed him that the Oracle of Delphi had said that "Socrates is the wisest man in Greece." Socrates had been so surprised by this statement, and so sure of its inaccuracy, that he set about
(40) disproving it by talking to the reputed wise men of Athens and showing how much more knowledge they possessed. Unfortunately, as he told the jury, those citizens reputed to be wise (politicians, businessmen, artists) turned out to be ignorant,
(45) either by knowing absolutely nothing, or by having limited knowledge in their fields of expertise and assuming knowledge of everything else. Of these, Socrates had to admit, "I am wiser, because although all of us have little knowledge, I am aware
(50) of my ignorance, while they are not." But this practice of revealing prominent citizens' ignorance and arrogance did not earn Socrates their affection, especially when the bright young men of Athens began following him around and delighting in the
(55) disgracing of their elders. Hence, in his view, the formal charges of "corrupting the youth" and "impiety" were a pretext to retaliate for the deeper offense of challenging the pretensions of the establishment.
(60) Although Socrates viewed the whole trial as a sham, he cleverly refuted the charges by using the same method of questioning that got him in trouble in the first place. Against the charges of corrupting the youth, Socrates asked his chief
(65) accuser, Meletus, if any wanted to arm himself, to which Meletus answered, "no." Then, Socrates asked if one's associates had an effect on one: Good people for good, and evil people for evil, to which Meletus answered, "yes." Next, Socrates asked if
(70) corrupting one's companions makes them better or worse, to which Meletus responded, "worse."

Finally Socrates set the trap by asking Meletus if Socrates had corrupted the youth intentionally or unintentionally. Meletus, wanting to make the
(75) charges as bad as possible, answered, "intentionally." Socrates showed the contradictory nature of the charge, since by intentionally corrupting his companions he made them worse, thereby bringing harm on himself. He also refuted
(80) the second charge of impiety in the same manner, by showing that its two components (teaching about strange gods and atheism) were inconsistent.

Although Socrates had logically refuted the charges against him, the Athenian jury found him
(85) guilty, and Meletus proposed the death penalty. The defendant Socrates was allowed to propose an alternative penalty and Socrates proposed a state pension, so he could continue his philosophical activity to the benefit of Athens. He stated that this
(90) is what he deserved. The Athenian jury, furious over his presumption, voted the death penalty and, thus, one of the great philosophers of the Western heritage was executed.

The **social science passage** may discuss such topics as psychology, archaeology, anthropology, economics, political science, sociology, and history. The following is an example of such a passage. It falls into the 400 to 550 word range.

Not only does music have the ability to entertain and enthrall, but it also has the capacity to heal. The following passage illustrates the recent indoctrination of music therapy.

Music's power to affect moods and stir emotions has been well known for as long as music has existed. Stories about the music of ancient
Line Greece tell of the healing powers of Greek music.
(5) Leopold Mozart, the father of Wolfgang, wrote that if the Greeks' music could heal the sick, then our music should be able to bring the dead back to life. Unfortunately, today's music cannot do quite that much.
(10) The healing power of music, taken for granted by ancient man and by many primitive societies, is only recently becoming accepted by medical professionals as a new way of healing the emotionally ill.
(15) Using musical activities involving patients, the music therapist seeks to restore mental and physical health. Music therapists usually work with emotionally disturbed patients as part of a team of therapists and doctors. Music therapists work
(20) together with physicians, psychiatrists, psychologists, physical therapists, nurses, teachers, recreation leaders, and families of patients.
The rehabilitation that a music therapist gives to

patients can be in the form of listening, performing,
(25) lessons on an instrument or even composing. A therapist may help a patient regain lost coordination by teaching the patient how to play an instrument. Speech defects can sometimes be helped by singing activities. Some patients need the social awareness
(30) of group activities, but others may need individual attention to build self-confidence. The music therapist must learn what kinds of activities are best for each patient.
In addition to working with patients, the music
(35) therapist has to attend meetings with other therapists and doctors that work with the same patients to discuss progress and plan new activities. Written reports to doctors about patients' responses to treatment are another facet of the music
(40) therapist's work.
Hospitals, schools, retirement homes, and community agencies and clinics are some of the sites where music therapists work. Some music therapists work in private studies with patients who
(45) are sent to them by medical doctors, psychologists, and psychiatrists. Music therapy can be done in studios, recreation rooms, hospital wards, or classrooms depending on the type of activity and needs of the patients.
(50) Qualified music therapists have followed a four-year course with a major emphasis in music plus courses in biological science, anthropology, sociology, psychology, and music therapy. General studies in English, history, speech, and government
(55) complete the requirements for a Bachelor of Music

Therapy. After college training, a music therapist must participate in a six-month training internship under the guidance of a registered music therapist.

(60)   Students who have completed college courses and have demonstrated their ability during the six-month internship can become registered music therapists by applying to the National Association for Music Therapy, Inc. New methods and techniques of music therapy are always being (65) developed, so the trained therapist must continue to study new articles, books, and reports throughout his/her career.

The **natural science passage** may discuss such topics as biology, geology, astronomy, chemistry, and physics. The following is an example of such a passage. It falls into the 550 to 700 word range.

The following article was written by a physical chemist and recounts the conflict between volcanic matter in the atmosphere and airplane windows. It was published in a scientific periodical in 1989.

Reprinted by permission of *American Heritage Magazine*, © Forbes Inc., 1989.

Several years ago the airlines discovered a new kind of problem—a window problem. The acrylic windows on some of their 747s were getting hazy
Line and dirty-looking. Suspicious travelers thought the
(5) airlines might have stopped cleaning them, but the windows were not dirty; they were inexplicably deteriorating within as little as 390 hours of flight time, even though they were supposed to last for five to ten years. Boeing looked into it.
(10)   At first the company thought the culprit might be one well known in modern technology, the component supplier who changes materials without telling the customer. Boeing quickly learned this was not the case, so there followed an
(15) extensive investigation that eventually brought in the Air Transport Association, geologists, and specialists in upper-atmosphere chemistry, and the explanation turned out to be not nearly so mundane. Indeed, it began to look like a grand
(20) reenactment of an ancient Aztec myth: the struggle between the eagle and the serpent, which is depicted on the Mexican flag.

   The serpent in this case is an angry Mexican volcano, El Chichon. Like its reptilian counterpart,
(25) it knows how to spit venom at the eyes of its adversary. In March and April of 1982 the volcano, in an unusual eruption pattern, ejected millions of tons of sulfur-rich material directly into the stratosphere. In less than a year, a stratospheric (30) cloud had blanketed the entire Northern Hemisphere. Soon the photochemistry of the upper atmosphere converted much of the sulfur into tiny droplets of concentrated sulfuric acid.

   The eagle in the story is the 747, poking
(35) occasionally into the lower part of the stratosphere in hundreds of passenger flights daily. Its two hundred windows are made from an acrylic polymer, which makes beautifully clear, strong windows but was never intended to withstand
(40) attack by strong acids.

   The stratosphere is very different from our familiar troposphere environment. Down here the air is humid, with a lot of vertical convection to carry things up and down; the stratosphere is bone-
(45) dry, home to the continent-striding jet stream, with unceasing horizontal winds at an average of 120 miles per hour. A mist of acid droplets that accumulated gradually near the lower edge of the stratosphere, settling there at a thickness of about a
(50) mile a year, was able to wait for planes to come along.

   As for sulfuric acid, most people know only the relatively benign liquid in a car battery: 80 percent water and 20 percent acid. The stratosphere
(55) dehydrated the sulfuric acid into a persistent, corrosive mist 75 percent pure acid, an extremely aggressive liquid. Every time the 747 poked into the stratosphere—on almost every long flight—acid droplets struck the windows and began to react
(60) with their outer surface, causing it to swell. This built up stresses between the softened outer layer and the underlying material. Finally, parallel hairline cracks developed, creating the hazy appearance. The hazing was sped up by the
(65) mechanical stresses always present in the windows of a pressurized cabin.

   The airlines suffered through more than a year of window replacements before the acid cloud

finally dissipated. Ultimately the drops reached the
(70) lower edge of the stratosphere, were carried away
into the lower atmosphere, and finally came down
in the rain. In the meantime, more resistant
window materials and coatings were developed. (As
for the man-made sulfur dioxide that causes acid
(75) rain, it never gets concentrated enough to attack the
window material. El Chichon was unusual in its
ejection of sulfur directly into the stratosphere, and
the 747 is unusual in its frequent entrance into the
stratosphere.)
(80)　　As for the designers of those windows, it is hard
to avoid the conclusion that a perfectly adequate
engineering design was defeated by bad luck. After
all, this was the only time since the invention of
the airplane that there were acid droplets of this
(85) concentration in the upper atmosphere. But
reliability engineers, an eminently rational breed,
are very uncomfortable when asked to talk about
luck. In principle it should be possible to
anticipate events, and the failure to do so
(90) somehow seems like a professional failure. The
cosmos of the engineer has no room for
poltergeists, demons, or other mystic elements.
But might it accommodate the inexorable scenario
of an ancient Aztec myth?

A **narrative passage dealing with fictional material** may be in the form of dialogue between characters, or one character speaking to the reader. The following is an example of the latter. It falls into the 700 to 850 word range.

In this passage, the narrator discovers that he has been transported to King Arthur's court in the year 528 A.D.

The moment I got a chance I slipped aside
privately and touched an ancient common-looking
man on the shoulder and said, in an insinuating,
Line confidential way—
(5)　　"Friend, do me a kindness. Do you belong to
the asylum, or are you just here on a visit or
something like that?"
　　He looked me over stupidly, and said—
　　"Marry, fair sir, me seemeth—"
(10)　　"That will do," I said; "I reckon you are a
patient."
　　I moved away, cogitating, and at the same time
keeping an eye out for any chance passenger in his
right mind that might come along and give me
(15) some light. I judged I had found one, presently; so I
drew him aside and said in his ear—
　　"If I could see the head keeper a minute—only
just a minute—"
　　"Prithee do not let me."
(20)　　"Let you *what*?"
　　"*Hinder* me, then, if the word please thee
better." Then he went on to say he was an under-
cook and could not stop to gossip, though he would
like it another time; for it would comfort his very
(25) liver to know where I got my clothes. As he started
away he pointed and said yonder was one who was
idle enough for my purpose, and was seeking me
besides, no doubt. This was an airy slim boy in
shrimp-colored tights that made him look like a
(30) forked carrot; the rest of his gear was blue silk and
dainty laces and ruffles; and he had long yellow
curls, and wore a plumed pink satin cap tilted
complacently over his ear. By his look, he was good-
natured; by his gait, he was satisfied with himself.
(35) He was pretty enough to frame. He arrived, looked
me over with a smiling and impudent curiosity; said
he had come for me, and informed me that he was a
page.
　　"Go 'long," I said; "you ain't more than a
(40) paragraph."
　　It was pretty severe, but I was nettled. However,
it never phazed him; he didn't appear to know he
was hurt. He began to talk and laugh, in happy,
thoughtless, boyish fashion, as we walked along,
(45) and made himself old friends with me at once;
asked me all sorts of questions about myself and
about my clothes, but never waited for an answer—
always chattered straight ahead, as if he didn't
know he had asked a question and wasn't expecting
(50) any reply, until at last he happened to mention that
he was born in the beginning of the year 513.
　　It made the cold chills creep over me! I stopped,
and said, a little faintly:
　　"Maybe I didn't hear you just right. Say it
(55) again—and say it slow. What year was it?"
　　"513."
　　"513! You don't look it! Come, my boy, I am a
stranger and friendless: be honest and honorable
with me. Are you in your right mind?"

(60)   He said he was.

"Are these other people in their right minds?"

He said they were.

"And this isn't an asylum? I mean, it isn't a place where they cure crazy people?"

(65)   He said it wasn't.

"Well, then," I said, "either I am a lunatic, or something just as awful has happened. Now tell me, honest and true, where am I?"

"In King Arthur's Court."

(70)   I waited a minute, to let that idea shudder its way home, and then said:

"And according to your notions, what year is it now?"

"528—nineteenth of June."

(75)   I felt a mournful sinking at the heart, and muttered: "I shall never see my friends again— never, never again. They will not be born for more than thirteen hundred years yet."

I seemed to believe the boy, I didn't know why.

(80)   *Something* in me seemed to believe him—my consciousness, as you may say; but my reason didn't. My reason straightway began to clamor; that was natural. I didn't know how to go about satisfying it, because I knew that the testimony of

(85)   men wouldn't serve—my reason would say they were lunatics, and throw out their evidence. But all of a sudden I stumbled on the very thing, just by luck. I knew that the only total eclipse of the sun in the first half of the sixth century occurred on the

(90)   21st of June, A. D. 528, O. S., and began at 3 minutes after 12 noon. I also knew that no total eclipse of the sun was due in what to *me* was the present year— *i.e.*, 1879. So, if I could keep my anxiety and curiosity from eating the heart out of me for forty-

(95)   eight hours, I should then find out for certain whether this boy was telling me the truth or not.

A **narrative passage** dealing with nonfiction material may appear in the form of a speech or any such discourse in which one person speaks to a group of people or to the reader. The following two selections are examples of nonfiction narratives. Together, they are also an example of a double passage, in which the subject matter in the selections can be either compared or contrasted. As you will recall, the two selections will total 700 to 850.

The following passages are excerpts from two different Presidential Inaugural Addresses. Passage 2 was given by President Franklin D. Roosevelt on March 4, 1933. Passage 1 comes from President John F. Kennedy's Inaugural Address, given on January 20, 1961.

Passage 1

Let every nation know, whether it wishes us well or ill, that we shall pay any price, bear any burden, meet any hardship, support any friend,

Line   oppose any foe to assure the survival and the

(5)   success of liberty.

This much we pledge—and more.

To those old allies whose cultural and spiritual origins we share, we pledge the loyalty of faithful friends. United, there is little we cannot do in a host

(10)   of co-operative ventures. Divided, there is little we can do, for we dare not meet a powerful challenge at odds and split asunder.

To those new states whom we welcome to the ranks of the free, we pledge our word that one form

(15)   of colonial control shall not have passed away merely to be replaced by a far more iron tyranny. We shall not always expect to find them supporting our view. But we shall always hope to find them strongly supporting their own freedom, and to

(20)   remember that, in the past, those who foolishly sought power by riding the back of the tiger ended up inside.

To those peoples in the huts and villages of half the globe struggling to break the bonds of mass

(25)   misery, we pledge our best efforts to help them help themselves, for whatever period is required, not because the Communists may be doing it, not because we seek their votes, but because it is right. If a free society cannot help the many who are poor,

(30)   it cannot save the few who are rich.

Passage 2

This is pre-eminently the time to speak the truth, the whole truth, frankly and boldly. Nor need we shrink from honestly facing conditions in our country today. This great nation will endure as it
(35) has endured, will revive, and will prosper.

So first of all let me assert my firm belief that the only thing we have to fear is fear itself—nameless, unreasoning, unjustified terror, which paralyzes needed efforts to convert retreat into
(40) advance.

In every dark hour of our national life a leadership of frankness and vigor has met with that understanding and support of the people themselves which is essential to victory. I am
(45) convinced that you will again give that support to leadership in these critical days.

In such a spirit on my part and yours we face our common difficulties. They concern, thank God, only material things. Values have shrunken to
(50) fantastic levels; taxes have risen; our ability to pay has fallen; government of all kinds is faced by serious curtailment of income; the means of exchange are frozen in the currents of trade; the withered leaves of industrial enterprise lie on every
(55) side; farmers find no markets for their produce; the savings of many years in thousands of families are gone.

More important, a host of unemployed citizens face the grim problem of existence, and an equally
(60) great number toil with little return. Only a foolish optimist can deny the dark realities of the moment.

Yet our distress comes from no failure of substance. We are stricken by no plague of locusts. Compared with the perils which our forefathers
(65) conquered because they believed and were not afraid, we have still much to be thankful for. Nature still offers her bounty, and human efforts have multiplied it. Plenty is at our doorstep, but a generous use of it languishes in the very sight of the
(70) supply.

Primarily, this is because the rulers of the exchange of mankind's goods have failed through their own stubbornness and their own incompetence, have admitted their failure and
(75) abdicated. Practices of the unscrupulous money-changers stand indicted in the court of public opinion, rejected by the hearts and minds of men.

About the Questions

As previously mentioned, there are four major question types which appear in the Critical Reading section. The following explains what these questions will cover.

Important Information!

Question Type 1: SYNTHESIS/ANALYSIS

Synthesis/Analysis questions deal with the structure of the passage and how one part relates to another part or to the text as a whole. These questions may ask you to look at passage details and from them, point out general themes or concepts. They might ask you to trace problems, causes, effects, and solutions or to understand the points of an argument or persuasive passage. They might ask you to compare or contrast different aspects of the passage. Synthesis/Analysis questions may also involve inferences, asking you to decide what the details of the passage imply about the author's general tone or attitude. Key terms in Synthesis/Analysis questions are example, difference, general, compare, contrast, cause, effect, and result.

Question Type 2: EVALUATION

Evaluation questions involve judgments about the worth of the essay as a whole. You may be asked to consider concepts the author assumes rather than factually proves and to judge whether or not the author presents a logically consistent case. Does he/she prove the points through generalization, citing an authority, use of example, implication, personal experience, or factual data? You'll need to be able to distinguish the supportive bases for the argumentative theme. Almost as a book reviewer, you'll also be asked to pinpoint the author's writing techniques. What is the style, the tone? Who is the intended audience? How might the author's points relate to information outside the essay, itself? Key terms you'll often see in Evaluation questions and answer choices are generalization, implication, and support.

Important Information!

Question Type 3: VOCABULARY-IN-CONTEXT

Vocabulary-in-Context questions occur in several formats. You'll be given easy words with challenging choices or the reverse. You'll need to know multiple meanings of words. You'll encounter difficult words and difficult choices. In some cases, your knowledge of prefixes-roots-suffixes will give you a clear advantage. In addition, connotations will be the means of deciding, in some cases, which answer is the best. Of course, how the term works in the textual context is the key to the issue.

Question Type 4: INTERPRETATION

Interpretation questions ask you to decide on a valid explanation or clarification of the author's points. Based on the text, you'll be asked to distinguish probable motivations and effects or actions not stated outright in the essay. Furthermore, you'll need to be familiar with clichés, euphemisms, catch phrases, colloquialisms, metaphors, and similes, and be able to explain them in straightforward language. Interpretation question stems usually have a word or phrase enclosed in quotation marks.

Important Information!

Keep in mind that being able to categorize the type of Reading Comprehension question accurately is not of prime importance. What is important, however, is that you are familiar with all the types of information you will be asked and that you have a set of basic strategies to use when answering questions. The remainder of this review will give you these skills.

Points to Remember

On Target!

✔   Do not spend too much time answering any one question.

✔   Vocabulary plays a large part in successful critical reading. See the chapter on building your SAT vocabulary. As a long-term approach to improving your ability and therefore your test scores, read as much as you can of any type of material. Your speed, comprehension, and vocabulary will grow.

✔   Be an engaged reader. Don't let your mind wander. Focus through annotation and key terms.

✔   Time is an important factor on the SAT. Therefore, the rate at which you are reading is very important. If you are concerned that you may be reading too slowly, try to compete with yourself. For example, if you are reading at 120 words per minute, try to improve your speed to 250 words per minute (without decreasing your understanding). Remember that improving reading speed is not a means in itself. Improved comprehension with fewer regressions must accompany this speed increase. Make sure to read, read, read. The more you read, the more you will sharpen your skills.

Answering Critical Reading Questions

You should follow these steps as you begin each Critical Reading passage. They will act as a guide when answering the questions.

STEP 1 | **Attack the easiest and most interesting passages first.**

Critical Reading passages are not automatically presented in the order of least-to-most difficult. The difficulty or ease of a reading selection is an individual matter, determined by the reader's own specific interests and past experience, so what you might consider easy, someone else might consider hard, and *vice-versa.* But be sure to look at passages in only the first 2/3 of the questions. Save the hard questions for last. Again, time is an issue, so you need to begin with something you can quickly understand in order to get to the questions, but since every question is worth the same amount of points, answer all the easy and medium–difficulty questions in each section before attacking the hard ones.

Look!

Important Strategy

STEP 2 | First, read the question stems following the passage, making sure to block out the answer choices with your free hand. (You don't want to be misled by incorrect choices.)

In question stems, underline key words, phrases, and dates. For example:

Important Strategy

1. In line 27, "stand" means:

2. From 1776 to 1812, King George did:

3. Lincoln was similar to Pericles in that:

The act of underlining takes little time and will force you to focus first on the main ideas in the questions, then in the passages.

You will notice that questions often note a line number for reference. Place a small mark by the appropriate lines in the essay itself to remind yourself to read those parts very carefully. You'll still have to refer to these lines upon answering the questions, but you'll be able to find them quickly.

STEP 3 | If the passage is not divided into paragraphs, read the first 10 lines. If the passage is divided into manageable paragraphs, read the first paragraph. Make sure to read at a moderate pace, as fast skimming will not be sufficient for comprehension, while slow, forced reading will take too much time and yield too little understanding of the overall passage.

In the margin of your test booklet, using two or three words, note the main point of the paragraph/section. Don't labor long over the exact wording. Underline key terms, phrases, or ideas when you notice them. If a sentence is particularly difficult, don't spend too much time trying to figure it out. Bracket it, though, for easy reference in the remote instance that it might serve as the basis for a question.

You should proceed through each paragraph/section in a similar manner. Don't read the whole passage with the intention of going back and filling in the main points. Read carefully and consistently, annotating and underlining to keep your mind on the context.

Important Strategy

Upon finishing the entire passage, quickly review your notes in the margin. They should give you main ideas and passage structure (chronological, cause and effect, process, comparison-contrast). Ask yourself what the author's attitude is toward his/her subject. What might you infer from the selection? What might the author say next? Some of these questions may appear, and you'll be immediately prepared to answer.

STEP 4 | **Start with the first question and work through to the last question. The order in which the questions are presented follows the order of the passage, so going for the "easy" questions first rather than answering the questions consecutively will cost you valuable time in searching and backtracking.**

Be sure to block the answer choices for each question before you read the question, itself. Again, you don't want to be misled.

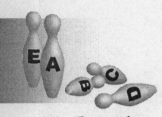

*Eliminating
Answer
Choices*

If a line number is mentioned, quickly re-read that section. In addition, circle your own answer to the question *before* viewing the choices. Then, carefully examine each answer choice, eliminating those which are obviously incorrect. If you find a close match to your own answer, don't assume that it is the best answer, as an even better one may be among the last choices. Remember, in the SAT, only one answer is correct, and it is the *best* one, not simply one that will work.

Once you've proceeded through all the choices, eliminating incorrect answers as you go, choose from among those remaining. If the choice is not clear, re-read the question stem and the referenced passage lines to seek tone or content you might have missed. If the answer now is not readily obvious and you have reduced your choices by eliminating at least one, then simply choose one of the remaining and proceed to the next question. Place a small mark in your test booklet to remind you, should you have time at the end of this test section, to review the question and seek a more accurate answer.

Now, let's go back to our natural sciences passage. Read the passage, and then answer the questions which follow using the skills gained through this review.

The following article was written by a physical chemist and recounts the conflict between volcanic matter in the atmosphere and airplane windows. It was published in a scientific periodical in 1989.

Reprinted by permission of *American Heritage Magazine,*© Forbes Inc., 1989.

Several years ago the airlines discovered a new kind of problem—a window problem. The acrylic windows on some of their 747s were getting hazy
Line and dirty-looking. Suspicious travelers thought the
(5) airlines might have stopped cleaning them, but the windows were not dirty; they were inexplicably deteriorating within as little as 390 hours of flight time, even though they were supposed to last for five to ten years. Boeing looked into it.
(10)   At first the company thought the culprit might be one well known in modern technology, the component supplier who changes materials without telling the customer. Boeing quickly learned this was not the case, so there followed an
(15) extensive investigation that eventually brought in the Air Transport Association, geologists, and specialists in upper-atmosphere chemistry, and the explanation turned out to be not nearly so mundane. Indeed, it began to look like a grand
(20) reenactment of an ancient Aztec myth: the struggle between the eagle and the serpent, which is depicted on the Mexican flag.
    The serpent in this case is an angry Mexican volcano, El Chichon. Like its reptilian counterpart,
(25) it knows how to spit venom at the eyes of its

adversary. In March and April of 1982 the volcano, in an unusual eruption pattern, ejected millions of tons of sulfur-rich material directly into the stratosphere. In less than a year, a stratospheric

(30) cloud had blanketed the entire Northern Hemisphere. Soon the photochemistry of the upper atmosphere converted much of the sulfur into tiny droplets of concentrated sulfuric acid.

The eagle in the story is the 747, poking

(35) occasionally into the lower part of the stratosphere in hundreds of passenger flights daily. Its two hundred windows are made from an acrylic polymer, which makes beautifully clear, strong windows but was never intended to withstand

(40) attack by strong acids.

The stratosphere is very different from our familiar troposphere environment. Down here the air is humid, with a lot of vertical convection to carry things up and down; the stratosphere is bone-

(45) dry, home to the continent-striding jet stream, with unceasing horizontal winds at an average of 120 miles per hour. A mist of acid droplets that accumulated gradually near the lower edge of the stratosphere, settling there at a thickness of about a

(50) mile a year, was able to wait for planes to come along.

As for sulfuric acid, most people know only the relatively benign liquid in a car battery: 80 percent water and 20 percent acid. The stratosphere

(55) dehydrated the sulfuric acid into a persistent, corrosive mist 75 percent pure acid, an extremely aggressive liquid. Every time the 747 poked into the stratosphere—on almost every long flight—acid droplets struck the windows and began to react

(60) with their outer surface, causing it to swell. This built up stresses between the softened outer layer and the underlying material. Finally, parallel hairline cracks developed, creating the hazy appearance. The hazing was sped up by the

(65) mechanical stresses always present in the windows of a pressurized cabin.

The airlines suffered through more than a year of window replacements before the acid cloud finally dissipated. Ultimately the drops reached the

(70) lower edge of the stratosphere, were carried away into the lower atmosphere, and finally came down in the rain. In the meantime, more resistant window materials and coatings were developed. (As for the man-made sulfur dioxide that causes acid

(75) rain, it never gets concentrated enough to attack the window material. El Chichon was unusual in its ejection of sulfur directly into the stratosphere, and the 747 is unusual in its frequent entrance into the stratosphere.)

(80) As for the designers of those windows, it is hard to avoid the conclusion that a perfectly adequate

engineering design was defeated by bad luck. After all, this was the only time since the invention of the airplane that there were acid droplets of this

(85) concentration in the upper atmosphere. But reliability engineers, an eminently rational breed, are very uncomfortable when asked to talk about luck. In principle it should be possible to anticipate events, and the failure to do so somehow seems like

(90) a professional failure. The cosmos of the engineer has no room for poltergeists, demons, or other mystic elements. But might it accommodate the inexorable scenario of an ancient Aztec myth?

1 Initially the hazy windows were thought by the company to be a result of

(A) small particles of volcanic glass abrading their surfaces.
(B) substandard window material substituted by the parts supplier.
(C) ineffectual cleaning products used by the maintenance crew.
(D) a build-up of the man-made sulfur dioxide that also causes acid rain.
(E) the humidity.

2 When first seeking a reason for the abraded windows, both the passengers and Boeing management exhibited attitudes of

(A) disbelief.   (D) pacifism.
(B) optimism.   (E) disregard.
(C) cynicism.

3 In line 19, "mundane" means

(A) simple.   (D) ordinary.
(B) complicated.   (E) important.
(C) far-reaching.

4 In what ways is El Chichon like the serpent on the Mexican flag, knowing how to "spit venom at the eyes of its adversary" (lines 25-26)?

(A) It seeks to poison its adversary with its bite.
(B) It carefully plans its attack on an awaited intruder.
(C) It ejects tons of destructive sulfuric acid to damage jet windows.
(D) It angrily blankets the Northern Hemisphere with sulfuric acid.
(E) It protects itself with the acid rain it produces.

5 The term "photochemistry" in line 31 refers to a chemical change caused by

(A) the proximity of the sun.
(B) the drop in temperature at stratospheric altitudes.
(C) the jet stream's "unceasing horizontal winds."
(D) the vertical convection of the troposphere.
(E) the amount of sulfur present in the atmosphere.

6 Unlike the troposphere, the stratosphere

(A) is extremely humid as it is home to the jet stream.
(B) contains primarily vertical convections to cause air particles to rise and fall rapidly.
(C) is approximately one mile thick.
(D) contains powerful horizontal winds resulting in an excessively dry atmosphere.
(E) contains very little wind activity.

7 In line 57, "aggressive" means

(A) exasperating.   (D) assertive.
(B) enterprising.   (E) surprising.
(C) prone to attack.

8 As the eagle triumphed over the serpent in the Mexican flag,

(A) El Chichon triumphed over the plane as the 747s had to change their flight altitudes.
(B) the newly designed window material deflected the damaging acid droplets.
(C) the 747 was able to fly unchallenged by acid droplets a year later as they drifted away to the lower atmosphere.
(D) the reliability engineers are now prepared for any run of "bad luck" which may approach their aircraft.
(E) the component supplier of the windows changed materials without telling the customers.

9 The reliability engineers are typified as people who

(A) are uncomfortable considering natural disasters.
(B) believe that all events are predictable through scientific methodology.
(C) accept luck as an inevitable and unpredictable part of life.
(D) easily accept their failure to predict and protect against nature's surprises.
(E) are extremely irrational and are comfortable speaking about luck.

Answers to Drill Questions: 1. (B)   2. (C)   3. (D)   4. (C)   5. (A)   6. (D)   7. (C)   8. (C)   9. (B)

The questions following the passage which you just read are typical of those in the Critical Reading section. After carefully reading the passage, you can begin to answer these questions. Let's look again at the questions.

1 Initially the hazy windows were thought by the company to be a result of

(A)   small particles of volcanic glass abrading their surfaces.
(B)   substandard window material substituted by the parts supplier.

(C)   ineffectual cleaning products used by the
maintenance crew.

(D)   a build-up of the man-made sulfur dioxide
that also causes acid rain.

(E)   the humidity.

As you read the question stem, blocking the answer choices, you'll note the key term "result" which should alert you to the question category **Synthesis/Analysis. Argument structure is the focus here**. Ask yourself what part of the argument is being questioned: cause, problem, result, or solution. Careful reading of the stem and perhaps mental rewording to "_____ caused hazy windows" reveals cause is the issue. Once you're clear on the stem, proceed to the choices.

Important Information!

The word "initially" clues you in to the fact that the correct answer should be the first cause considered. Answer choice (B) is the correct response, as "substandard window material" was the *company's* first (initial) culprit, as explained in the first sentence of the second paragraph. They had no hint of (A) a volcanic eruption's ability to cause such damage. In addition, they were not concerned, as were the *passengers*, that (C) the windows were not properly cleaned. Answer (D) is not correct since scientists had yet to consider testing the atmosphere. Along the same lines, answer choice (E) is incorrect.

Bust it!

2   When first seeking a reason for the abraded windows,
both the passengers and Boeing management exhibited
attitudes of

(A)   disbelief.   (D)   pacifism.
(B)   optimism.   (E)   disregard.
(C)   cynicism.

As you read the stem before viewing the choices, you'll know you're being asked to judge or **Evaluate the tone** of a passage.

Bust it!

The tone is not stated outright, so you'll need to rely on your perception as you re-read that section, if necessary. Remember, questions follow the order of the passage, so you know to look after the initial company reaction to the windows, but not far after, as many more questions are to follow. Now, formulate your own word for the attitude of the passengers and employees. "Skepticism" or "criticism" work well. If you can't come up with a term, at least note if the tone is negative or positive. In this case, negative is clearly indicated as the passengers are distrustful of the maintenance crew and the company mistrusts the window supplier. Proceed to each choice, seeking the closest match to your term and/or eliminating words with positive connotations.

Choice (C) is correct because "cynicism" best describes the skepticism and distrust with which the passengers view the cleaning company and the parts suppliers. Choice (A) is not correct because both Boeing and the passengers believed the windows were hazy, they just didn't know why. Choice (B) is not correct because people were somewhat agitated that the windows were hazy—certainly not "optimistic." Choice (D), "pacifism," has a rather positive connotation, which the tone of the section does not. Choice (E) is incorrect because the people involved took notice of the situation and did not disregard it. In addition to the ability to discern tone, of course, your vocabulary knowledge is being tested. "Cynicism," should you be unsure of the term, can be viewed in its root, "cynic," which may trigger you to remember that it is negative, and therefore, appropriate in tone.

3   **In line 19, "mundane" means**

(A)   simple.   (D)   ordinary.
(B)   complicated.   (E)   important.
(C)   far-reaching.

This question obviously tests *Vocabulary-in-Context*. Your strategy here should be quickly to view line 12 to confirm usage, block answer choices while devising your own synonym for "mundane," perhaps "common," and then viewing each choice separately, looking for the closest match. Although you might not be familiar with "mundane," the choices are all relatively simple terms. Look for contextual clues in the passage if you can't define the term outright. While the "component supplies" explanation is "mundane," the Aztec myth is not. Perhaps, you could then look for an opposite of mythical; "real" or "down-to-earth" comes to mind.

Choice (D), "ordinary," fits best as it is clearly the opposite of the extraordinary Aztec myth of the serpent and the eagle, which is not as common as a supplier switching materials. Choice (A), "simple," works contextually, but not as an accurate synonym for the word "mundane"; it does not deal with "mundane's" "down-to-earth" definition. Choice (B), "complicated," is inaccurate because the parts switch is anything but complicated. Choice (C), "far-reaching," is not better as it would apply to the myth rather than the common, everyday action of switching parts. Choice (E), "important," does not work either, because the explanation was an integral part of solving the problem. Had you eliminated (B), (C), and (E) due to contextual inappropriateness, you were left with "ordinary" and "simple." A quick re-reading of the section, then, should clarify the better choice. But, if the re-reading did not clarify the better choice, your strategy would be to choose one answer, place a small mark in the booklet, and proceed to the next question. If time is left at the end of the test, you can then review your answer choice.

Bust it!

4 In what ways is El Chichon like the serpent on the Mexican flag, knowing how to "spit venom at the eyes of its adversary" (lines 25-26)?

(A)   It seeks to poison its adversary with its bite.

(B)   It carefully plans its attack on an awaited intruder.

(C)   It ejects tons of destructive sulfuric acid to damage jet windows.

(D)   It angrily blankets the Northern Hemisphere with sulfuric acid.

(E)   It protects itself with the acid rain it produces.

As you view the question, note the word **"like" indicates a comparison is being made**. The quoted simile forms the comparative basis of the question, and you must *Interpret* that phrase with respect to the actual process. You must carefully seek to duplicate the tenor of the terms, coming close to the spitting action in which a harmful substance is expelled in the direction of an object similar to the eyes of an opponent. Look for key words when comparing images. "Spit," "venom," "eyes," and "adversary" are these keys.

Bust it!

In choice (C), the verb that is most similar to the serpent's "spitting" venom is the sulfuric acid "ejected" from the Mexican volcano, El Chichon. Also, the jet windows most closely resemble the "eyes of the adversary" that are struck by El Chichon. Being a volcano, El Chichon is certainly incapable of injecting poison into an adversary, as in choice (A), or planning an attack on an intruder, as in choice (B). In choice (D), although the volcano does indeed "blanket the Northern Hemisphere" with sulfuric acid, this image does not coincide with the "spitting" image of the serpent. Finally, in choice (E), although a volcano can indirectly cause acid rain, it cannot produce acid rain on its own and then spew it out into the atmosphere.

5   The term "photochemistry" in line 31 refers to a chemical change caused by

(A)   the proximity of the sun.

(B)   the drop in temperature at stratospheric altitudes.

(C)   the jet stream's "unceasing horizontal winds."

(D)   the vertical convection of the troposphere.

(E)   the amount of sulfur present in the atmosphere.

Even if you are unfamiliar with the term "photochemistry," you probably know its root or its prefix. Clearly, this question fits in the **Vocabulary-in-Context** mode. Your first step may be a quick reference to line 31. If you don't know the term, context may provide you a clue. The conversion of sulfur-rich *upper* atmosphere into droplets may help. If context does not yield information, look at the term "photochemistry," itself. "Photo" has to do with light or sun, as in photosynthesis. Chemistry deals with substance composition and change. Knowing these two parts can take you a long way toward a correct answer.

Bust it!

Answer choice (A) is the correct response, as the light of the sun closely compares with the prefix "photo." Although choice (B), "the drop in temperature," might lead you to associate the droplet formation with condensation, light is not a factor here, nor is it in choice (C), "the jet stream's winds"; choice (D), "the vertical convection"; or choice (E), "the amount of sulfur present."

6   Unlike the troposphere, the stratosphere

(A)   is extremely humid as it is home to the jet stream.

(B)   contains primarily vertical convections to cause air particles to rise and fall rapidly.

(C)   is approximately one mile thick.

(D)   contains powerful horizontal winds resulting in an excessively dry atmosphere.

(E)   contains very little wind activity.

"Unlike" should immediately alert you to a **Synthesis/Analysis** question asking you to contrast specific parts of the text. Your margin notes should take you right to the section contrasting the atmospheres. Quickly scan it before considering the answers. Usually you won't remember this broad type of comparison from your first passage reading. Don't spend much time, though, on the scan before beginning to answer, as time is still a factor.

Bust it!

This question is tricky because all the answer choices contain key elements/phrases in the passage, but again, a quick, careful scan will yield results. Answer (D) proves the best choice as the "horizontal winds" dry the air of the stratosphere. Choices (A), (B), (C), and (E) are all characteristic of the troposphere, while only the acid droplets accumulate at the rate of one mile per year within the much larger stratosphere. As you answer such questions, remember to eliminate incorrect choices as you go; don't be misled by what seems familiar, yet isn't accurate—read all the answer choices.

7   In line 57, "aggressive" means

(A)   exasperating.   (D)   assertive.
(B)   enterprising.   (E)   surprising.
(C)   prone to attack.

Bust it!

Another *Vocabulary-in-Context* surfaces here; yet, this time, the word is probably familiar to you. Again, before forming a synonym, quickly refer to the line number, aware that perhaps a secondary meaning is appropriate as the term already is a familiar one. Upon reading the line, you'll note "persistent" and "corrosive," both strong terms, the latter being quite negative in its destruction. Now, form an appropriate synonym for aggressive, one that has a negative connotation. "Hostile" might come to mind. You are ready at this point to view all choices for a match.

Using your vocabulary knowledge, you can answer this question. "Hostile" most closely resembles choice (C), "prone to attack," and is therefore the correct response. Choice (A), "exasperating," or irritating, is too weak a term, while choice (B), "enterprising," and (D), "assertive," are too positive. Choice (E), "surprising," is not a synonym for "aggressive."

8 As the eagle triumphed over the serpent in the Mexican flag,

(A)   El Chichon triumphed over the plane as the 747s had to change their flight altitudes.

(B)   the newly designed window material deflected the damaging acid droplets.

(C)   the 747 was able to fly unchallenged by acid droplets a year later as they drifted away to the lower atmosphere.

(D)   the reliability engineers are now prepared for any run of "bad luck" which may approach their aircraft.

(E)   the component supplier of the windows changed materials without telling the customer.

This question asks you to compare the eagle's triumph over the serpent to another part of the text. "As" often signals comparative relationships, so you are forewarned of the **Synthesis/ Analysis question**. You are also dealing again with a simile, so, of course, the question can also be categorized as **Interpretation**. The eagle-serpent issue is a major theme in the text. You are being asked, as you will soon discover in the answer choices, what this general theme is. Look at the stem keys: eagle, triumphed, and serpent. Ask yourself to what each corresponds. You'll arrive at the eagle and the 747, some sort of victory, and the volcano or its sulfur. Now that you've formed that corresponding image in your own mind, you're ready to view the choices.

Bust it!

Choice (C) is the correct choice because we know the statement "the 747 was able to fly unchallenged . . . " to be true. Not only do the remaining choices fail to reflect the eagle-triumphs-over-serpent image, but choice (A) is inaccurate because the 747 did not "change its flight altitudes." In choice (B), the windows did not deflect "the damaging acid droplets." Furthermore, in choice (D), "the reliability engineers" cannot be correct because they cannot possibly predict the future, and therefore, cannot anticipate what could go wrong in the future. Finally, we know that in (E) the window materials were never changed.

9   **The reliability engineers are typified as people who**

(A)   **are uncomfortable considering natural disasters.**
(B)   **believe that all events are predictable through scientific methodology.**
(C)   **accept luck as an inevitable and unpredictable part of life.**
(D)   **easily accept their failure to predict and protect against nature's surprises.**
(E)   **are extremely irrational and are comfortable speaking about luck.**

When the question involves such terms as type, kind, example, or typified, be aware of possible ***Synthesis/Analysis*** or ***Interpretation*** issues. Here the question deals with implications: what the author means but doesn't state outright. "Types" can also lead you to situations which ask you to make an unstated generalization based on specifically stated details. In fact, this question could even be categorized as ***Evaluation*** because specific detail to generalization is a type of argument/essay structure. In any case, before viewing the answer choices, ask yourself what general traits the reliability engineers portray. You may need to check back in the text for typical characteristics. You'll find the engineers to be rational unbelievers in luck. These key characteristics will help you to make a step toward a correct answer.

Bust it!

Choice (B) is the correct answer because the passage specifically states that the reliability engineers "are very uncomfortable when asked to talk about luck" and believe "it should be possible to anticipate events" scientifically. The engineers might be uncomfortable, as in choice (A), but this is not a main concern in the passage. Choice (C) is obviously incorrect, because the engineers do not believe in luck at all, and choice (D) is not correct because "professional failure" is certainly unacceptable to these scientists. There is no indication in the passage that (E) the scientists are "irrational and are comfortable speaking about luck."

The following drill should be used to test what you have just learned. Read the passages and answer the questions. If you are unsure of an answer, refer back to the review for help.

Drill: Critical Reading

In this excerpt from Dickens's Oliver Twist, we read the early account of Oliver's birth and the beginning of his impoverished life.

Although I am not disposed to maintain that the being born in a workhouse, is in itself the most fortunate and enviable circumstance that can
Line possibly befall a human being, I do mean to say that
(5) in this particular instance, it was the best thing for Oliver Twist that could by possibility have occurred. The fact is, that there was considerable difficulty in inducing Oliver to take upon himself the office of respiration,—a troublesome practice, but one which
(10) custom has rendered necessary to our easy existence; and for some time he lay gasping on a little flock mattress, rather unequally poised between this world and the next: the balance being decidedly in favour of the latter. Now, if, during this
(15) brief period, Oliver had been surrounded by careful grandmothers, anxious aunts, experienced nurses, and doctors of profound wisdom, he would most inevitably and indubitably have been killed in no time. There being nobody by, however, but a pauper
(20) old woman, who was rendered rather misty by an unwonted allowance of beer; and a parish surgeon who did such matters by contract; Oliver and Nature fought out the point between them. The result was, that, after a few struggles, Oliver breathed, sneezed,
(25) and proceeded to advertise to the inmates of the workhouse the fact of a new burden having been imposed upon the parish, by setting up as loud a cry as could reasonably have been expected from a male infant who had not been possessed of that very
(30) useful appendage, a voice, for a much longer space of time than three minutes and a quarter. . . .

For the next eight or ten months, Oliver was the victim of a systematic course of treachery and deception. He was brought up by hand. The hungry
(35) and destitute situation of the infant orphan was duly reported by the workhouse authorities to the parish authorities. The parish authorities inquired with dignity of the workhouse authorities, whether there was no female then domiciled in 'the house' who
(40) was in a situation to impart to Oliver Twist, the consolation and nourishment of which he stood in need. The workhouse authorities replied with humility, that there was not. Upon this, the parish authorities magnanimously and humanely resolved,
(45) that Oliver should be 'farmed,' or, in other words, that he should be despatched to a branchworkhouse some three miles off, where twenty or thirty other juvenile offenders against the poor-laws, rolled about the floor all day, without the inconvenience of
(50) too much food or too much clothing, under the parental superintendence of an elderly female, who received the culprits at and for the consideration of sevenpence-halfpenny per small head per week. Sevenpence-halfpenny's worth per week is a good
(55) round diet for a child; a great deal may be got for sevenpence-halfpenny: quite enough to overload its stomach, and make it uncomfortable. The elderly female was a woman of wisdom and experience; she knew what was good for children; and she had a very
(60) accurate perception of what was good for herself. So, she appropriated the greater part of the weekly stipend to her own use, and consigned the rising parochial generation to even a shorter allowance than was originally provided for them. Thereby
(65) finding in the lowest depth a deeper still; and proving herself a very great experimental philosopher.

Everybody knows the story of another experimental philosopher, who had a great theory
(70) about a horse being able to live without eating, and who demonstrated it so well, that he got his own horse down to a straw a day, and would most unquestionably have rendered him a very spirited and rampacious animal on nothing at all, if he had
(75) not died, just four-and-twenty hours before he was to have had his first comfortable bait of air. Unfortunately for the experimental philosophy of the female to whose protecting care Oliver Twist was delivered over, a similar result usually attended the
(80) operation of *her* system . . .

It cannot be expected that this system of farming would produce any very extraordinary or luxuriant crop. Oliver Twist's ninth birth-day found him a pale thin child, somewhat diminutive in
(85) stature, and decidedly small in circumference. But nature or inheritance had implanted a good sturdy

spirit in Oliver's breast. It had had plenty of room to expand, thanks to the spare diet of the establishment; and perhaps to this circumstance may be attributed (90) his having any ninth birth-day at all.

1 After Oliver was born, he had an immediate problem with his

(A) heart rate.   (D) hearing.
(B) breathing.   (E) memory.
(C) vision.

2 What are the two worlds that Oliver stands "unequally poised between" in lines 12-13?

(A) Poverty and riches
(B) Infancy and childhood
(C) Childhood and adolescence
(D) Love and hatred
(E) Life and death

3 What does the author imply about "careful grandmothers, anxious aunts, experienced nurses, and doctors of profound wisdom" in lines 15-17?

(A) They can help nurse sick children back to health.
(B) They are necessary for every being's survival.
(C) They are the pride of the human race.
(D) They tend to adversely affect the early years of children.
(E) Their involvement in Oliver's birth would have had no outcome on his survival.

4 What is the outcome of Oliver's bout with Nature?

(A) He is unable to overcome Nature's fierceness.
(B) He loses, but gains some dignity from his will to fight.
(C) It initially appears that Oliver has won, but moments later he cries out in crushing defeat.
(D) Oliver cries out with the breath of life in his lungs.
(E) There is no way of knowing who won the struggle.

5 What is the "systematic course of treachery and deception" that Oliver falls victim to in the early months of his life?

(A) He is thrown out into the streets.
(B) His inheritance is stolen by caretakers of the workhouse.
(C) He is relocated by the uncaring authorities of the workhouse and the parish.
(D) The records of his birth are either lost or destroyed.
(E) He is publicly humiliated by the parish authorities.

6 What is meant when the residents of the branch workhouse are referred to by the phrase "juvenile offenders against the poor-laws" (line 48)?

(A) They are children who have learned to steal early in life.
(B) They are adolescents who work on probation.
(C) They are infants who have no money to support them.
(D) They are infants whose parents were law offenders.
(E) They are adults who have continuously broken the law.

7 What is the author's tone when he writes that the elderly caretaker "knew what was good for children" (line 59)?

(A) Sarcastic   (D) Astonished
(B) Complimentary   (E) Outraged
(C) Impressed

8 What does the author imply when he further writes that the elderly caretaker "had a very accurate perception of what was good for herself" (lines 59-60)?

(A) She knew how to keep herself groomed and clean.
(B) She knew how to revenge herself on her enemies.
(C) She had a sense of confidence that inspired others.
(D) She really had no idea how to take care of herself.
(E) She knew how to selfishly benefit herself despite the cost to others.

9 Why is the elderly caretaker considered "a very great experimental philosopher" (lines 66-67)?

(A) She was scientifically weaning the children off of food trying to create stronger humans.
(B) She experimented with the survival of the children in her care.
(C) She thought children were the key to a meaningful life.
(D) She made sure that the children received adequate training in philosophy.
(E) She often engaged in parochial and philosophical discussions.

10 In line 76, "bait" most nearly means

(A) worms.
(B) a hook.
(C) a breeze.
(D) a trap.
(E) a meal.

11 To what does the author attribute Oliver's survival to his ninth year?

(A) A strong, healthy diet
(B) Money from an anonymous donor
(C) Sheer luck
(D) His diminutive stature
(E) His sturdy spirit

12 Based upon the passage, what is the author's overall attitude concerning the city where Oliver lives?

(A) It is the best of all possible worlds.
(B) It should be the prototype for future cities.
(C) It is a dark place filled with greedy, selfish people.
(D) Although impoverished, most of its citizens are kind.
(E) It is a flawed place, but many good things often happen there.

The following passage analyzes the legal and political philosophy of John Marshall, a chief justice of the Supreme Court in the nineteenth century.

As chief justice of the Supreme Court from 1801 until his death in 1835, John Marshall was a staunch nationalist and upholder of property rights. He was
Line not, however, as the folklore of American politics
(5) would have it, the lonely and embattled Federalist defending these values against the hostile forces of Jeffersonian democracy. On the contrary, Marshall's opinions dealing with federalism, property rights, and national economic
(10) development were consistent with the policies of the Republican Party in its mercantilist phase from 1815 to 1828. Never an extreme Federalist, Marshall opposed his party's reactionary wing in the crisis of 1798-1800. Like almost all Americans of his day,
(15) Marshall was a Lockean republican who valued property not as an economic end in itself, but rather as the foundation of civil liberty and a free society. Property was the source both of individual happiness and social stability and progress.
(20) Marshall evinced strong centralizing tendencies in his theory of federalism and completely rejected the compact theory of the Union expressed in the Virginia and Kentucky Resolutions. Yet his outlook was compatible with
(25) the Unionism that formed the basis of the post-1815 American System of the Republican Party. Not that Marshall shared the democratic sensibilities of the Republicans; like his fellow Federalists, he tended to distrust the common people and saw in
(30) legislative majoritarianism a force that was potentially hostile to constitutionalism and the rule of law. But aversion to democracy was not the hallmark of Marshall's constitutional jurisprudence. Its central features rather were a commitment to
(35) federal authority versus states' rights and a socially productive and economically dynamic conception of property rights. Marshall's support of these principles placed him near the mainstream of American politics in the years between the War of
(40) 1812 and the conquest of Jacksonian Democracy.
In the long run, the most important decisions of the Marshall Court were those upholding the authority of the federal government against the states. *Marbury v. Madison* provided a
(45) jurisprudential basis for this undertaking, but the practical significance of judicial review in the Marshall era concerned the state legislatures rather than Congress. The most serious challenge to national authority resulted from state attempts to
(50) administer their judicial systems independent of the Supreme Court's appellate supervisions as directed by the Judiciary Act of 1789. In successfully resisting this challenge, the Marshall Court not only averted a practical disruption of the
(55) federal system, but it also evolved doctrines of national supremacy which helped preserve the Union during the Civil War.

13 The primary purpose of this passage is to

(A) describe Marshall's political jurisprudence.
(B) discuss the importance of centralization to the preservation of the Union.
(C) criticize Marshall for being disloyal to his party.
(D) examine the role of the Supreme Court in national politics.
(E) chronicle Marshall's tenure on the Supreme Court.

14 According to the author, Marshall viewed property as

(A) an investment.
(B) irrelevant to constitutional liberties.
(C) the basis of a stable society.
(D) inherent to the upper class.
(E) an important centralizing incentive.

15 In line 22, the "compact theory" was most likely a theory

(A) supporting states' rights.
(B) of the extreme Federalists.
(C) of the Marshall Court's approach to the Civil War.
(D) supporting centralization.
(E) advocating jurisprudential activism.

16 According to the author, Marshall's attitude toward mass democratic politics can best be described as

(A) hostile.   (D) nurturing.
(B) supportive.   (E) distrustful.
(C) indifferent.

17 In line 32, the word "aversion" means

(A) loathing.   (D) forbidding.
(B) acceptance.   (E) misdirection.
(C) fondness.

18 The author argues the Marshall Court

(A) failed to achieve its centralizing policies.
(B) failed to achieve its decentralizing policies.
(C) helped to bring on the Civil War.
(D) supported federalism via judicial review.
(E) had its greatest impact on Congress.

19 According to the author, Marshall's politics were

(A) extremist.   (D) moderate.
(B) right-wing.   (E) majoritarian.
(C) democratic.

In this passage, the author discusses the properties and uses of selenium cells, which convert sunlight to energy, creating solar power.

The physical phenomenon responsible for converting light to electricity—the photovoltaic effect—was first observed in 1839 by the renowned
Line French physicist, Edmund Becquerel. Becquerel
(5) noted that a voltage appeared when one of two identical electrodes in a weak conducting solution was illuminated. The PV effect was first studied in solids, such as selenium, in the 1870s. In the 1880s, selenium photovoltaic cells were built that exhibited
(10) 1%-2% efficiency in converting light to electricity. Selenium converts light in the visible part of the sun's spectrum; for this reason, it was quickly adopted by the then merging field of photography for photometric (light-measuring) devices. Even
(15) today, the light-sensitive cells on cameras used for adjusting shutter speed to match illumination are made of selenium.

Selenium cells have never become practical as energy converters because their cost is too high
(20) relative to the tiny amount of power they produce (at 1% efficiency). Meanwhile, work on the physics of PV phenomena has expanded. In the 1920s and 1930s, quantum mechanics laid the theoretical foundation for our present understanding of PV. A
(25) major step forward in solar-cell technology came in the 1940s and early 1950s when a new method (called the Czochralski method) was developed for producing highly pure crystalline silicon. In 1954, work at Bell Telephone Laboratories resulted in a
(30) silicon photovoltaic cell with a 4% efficiency. Bell Labs soon bettered this to a 6% and then 11% efficiency, heralding an entirely new era of power-producing cells.

A few schemes were tried in the 1950s to use
(35) silicon PV cells commercially. Most were for cells in regions geographically isolated from electric utility lines. But an unexpected boom in PV technology came from a different quarter. In 1958, the U.S. Vanguard space satellite used a small (less than one-
(40) watt) array of cells to power its radio. The cells worked so well that space scientists soon realized the PV could be an effective power source for many space missions. Technology development of the solar cell has been a part of the space program ever
(45) since.

Today, photovoltaic systems are capable of transforming one kilowatt of solar energy falling on one square meter into about a hundred watts of electricity. One hundred watts can power most
(50) household appliances: a television, a stereo, an electric typewriter, or a lamp. In fact, standard solar cells covering the sun-facing roof space of a typical home can provide about 8,500-kilowatt-hours of electricity annually, which is about the average
(55) household's yearly electric consumption. By comparison, a modern, 200-ton electric-arc steel furnace, demanding 50,000 kilowatts of electricity, would require about a square kilometer of land for a PV power supply.
(60) Certain factors make capturing solar energy difficult. Besides the sun's low illuminating power per square meter, sunlight is intermittent, affected by time of day, climate, pollution, and season. Power sources based on photovoltaics require either
(65) back-up from other sources or storage for times when the sun is obscured.

In addition, the cost of a photovoltaic system is far from negligible (electricity from PV systems in 1980 cost about 20 times more than that from
(70) conventional fossil-fuel-powered systems).

Thus, solar energy for photovoltaic conversion into electricity is abundant, inexhaustible, and clean; yet, it also requires special techniques to gather enough of it effectively.

20 To the author, Edmund Becquerel's research was

(A) unimportant.
(B) of some significance.
(C) not recognized in its time.
(D) weak.
(E) an important breakthrough.

21 In the first paragraph, it can be concluded that the photovoltaic effect is the result of

(A) two identical negative electrodes.
(B) one weak solution and two negative electrodes.
(C) two positive electrodes of different qualities.
(D) positive electrodes interacting in a weak environment.
(E) one negative electrode and one weak solution.

22 The author establishes that selenium was used for photometric devices because

(A) selenium was the first solid to be observed to have the PV effect.
(B) selenium is inexpensive.
(C) selenium converts the visible part of the sun's spectrum.
(D) selenium can adjust shutter speeds on cameras.
(E) selenium is abundant.

23 Which of the following can be concluded from the passage?

(A) Solar energy is still limited by problems of technological efficiency.
(B) Solar energy is the most efficient source of heat for most families.
(C) Solar energy represents the PV effect in its most complicated form.
(D) Solar energy is 20 percent cheaper than fossil-fuel-powered systems.
(E) Solar energy is 40 percent more expensive than fossil-fuel-powered systems.

24 In line 32, the word "heralding" most nearly means

(A) celebrating.   (D) anticipating.
(B) observing.   (E) introducing.
(C) commemorating.

25 According to the passage, commercially used PV cells have powered

(A) car radios.   (D) electric utility lines.
(B) space satellite radios.   (E) space stations.
(C) telephones.

26 Through the information in lines 46-49, it can be inferred that two kilowatts of solar energy transformed by a PV system equal

(A) 200 watts of electricity.
(B) 100 watts of electricity.
(C) no electricity.
(D) two square meters.
(E) 2,000 watts of electricity.

27 Sunlight is difficult to procure for transformation into solar energy. Which of the following statements most accurately supports this belief derived from the passage?

(A) Sunlight is erratic and subject to variables.
(B) Sunlight is steady but never available.
(C) Sunlight is not visible because of pollution.
(D) Sunlight would have to be artificially produced.
(E) Sunlight is never erratic.

28 The author's concluding paragraph would be best supported with additional information regarding

(A) specific benefits of solar energy for photovoltaic conversion into electricity.
(B) the negative effects of solar energy for photovoltaic conversion into electricity.
(C) the negative effects of photovoltaic conversion.
(D) why solar energy is clean.
(E) why solar energy is abundant.

In Passage 1, the author writes a general summary about the nature of comedy. In Passage 2, the author sums up the essentials of tragedy.

Passage 1

The primary aim of comedy is to amuse us with a happy ending, although comedies can vary according to the attitudes they project, which can
Line be broadly identified as either high or low, terms
(5) having nothing to do with an evaluation of the play's merit. Generally, the amusement found in comedy comes from an eventual victory over threats or ill fortune. Much of the dialogue and plot development might be laughable, yet a play need
(10) not be funny to be comic. In fact, some critics in the Renaissance era thought that the highest form of comedy should elicit no laughter at all from its audience. A comedy that forced its audience into laughter failed in the highest comic endeavor,
(15) whose purpose was to amuse as subtly as possible. Note that Shakespeare's comedies themselves were often under attack for their appeal to laughter.

Farce is low comedy intended to make us laugh by means of a series of exaggerated, unlikely
(20) situations that depend less on plot and character than on gross absurdities, sight gags, and coarse dialogue. The "higher" a comedy goes, the more natural the characters seem and the less boisterous their behavior. The plots become more sustained,
(25) and the dialogue shows more weighty thought. As with all dramas, comedies are about things that go wrong. Accordingly, comedies create deviations from accepted normalcy, presenting problems which we might or might not see as harmless. If
(30) these problems make us judgmental about the involved characters and events, the play takes on the features of satire, a rather high comic form implying that humanity and human institutions are in need of reform. If the action triggers our
(35) sympathy for the characters, we feel even less protected from the incongruities as the play tilts more in the direction of tragicomedy. In other words, the action determines a figurative distance between the audience and the play. Such factors as
(40) characters' personalities and the plot's predictability influence this distance. The farther away we sit, the more protected we feel and usually the funnier the play becomes. Closer proximity to believability in the script draws us nearer to the
(45) conflict, making us feel more involved in the action and less safe in its presence.

Passage 2

The term "tragedy" when used to define a play has historically meant something very precise, not simply a drama which ends with unfortunate
(50) consequences. This definition originated with Aristotle, who insisted that the play be an imitation of complex actions which should arouse an emotional response combining fear and pity. Aristotle believed that only a certain kind of plot
(55) could generate such a powerful reaction. Comedy shows us a progression from adversity to prosperity. Tragedy must show the reverse; moreover, this progression must be experienced by a certain kind of character, says Aristotle, someone whom we can
(60) designate as the tragic hero. This central figure must be basically good and noble: "good" because we will not be aroused to fear and pity over the misfortunes of a villain, and "noble" both by social position and moral stature because the fall to
(65) misfortune would not otherwise be great enough for tragic impact. These virtues do not make the tragic hero perfect, however, for he must also possess hamartia—a tragic flaw—the weakness which leads him to make an error in judgment
(70) which initiates the reversal in his fortunes, causing his death or the death of others or both. These dire consequences become the hero's catastrophe. The most common tragic flaw is hubris, an excessive pride that adversely influences the protagonist's
(75) judgment.

Often the catastrophic consequences involve an entire nation because the tragic hero's social rank carries great responsibilities. Witnessing these events produces the emotional reaction Aristotle
(80) believed the audience should experience, the catharsis. Although tragedy must arouse our pity for the tragic hero as he endures his catastrophe and must frighten us as we witness the consequences of a flawed behavior which anyone could exhibit,

(85) there must also be a purgation, "a cleansing," of these emotions which should leave the audience feeling not depressed but relieved and almost elated. The assumption is that while the tragic hero endures a crushing reversal, somehow he is not
(90) thoroughly defeated as he gains new stature through suffering and the knowledge that comes with suffering. Classical tragedy insists that the universe is ordered. If truth or universal law is ignored, the results are devastating, causing the
(100) audience to react emotionally; simultaneously, the tragic results prove the existence of truth, thereby reassuring our faith that existence is sensible.

29 In Passage 1, the term "laughable" (line 9) suggests that on occasion comic dialogue and plot development can be

(A) senselessly ridiculous.
(B) foolishly stupid.
(C) amusingly droll.
(D) theoretically depressing.
(E) critically unsavory.

30 The author of Passage 1 makes an example of Shakespeare (lines 16-17) in order to

(A) make the playwright look much poorer in our eyes.
(B) emphasize that he wrote the highest form of comedy.
(C) degrade higher forms of comedy.
(D) suggest the foolishness of Renaissance critics.
(E) show that even great authors do not always use high comedy.

31 The protagonist in a play discovers he has won the lottery, only to misplace the winning ticket. According to the author's definition, this situation would be an example of which type of comedy?

(A) Satire   (D) Sarcasm
(B) Farce   (E) Slapstick
(C) Tragicomedy

32 In line 38, the phrase "figurative distance" suggests

(A) the distance between the seats in the theater and the stage.
(B) the lengths the comedy will go to elicit laughter.
(C) the years separating the composition of the play and the time of its performance.
(D) the degree to which an audience relates with the play's action.
(E) that the play's matter is too high for the audience to grasp.

33 What is the author trying to espouse in lines 41-46?

(A) He warns us not to get too involved with the action of the drama.
(B) He wants the audience to immerse itself in the world of the drama.
(C) He wants us to feel safe in the presence of the drama.
(D) He wants us to be critical of the drama's integrity.
(E) He feels that we should not enjoy the drama overly much.

34 In Passage 2, the author introduces Aristotle as a leading source for the definition of tragedy. He does this

(A) to emphasize how outdated the tragedy is for the modern audience.
(B) because Greek philosophy is the only way to truly understand the world of the theater.
(C) because Aristotle was one of Greece's greatest actors.
(D) because Aristotle instituted the definition of tragedy still used widely today.
(E) in order to prove that Aristotle's sense of tragedy was based on false conclusions.

35 In line 61, "noble" most nearly means

(A) of high degree and superior virtue.
(B) of great wealth and self-esteem.
(C) of quick wit and high intelligence.
(D) of manly courage and great strength.
(E) of handsome features and social charm.

36 Which of the following is an example of *hamartia* (line 68)?

(A) Courtesy to the lower class
(B) The ability to communicate freely with others
(C) A refusal to acknowledge the power of the gods
(D) A weak, miserly peasant
(E) A desire to do penance for one's crimes

37 Which of the following best summarizes the idea of *catharsis* explained in lines 81-88?

(A) All of the tragic consequences are reversed at the last moment; the hero is rescued from certain doom and is allowed to live happily for the rest of his life.
(B) The audience gains a perverse pleasure from watching another's suffering.
(C) The play's action ends immediately, unresolved, and the audience is left in a state of blissful confusion.
(D) When the play ends, the audience is happy to escape the drudgery of the tragedy's depressing conclusion.
(E) The audience lifts itself from a state of fear and pity for the tragic hero to a sense of renewal and absolution for the hero's endurance of great suffering.

38 The authors of both passages make an attempt to

(A) ridicule their subject matter.
(B) outline the general terms and guidelines of a particular aspect of drama.
(C) thrill their readers with sensational information.
(D) draw upon Shakespeare as an authority to back up their work.
(E) persuade their readers to study only one or the other type of drama (i.e., comedy or tragedy).

39 Which of the following best describes the differences between the structure of both passages?

(A) Passage 1 is concerned primarily with the Renaissance era. Passage 2 is concerned primarily with Classical Greece.
(B) Passage 1 is concerned with dividing its subject into subcategories. Passage 2 is concerned with extracting its subject's individual elements.
(C) Passage 1 makes fun of its subject matter. Passage 2 treats its subject matter very solemnly.
(D) Passage 1 draws upon a series of plays that serve as examples. Passage 2 draws upon no outside sources.
(E) Passage 1 introduces special vocabulary to illuminate the subject matter; Passage 2 fails to do this.

40 What assumption do both passages seem to draw upon?

(A) Tragedy is a higher form of drama than comedy.
(B) Tragedy is on the decline in modern society; comedy, however, is on the rise.
(C) *Catharsis* is an integral part of both comedy and tragedy.
(D) An audience's role in the performance of either comedy or tragedy is a vital one.
(E) The tragicomedy is a form that is considered greater than drama that is merely comic or tragic.

Critical Reading Drill
ANSWER KEY

1. (B)	21. (D)
2. (E)	22. (C)
3. (D)	23. (A)
4. (D)	24. (E)
5. (C)	25. (B)
6. (C)	26. (A)
7. (A)	27. (A)
8. (E)	28. (A)
9. (B)	29. (C)
10. (E)	30. (E)
11. (E)	31. (C)
12. (C)	32. (D)
13. (A)	33. (B)
14. (C)	34. (D)
15. (A)	35. (A)
16. (E)	36. (C)
17. (A)	37. (E)
18. (D)	38. (B)
19. (D)	39. (B)
20. (E)	40. (D)

Attacking Regular Multiple-Choice Math Questions

The next three chapters of this book are devoted to teaching you how to bust SAT Math. As discussed in Chapter 1, there are three kinds of math questions on the SAT:

1)   regular multiple-choice questions;

2)   quantitative comparisons; and

3)   student-produced responses (grid-ins).

Bust it!

All of the math sections on the SAT will present questions in **arithmetic, algebra and geometry.** The good news is that SAT math requires only the use of basic mathematical rules and formulas. You will not have to use complex formulas or advanced principles. But there is still a lot of work cut out for you and this chapter will teach you how to successfully attack the regular multiple-choice questions on the SAT. Since you are already familiar with many of the basic rules of math, your mission is to learn how to use these rules quicker and easier! We will also teach you the types of questions that you will encounter and the techniques and tricks that will help you answer these questions.

Multiple-Choice Math

Important Information!

There are a number of advantages and disadvantages associated with multiple-choice math tests. The greatest advantage of a multiple-choice test is that the right answer is always given to you. This means that you may be able to spot the right answer even if you don't understand a problem completely or don't have time to finish it. It means that you may be able to pick the right answer by simply guessing intelligently. It also means that you may be saved from answering a question incorrectly if the answer you obtain is not among the answer choices.

Unfortunately, there are also disadvantages. One of the biggest disadvantages is that every question presents you with four wrong answers. These wrong answers are not randomly chosen numbers—they are the answers that you are most likely to get if you make certain mistakes. **These wrong answers also tend to be choices that "look right" if you don't know how to solve the problem.** Thus, on a particular question, you may be relieved to find "your" answer among the answer choices, only to discover later that you fell into a common error trap. Wrong answer choices can also distract or confuse you when you are attempting to solve a problem correctly, causing you to question your answer even though it is right.

Working from Easiest to Hardest

The testbusting technique of working from the easiest questions to the hardest will help you the most in the multiple-choice math sections. You'll remember from Chapter 2 that all SAT questions are presented from easiest to hardest in each section. You should also remember that every SAT question is worth an equal amount of points. Since each question is worth the same amount of points, why not answer all the easy questions first, thus gaining the most points in the easiest and quickest manner possible? This is going to be your key to success on the regular multiple-choice math questions!

Easy to Difficult

Whenever you start a multiple-choice math section, tell yourself to spend the most amount of time and the greatest effort on the first two-thirds of the questions. The first two-thirds of the section are the easy and medium questions. The writers of the SAT expect that you will get most of these questions right, so make sure you do. Answer each question carefully to avoid making careless errors. If you are expected to get these easy and medium questions correct, you had better do everything you can to get them right. You need to get the points on the easy and medium questions because the SAT writers have made the hard questions (the final third of the section) extremely difficult—not only because of the math involved, but also because of the traps they've laid for you.

Look!

Important Strategy

"What traps?" you might be asking. The traps in the answer choices. Remember our discussion of using the answer choices and the process of elimination to attack easy questions, medium questions, and hard questions? You should remember how we told you the easy questions will have a correct answer choice that looks right and incorrect answer choices that look wrong. You should also remember that the hard questions will have incorrect answer choices that look right and the correct answer choice will almost always look wrong (this is because the SAT writers want you to get these questions wrong). Well, in no section on the entire SAT will the traps in the answer choices be more deadly than in the regular multiple-choice math sections.

"Why?" you probably ask. Because the nature of mathematics enables the writers of the SAT to anticipate the simple errors you will make in a complex question and present an answer choice with the result you would get by making these simple errors.

Here's an example:

What square root is 35% greater than 60?

(A) 81   (D) 40.5

(B) 12   (E) 95

(C) 9

You may or may not consider this a difficult math question, but that doesn't matter. What matters is that the SAT writers have deemed this a hard question and will try and trap you into selecting the wrong answer choice.

Let's look at choice (A). Even if you knew how to answer this question, you may still have fallen victim to this trap. Yes, choice (A) is a trap answer choice. It's a trap because if you pick this choice you didn't work the problem through to its completion. To illustrate, let's take the problem step by step:

To answer this question, you should know that the first step is to reword the problem to make it easier to understand: "What square root is 35% greater than 60?" can be thought of as "What square root is 21 greater than 60." Why? Because 35% of 60 is 21:

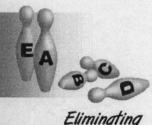

Eliminating Answer Choices

$$35\% \times 60 = 21$$

or

$$.35 \times 60 = 21$$

So, you must determine what is 21 greater than 60. Right, 81! Simply add 21 and 60 to get 81.

Now if you had stopped there and selected choice (A), you would have fallen into the trap because you didn't complete the question. Notice that you are being asked "What *square root* is 21 greater than 60?" You need to determine the square root of 81 to find the correct answer. What's the correct answer? That's right, choice (C), because the square root of 81 is 9.

But choice (A) is not the only trap in this question! Let's say you know how to answer this type of question up to getting the number 81, but didn't know how to determine a square root. You might have known you had to find its square root, but incorrectly thought that the square root is the number divided by 2. Well, there's the trap waiting for you! Answer choice (D), 40.5, was placed there by the SAT writers exactly because of the chance that test-takers might mistakenly think that the square root of a number is its half. They've placed two traps into this question.

And it's not over yet! If you didn't know how to answer this type of question, but were determined to figure it out through the answer choices, you might pick choice (E), 95, because 35 plus 60 equals 95. A hasty decision on your part, in addition to not knowing how to solve the problem, may place you directly in the path of this trap.

So you can see that it is extremely simple for the writers of the SAT to write hard questions with a high level of difficulty and include multiple traps to trick you into selecting the wrong answer.

Look!

Important Strategy

By spending most of your time and effort on the easy and medium questions, you will get a triple benefit: First, you will probably know how to answer these questions quickly because they ask you to use the math skills you should know pretty well. The hard questions will require more reasoning and steps, and the chance that you will know the steps to solve these hard problems is much less than in easy or medium questions. Second, because you probably know how to solve the easy and medium questions, you will be able to spend less time on each of them, thus giving you a better chance to answer more questions. And if you answer more questions correctly, you score more points. Even by taking your time and double-checking your work to avoid careless errors, you will probably go through the easy and medium questions quicker than if you sat and tried to figure out how to solve only a few hard questions. Finally, the easy and medium questions will have correct answer choices that seem right to you. You will be less likely to fall into one the traps that are so very easy to place in difficult regular multiple-choice math questions, as you've just seen.

Easy to
Difficult

Calculators and the Regular Multiple-Choice Math Section

Use
Cautiously

Using a calculator is permitted for any of the math sections of the SAT. This is a huge advantage for you. A calculator will help you solve some regular multiple-choice math questions quicker and with more accuracy. But you must know when to use your calculator and when you shouldn't.

Don't be tempted to use your calculator for every problem. Some problems can actually be solved quicker without a calculator. You need to use your calculator only when it will work to your advantage.

Use Cautiously

There are several types of questions (which you'll learn about later in this chapter) **that are perfect for using your calculator effectively:**

---

1. **Arithmetic calculations** (adding, subtracting, dividing, or multiplying)

---

2. **Converting fractions to decimals and comparing fraction values**

---

3. **Determining square roots**

---

4. **Working with percentages**

If you find yourself faced with one of these types of questions, you are in a prime position to use your calculator. But first, you must know how to solve the question. Once you know how to solve the question, then, and only then, can your calculator help you.

Your next step is to determine if taking the time to punch in the numbers will save you time or if working the calculations out in the margin of your test booklet would be faster. Another advantage, besides saving time, to using the margin of your test booklet is that it will give you a record of your calculations that you can look over and use if you have to rework the problem. The only way to gain the skill in knowing when to use your calculator is through practice, practice, and more practice!

Once you've decided to use your calculator, you should follow the following guidelines:

> 1.   Be sure you've punched in the proper numbers; double-check your display before hitting the function key.
>
> 2.   Once you've finished a question, be sure to hit the clear key or turn the calculator off and then on. Doing so will avoid having calculations from your last question messing up the calculations on your current problem.
>
> 3.   Avoid the memory functions on your calculator. You will have trouble remembering what question you used the memory function for and the figure in the memory may accidentally appear in calculations for the wrong questions. If you want to remember a figure, write it down in your test booklet's margin next to the question it belongs to.
>
> 4.   Pay attention to the order of operations when using your calculator. It is much harder to keep track of the order of operations on a calculator. In fact, you might think about not even using your calculator for questions that have order of operations issues.

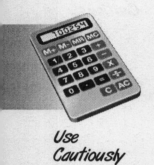

Use Cautiously

About the Directions

The directions found at the beginning of each regular multiple-choice math section are simple—solve each problem, then mark the best of five answer choices on your answer sheet. Printed after these instructions, however, is important information that you should understand thoroughly and memorize before you attempt to take the test. This information includes definitions of standard symbols and formulas that you may need in order to solve regular multiple-choice math problems. The formulas are given so that you don't have to memorize them—however, in order to benefit from this information, you need to know what is and what is not printed in the test booklet. Otherwise, you may waste time looking for a formula that is not listed, or you may fail to look for a formula that is listed. The formulas given to you at the beginning of a regular multiple-choice math section include:

Important Information!

- **The number of degrees in a straight line**

- **Area and circumference of a circle; number of degrees in a circle**

- **Area of a triangle; Pythagorean Theorem for a right triangle; sum of angle measures of a triangle**

Printed after the formulas and definitions of symbols is a very important statement about the diagrams, or figures, that may accompany regular multiple-choice math questions. This statement tells you that, unless stated otherwise in a specific question, figures are drawn to scale. We will discuss the importance of figures being drawn to scale later, in the geometry section of this chapter.

About the Questions

Most regular multiple-choice math questions on the SAT fall into one of three categories: arithmetic, algebra, or geometry. This chapter will tell you the skills you'll need to answer each type of question. By studying the skills you'll need to know and completing the

Important Information!

Important Strategy

corresponding drills, you'll be able to identify your weak and strong areas. The purpose of identifying your weak and strong areas is to enable you to take extra time to study your weak areas. If you find you are having trouble with square roots, get out a math textbook and study square roots. If you have trouble rounding decimals, study that topic.

In the following three sections we will present the types of questions you will encounter on the SAT. Under each section, we will pinpoint the skills you need to know and then teach you specific ways to use these skills faster and easier.

Attacking SAT Arithmetic Questions

The arithmetic questions on the SAT fall into one of the following six question types:

1	FRACTIONS
2	DECIMALS
3	RATIOS
4	PERCENTAGES
5	AVERAGES
6	EXPONENTS AND RADICALS

Bust it!

In this section we'll introduce you to each of these six question types and teach you strategies and techniques for completing each type of question as quickly and easily as possible.

Question Type 1: FRACTIONS

There are many ways that the SAT will ask you to use fractions. The skills you need to have mastered in order to successfully attack fractions on the SAT include:

1. **Adding Fractions**

2. **Subtracting Fractions**

3. **Multiplying Fractions**

4. **Dividing Fractions**

5. **Reducing Fractions**

6. **Converting Mixed Numbers to Fractions**

Bust it!

Since the operations of fractions can be very confusing, we've given you a quick refresher on them:

A.   Parts and types of fractions:

In the fraction $\frac{a}{b}$, the *numerator* is a and the *denominator* is b. This fraction means that a is being divided by b. The denominator of a fraction can never be zero since a number divided by zero is not defined. If the numerator of a fraction is greater than the denominator, the fraction is called an *improper fraction*. A *mixed number* is the sum of a whole number and a fraction.

An example of a mixed number is:

$$4\frac{3}{8} = 4 + \frac{3}{8}$$

B.   Changing a mixed number to an improper fraction:

To change a mixed number to an improper fraction, simply multiply the whole number by the denominator of the fraction and add that to the numerator. Put this sum over the denominator. For example:

$$5\frac{2}{3} = \frac{(5 \times 3) + 2}{3} = \frac{15 + 2}{3} = \frac{17}{3}$$

C.   Changing an improper fraction to a mixed number:

Look!

Important Strategy

To change an improper fraction to a mixed number, simply divide the numerator by the denominator. The remainder becomes the numerator of the fractional part of the mixed number, and the denominator remains the same. For example:

$$\frac{35}{4} = 35 \div 4 = 8\frac{3}{4}$$

D.   Adding fractions that have a common denominator:

To find the sum of fractions having a common denominator, simply add together the numerators of the given fractions and put this sum over their common denominator. Do not add together the common denominators. For example:

$$\frac{11}{3} + \frac{5}{3} = \frac{11 + 5}{3} = \frac{16}{3}$$

E.   Subtracting fractions that have a common denominator:

To find the difference of fractions having a common

denominator, simply subtract the numerators of the given fractions and put this difference over their common denominator. Do not subtract the common denominators. For example:

$$\frac{11}{3} - \frac{5}{3} = \frac{11-5}{3} = \frac{6}{3} = 2$$

F.   Adding fractions that have different denominators:

To find the sum of fractions having different denominators, it is necessary to find the *lowest common denominator (LCD)* of the different denominators using a process called *factoring*.

Important Information!

To *factor* a number means to find two numbers that when multiplied together have a product equal to the original number. These two numbers are then said to be *factors* of the original number. For example, the factors of 6 are:

            1 and 6 since $1 \times 6 = 6$
and
            2 and 3 since $2 \times 3 = 6$

Every number is the product of itself and 1. A *prime factor* is a number that does not have any factors besides itself and 1. This is important when finding the LCD of fractions having different denominators.

To find the LCD of $\frac{11}{6}$ and $\frac{5}{16}$, we must first find the prime factors of each of the two denominators:

$$6 = 2 \times 3$$

$$16 = 2 \times 2 \times 2 \times 2$$

$$LCD = 2 \times 2 \times 2 \times 2 \times 3 = 48$$

Note that we do not repeat the 2 that appears in both the factors of 6 and 16.

Once we have determined the LCD of the denominators, each of the fractions must be converted into *equivalent fractions* having the LCD as the denominator.

Important Strategy

To convert the fractions $\frac{11}{6}$ and $\frac{5}{16}$ to equivalent fractions, you must rewrite them so that 48 is their denominator. To do this you must multiply the numerator and the denominator of each fraction by a number to make the denominators in both fractions 48. This can be done because the numerator and denominator of a fraction can be multiplied (or divided) by the same number without changing the value of the fraction. So, this is how to determine what number you should multiply $\frac{11}{6}$ and $\frac{5}{16}$ by so that their denominators become 48:

$$6 \times \, ? = 48$$
$$6 \times 8 = 48$$
$$16 \times \, ? = 48$$
$$16 \times 3 = 48$$

Therefore, to convert $\frac{11}{6}$ and $\frac{5}{16}$ to equivalent fractions:

$$\frac{11}{6} \times \frac{8}{8} = \frac{88}{48}$$

$$\frac{5}{16} \times \frac{3}{3} = \frac{15}{48}$$

Now add these fractions:

$$\frac{11}{6} + \frac{5}{16} = \frac{88}{48} + \frac{15}{48} = \frac{103}{48}$$

G. Subtracting fractions that have different denominators:

To find the difference of fractions having different denominators, follow the same steps as adding fractions with different denominators, only subtract the numerators once you have made them equivalent fractions. For example:

$$\frac{11}{6} - \frac{5}{16} = \frac{88}{48} - \frac{15}{48} = \frac{73}{48}$$

H.   Multiplying fractions:

To find the product of two or more fractions, simply multiply the numerators of the given fractions to find the numerator of the product and multiply the denominators of the given fractions to find the denominator of the product. For example:

$$\frac{2}{3} \times \frac{1}{5} \times \frac{4}{7} = \frac{2 \times 1 \times 4}{3 \times 5 \times 7} = \frac{8}{105}$$

Look!

Important Strategy

I.   Dividing fractions:

To find the quotient of two or more fractions, simply invert (or flip-over) the divisor and multiply. For example:

$$\frac{8}{9} \div \frac{1}{3} = \frac{8}{9} \times \frac{3}{1} = \frac{8 \times 3}{9 \times 1} = \frac{24}{9} = \frac{8}{3}$$

J.   Simplifying fractions:

To simplify a fraction is to convert it into a form in which the numerator and denominator have no common factor other than 1. For example:

$$\frac{12}{18} = \frac{12 \div 6}{18 \div 6} = \frac{2}{3}$$

K.   Simplifying complex fractions:

Complex fractions are fractions whose numerators and/or denominators are made up of fractions. To simplify a complex fraction, find the LCD of all the fractions. Then multiply both the numerator and denominator by this number and simplify as you would a normal fraction. For example:

$$\frac{4+\dfrac{4}{9}}{4-\dfrac{4}{7}}$$

Important Strategy

In order to combine terms, we must find the LCD of 9 and 7:

$$9 = 3 \times 3$$

$$7 = 7 \times 1$$

$$LCD = 3 \times 3 \times 7 = 63$$

Now multiply both the numerator and denominator by 63:

$$\frac{63\left(4+\dfrac{4}{9}\right)}{63\left(4-\dfrac{4}{7}\right)} = \frac{\left(\dfrac{63}{1}\right)\left(\dfrac{4}{1}\right)+\left(\dfrac{\overset{7}{\cancel{63}}}{1}\right)\left(\dfrac{4}{\cancel{9}}\right)1}{\left(\dfrac{63}{1}\right)\left(\dfrac{4}{1}\right)-\overset{9}{}\left(\dfrac{\cancel{63}}{1}\right)\left(\dfrac{4}{\cancel{7}}\right)1} = \frac{252+28}{252-36} = \frac{280}{216}$$

Finally, simplify the fraction:

$$\frac{280}{216} \div \frac{8}{8} = \frac{35}{27}$$

Testbusting Fractions Tip #1:
TURN FRACTIONS INTO DECIMALS

While it is important to know and understand the above rules for working with fractions, it often easier to solve problems on the SAT by converting fractions into decimals. The decimal value of any fraction can be found by dividing the numerator (the top number) by its denominator (the bottom number).

Converting fractions to decimals will help you on the SAT in three specific ways. First, and most importantly, by converting fractions to decimals you will have a much easier time comparing and working with values. Second, you can't use your calculator to work with fractions, but you can use your calculator to work with decimals. And third, you will encounter some questions that require you to convert fractions to decimals in order to answer the question.

As we just told you, probably the best reason for converting fractions to decimals is that it makes it easier to work with values. While there will be situations where you will need to work with quantities in their fractional form, most questions will be easier if you can convert them to decimals. So, be sure to review topics involving fractions so you are comfortable working with them when you have to, but also remember that converting fractions to decimals when possible will enable you to work quicker and with more accuracy (since you can use your calculator with decimals).

Comparing fractions is a common task on the SAT. You will encounter problems that ask you to compare one fraction with another. Converting fractions to decimals will make these questions a snap. The people who write the SAT like these questions because fractions are very difficult to compare. This is true because the rules that apply to fractions are confusing. A fraction may look greater than another on paper, but it is really less. For example, $\frac{3}{4}$ is greater than $\frac{2}{16}$. You may be fooled into thinking $\frac{2}{16}$ is greater than $\frac{3}{4}$ because the numbers are bigger. But if you convert the fractions to decimals you'll easily see that .75 $\left(\frac{3}{4}\right)$ is greater than .125 $\left(\frac{2}{16}\right)$.

Converting fractions to decimals will save you time if there is a lot of adding, subtracting, multiplying, and dividing needed to solve the question. The time it takes to convert fractions into decimals in order to add them is usually much less than the time it takes just to find the least common denominator. Working with decimals avoids having to find a least common denominator in order to add fractions. And working in decimals saves you the confusing and slow task of factoring a fraction in order to reduce it.

Testbusting Fractions Tip #2:
REDUCE LARGE FRACTIONS

If you encounter a fraction question that thoroughly confuses you because of the large fractions involved, and you can't convert them to decimals, try reducing the fractions.

The best way to reduce a fraction is to divide both the numerator and the denominator by the largest number that is a common factor. For example:

$$\frac{12}{48}$$

12 divides into both 12 (12 × 1) and 48 (12 × 4)

Divide both the numerator and the denominator by 12

$$\frac{12 \div 12}{48 \div 12} = \frac{1}{4}$$

By reducing fractions, you'll often find that a question that looks very hard is actually very simple.

Question Type 2: DECIMALS

You've already learned that decimals can be very helpful in dealing with fractions. But in order to work with decimals you will need to know how to perform the following operations:

1. Adding Decimals

2. Subtracting Decimals

3. Multiplying Decimals

Bust it!

4. Dividing Decimals

5. Comparing Decimals

Testbusting Decimals Tip #1:
USE YOUR CALCULATOR

We've discussed that working with decimals is easier than working with fractions. One of the reasons this is true is because you can add, subtract, multiply, and divide decimals with your calculator and you can't perform these same operations on fractions with a calculator. With this in mind, be sure to use your calculator!

Using your calculator to work out decimal problems is the easiest way to prevent careless errors. It will also usually be faster than working the question out by hand. There you have it: using your calculator for decimal problems is easier and quicker. What more could you ask for?

Testbusting Decimals Tip #2:
USING THE DECIMAL POINT

Another important strategy you can learn to use with decimals on the SAT is to master the decimal point. You will be asked to compare decimals on the SAT. The placement of the decimal point is essential to determining the value of a decimal; hence being able to compare it to another.

Here is a brief chart explaining how to determine a decimal's value:

$$2,330 = 2,000 + 300 + 30 + 0$$

$$233.0 = 233 = 200 + 30 + 3$$

$$23.30 = 23.3 = 20 + 3 + \frac{3}{10}$$

$$2.330 = 2.33 = 2 + \frac{3}{10} + \frac{3}{100}$$

$$0.2330 = 0.233 = \frac{2}{10} + \frac{3}{100} + \frac{3}{1,000}$$

$$.02330 = 0.0233 = \frac{0}{10} + \frac{2}{100} + \frac{3}{1,000} + \frac{3}{10,000}$$

From this chart you can see that decimals can contain fractions. You probably knew this had to be true even before you saw this chart because you know that every fraction can be made into a decimal. So the opposite must also be possible. To find a fraction from a decimal, simply put the number over its position past the decimal point. From our example, we could take .233 and turn it into the fraction $\frac{233}{1,000}$. Pretty simple, right?

Here are some more examples of converting decimals to fractions:

$$.40 = \frac{40}{100} = \frac{10}{25} = \frac{2}{5}$$

$$.3994 = \frac{3,994}{10,000} = \frac{1,997}{5,000}$$

$$.7 = \frac{7}{10}$$

Converting decimals to fractions is easy. But comparing decimals can be tricky. The easiest way to compare two decimals is to line up the decimal points and fill in any missing spaces with zeros. Here's an example:

Is 0.0089 greater than 0.07?

First line up the two numbers by their decimal points:

0.0089

0.07

Next, fill in the empty spaces with zeros:

0.0089

0.0700

Now compare the numbers. It's obvious that 700 is greater than 89. So now you can see that 0.07 is definitely greater than 0.0089.

You may have been confused by the number 89. Isn't 89 greater than 7, so 0.0089 has to be greater than 0.07? While understandable, your assumption is wrong and will make you lose points on the SAT. Every time you need to compare decimals, make sure that you stop and think, "Am I positive that my choice is greater than the other?" If you aren't positive, get out your scrap paper, line up the decimal points, fill in the spaces with zeros, and THEN compare the decimals.

Question Type 3: RATIOS

A ratio is simply a relationship which compares two quantities. If you have a bowl of 3 apples and 3 oranges, you can express this mixture of apples and oranges as 1:1. In this bowl there are as many apples as there are oranges. If there were 6 apples and 3 oranges, twice as many apples as oranges, you can express this as the ratio 2:1. This ratio translates as meaning there are two apples for every orange.

Bust it!

Since ratios can be also be written as fractions and many of the same rules that apply to fractions also apply to ratios, it is as easy to work with ratios as fractions. But remember fractions and ratios are not the same. To look at a ratio as a fraction, the ratio "two to five" would be the same as saying $\frac{2}{5}$. The traditional way of presenting this ratio is 2:5. All of this means that there are three ways of writing a ratio:

1. $\dfrac{2}{5}$

2. the ratio 2 to 5

3. 2:5

Testbusting Ratios Tip #1:
USING ESTIMATION AND LOGIC

Ratios are very easy to work with if you have a good understanding of what they are: a relationship between two quantities.

Here's an example of a ratio problem and a typical SAT question:

If a crowd has 10,000 people and the ratio of men to women is 1:3 how many women are present?

(A) 10,000   (D) 5,000

(B) 2,500   (E) 3,000

(C) 7,500

Eliminating Answer Choices

If this ratio was 1:1 there would be the same number of men and women in the crowd. If the ratio was 3:3 there would also be the same number of men and women in the crowd. This is true because a ratio is a relationship between quantities. The ratios 1:1 and 3:3 are equal in their relationship to each other, so the number of men and women that they represent must also be equal to one another. This eliminates choice (D) because if the number of men and women were equal, there must be 5,000 of each in a crowd of 10,000.

Since the ratio we are dealing with is 1:3, that means there is 1 man to every 3 women in the crowd. From this you can guess that there will be quite a few more women in the crowd than men. This would help you eliminate choices (B), 2,500, and (E) , 3,000, since the question is asking you how many women there are in the crowd and there will be more women (greater than half: 5,000) than men. You can also eliminate choice (A), 10,000, because a ratio of 1:3 means there are some men in the crowd, the crowd is not all women. So, if there are 10,000 people in the crowd, choice (A) cannot be correct.

This leaves choice (C), 7,500, as the correct answer. Logically, you must agree that if there are three women for every man in a crowd of 10,000, the number 7,500 would be about right for the number of women in the crowd.

Testbusting Ratios Tip #2: USING THE SUM OF THE PARTS

Unlike the example we just showed you, estimating and using logic to guess the correct answer won't work every time, so you need to learn how to *solve* ratio problems. In the previous example we used logic and the process of elimination to help answer a ratio problem. But in order to solve some SAT ratio questions you'll need to perform the mathematical steps in order arrive at the correct answer.

Let's look at our example problem again:

If a crowd has 10,000 people and the ratio of men to women is 1:3 how many women are present?

(A) 10,000   **(D) 5,000**

(B) 2,500   **(E) 3,000**

(C) 7,500

To get the answer using a mathematical process, we have to use the technique of summing up the parts of a ratio.

To sum up the parts, you should add the ratio together. Using our example, that would be 1 added to 3 equals 4. That's 1 part boys plus 3 parts girls. Now take that sum and divide it into the total number of people in the crowd (which works out to be $\frac{10,000}{4} = 2,500$). This tells us that the crowd is made up of 4 parts of 2,500 people. We know that the ratio of men to women is 1:3, so there is 1 group of 2,500 men and 3 groups of 2,500 women. That means there are 7,500 women in the crowd (3 × 2,500). So the answer is (C), 7,500.

Let's try a another one!

A moving company's fleet of trucks is made up of cargo vans and moving vans. The ratio of cargo vans to moving vans is 14:7. If there are 294 trucks in the entire fleet, how many are moving vans?

First simplify the ratio of 14:7 to 2:1 since it's the same thing and it's eaiser to work with smaller numbers. $\frac{14}{7}$ is equal to $\frac{2}{1}$.

Once again, to sum up the parts you should add the ratio together. This means 2 added to 1 equals 3. That's 2 parts cargo vans plus 1 part moving vans. Now take that sum and divide it into the total number of trucks in the fleet (which works out to be $\frac{294}{3} = 98$). This tells us that the trucks are made up of 3 parts of 98 trucks. We know that the ratio of cargo vans to moving vans is 2:1, so there are 2 groups of 98 cargo vans and 1 group of 98 moving vans. There are 98 moving vans in the fleet.

Testbusting Ratios Tip #3:
THINK OF PROPORTIONS AS RATIOS

Once in a while, you'll be given a question on the SAT that you think is a ratio problem, but doesn't come right out and call itself a ratio problem. Usually, this type of question reads like this:

If Mary can knit 7 sweaters with 280 feet of yarn, how many feet would it take for her to knit 25 sweaters?

You should treat this question as a ratio, even if a true ratio is never given. This is a ratio question disguised as a proportion question. You have all the information to complete the proportion except for once piece. Here is the proportion created as a ratio:

$$\frac{7 \text{ sweaters}}{280 \text{ feet of yarn}} = \frac{25 \text{ sweaters}}{x \text{ feet of yarn}}$$

Since ratios can be treated as fractions, we can cross multiply to find the value for x.

$$7x = 25 \times 280$$

$$7x = 7,000$$

$$x = 1000$$

It would take 1,000 feet of yarn for Mary to knit 25 sweaters.

Question Type 4: PERCENTAGES

Percentages are simply fractions with a denominator of 100. Every percentage, when placed in decimal form, will have 100 as its denominator.

$$56\% = \frac{56}{100} = .56$$

Bust it!

Percentage problems are very popular with the writers of the SAT because most people don't like percentages. But, if you apply some simple techniques, you won't have the least bit of trouble answering any percentage problem you encounter.

Testbusting Percentage Tip #1:
MEMORIZE COMMON PERCENTAGE CONVERSIONS

The easiest way to answer percentage questions quicker is to memorize common percentage conversions. This means knowing what a percentage converts to in decimals and fractions. Here is a short list of common percentages:

$$100 \text{ percent} = \frac{100}{100} = 1$$

$$75 \text{ percent} = \frac{3}{4} = 0.75$$

$$50 \text{ percent} = \frac{1}{2} = 0.50$$

$$25 \text{ percent} = \frac{1}{4} = 0.25$$

$$20 \text{ percent} = \frac{1}{5} = 0.20$$

$$10 \text{ percent} = \frac{1}{10} = 0.10$$

$$5 \text{ percent} = \frac{1}{20} = 0.05$$

$$1 \text{ percent} = \frac{1}{100} = .01$$

Testbusting Percentage Tip #2:
KNOW HOW TO CONVERT PERCENTAGES TO FRACTIONS AND DECIMALS

You will need to know how to convert percentages to fractions to decimals and back again. This skill is necessary and will prove to be an invaluable tool in attacking SAT percentage questions.

To convert a percentage to a decimal, simply move the decimal point two places to the left. This is the same as dividing the percentage by 100, but much easier and quicker! For example, 25% is equal to 0.25. And 245% is equal to 2.45.

To convert a decimal to a percentage, do the opposite: move the decimal point two places to the right! For example, 0.94 would become 94%. And 0.0043 equals 0.43%.

Unlike working with decimals, converting a percentage to a fraction takes a bit more work. To do so, place the percentage over a denominator of 100 and reduce the fraction. For example, a percentage of 28 would become $\frac{28}{100}$ and then reduce to $\frac{7}{25}$. Another example would be a percentage of 65 becoming the fraction $\frac{65}{100}$ and then reducing to $\frac{13}{20}$.

To get a percentage from a fraction, you first have to convert the fraction to a decimal. As you know, to get a decimal from a fraction, divide the numerator by the denominator. Once you get a decimal, you know to move the decimal point two places to the right. Use your calculator. For example: $\frac{3}{4}$ would become 0.75 and then 75%. Here's another example: $\frac{14}{35}$ would become 0.4 and then 40%.

 ### Testbusting Percentage Tip #3:
TAKING IT ONE STEP AT A TIME

There are percentage questions on the SAT that are specifically designed to confuse you. These types of questions usually appear as follows:

What number is 20% less than 55?

What? This may seem confusing at first glance, but it can be very easy to find the solution if you take it one step at a time.

First, what is 20 percent of 55? Now be careful. On the actual test you will surely see 11 as an answer choice. This is a trap. You might incorrectly pick this trap answer choice as the correct answer if you don't carefully read the question. While 11 *is* 20 percent of 55, it is *not* the correct answer to this question. You need to do some further work.

The next step is to reword the question: What number is 11 less than 55? Well, that should be easy: 44. So the correct answer is 44! Not too bad if you slow down, take a deep breath, and attack a question one step at a time.

Let's try another one, only this one will be harder:

A couple rents an apartment for $500 a year. A year later the rent is increased by 10 percent. And the year after that, another 10 percent. How much will the couple pay for the three years that they rent the apartment?

Wow! If there ever was a question that needs to be taken one step at a time, this is it! But let's take a deep breath and get started. We must first determine what we are being asked. The last sentence asks us to find out how much the couple will pay for all three years that they rent the apartment. This means we need to add the three years of rent to get the correct answer.

The next step is to find the rent for each year. You know the first year's rent is $500 because you've been told so. That means the second year's rent is $500 plus 10 percent. What's 10 percent of $500?

$500 × 10 percent = $500 × .10 = $50

That's right, $50.00 So you add that to $500 to get the second year's rent: $550.00 Now find out the third year's rent: $550 (the second year's rent) plus 10 percent.

550.00×10 percent $= \$550.00 \times .10 = \$55.00$

So the third year's rent is $550 + $55 = $605. Now we must determine the total of all three years' rent:

$500 + $550 + $605 = $1655

So the correct answer is $1655. Again, not too bad if you sit back and take the question one step at a time!

You must be very careful with these complex percent questions. The SAT uses them (and very well, we might add) to get you to select an answer choice that seems right but is actually wrong. So take your time and be very careful to read the questions closely.

Question Type 5:
AVERAGES: MEANS, MEDIANS, AND MODES

Bust it!

The writers of the SAT love to use averages in questions. Why? Because they can use averages in three different ways using four different terms to confuse you. Huh? It's simple: There are three different ways you will encounter averages on the SAT and four different words to describe them. Those four words are average, mean, median, and mode.

Let's look at the first word: average. In mathematics, an average is a term used to describe a way to represent a list of numbers. But, an average can also be used to define the sum of a list of values divided by the number of values in the list. Here's an example:

Find the mean salary for four company employees who make $5.00 per hour, $8.00 per hour, $12.00 per hour, and $15.00 per hour.

$$\frac{\$5 + \$8 + \$12 + \$15}{4} \text{ (the number of values in the list)} = \$\frac{40}{4} = \$10$$

The mean salary is $10.00 per hour.

If you encounter the word average on the SAT, you should know that the question is asking you to find the sum of a list of values divided by the number of values in the list.

$$\text{Average} = \frac{\text{Sum of the Values}}{\text{Number of Values}}$$

The second word you need to know is mean. A mean and average are exactly the same thing when the word average is used to find the sum of a list of values divided by the number of values in the list. If you are asked to find the mean of a list of values on the SAT, you must know that you are being asked to find the average of that list.

The third word is median. A median is different than an average or mean. A median is the value that is in the exact middle of a group of values when all the numbers are arranged in order. For example, in a list of values such as 2, 4, 9, 22, 104, 105, 229, the median would be 22 since there are three values before it in the list and three values after it.

And the fourth word is mode. A mode is the value that appears most in a list of values, when all the numbers are arranged in order. For example, if you are given 3, 4, 4, 8, 8, 8, 8, 13, 14, 15, 15, 19, the mode of that list is 8 since it appears in the list four times (more than any other value in the list).

Testbusting Averages Tip #1:
TO FIND THE MEAN, FIND THE NUMBER OF VALUES

Whenever you are asked to find the mean or average in a question, the first thing you need to determine is the number of values. Here's an example:

A teacher grades 5 papers in one night. The scores on those papers are 80, 94, 88, 72, and 79. On the second night, the teacher grades 5 more papers. The scores on

the second night's papers are 99, 68, 84, 93, and 91.
What is the mean of all of the scores?

The first step, as we've told you, is to determine the number of values you are being asked to find the mean for. In this case there are 10 papers that were graded on two nights. The next step is to add all of the papers' scores together:

80 + 94 + 88 + 72 + 79 + 99 + 68 + 84 + 93 + 91 = 848

Then divide the sum of all the scores by the number of scores:

848 ÷ 10 = 84.8

This means the mean of all the scores is 84.8. Pretty simple, but you had to find the number of values before you could do anything else. Remember to do this first when you are being asked to find the average or mean.

Testbusting Averages Tip #2:
TAKE IT ONE STEP AT A TIME

Just like in percent questions, in complex average questions you need to attack the question one step at a time. Here's an example of how to attack a very hard average question:

A group of 20 farmers had an average truckload of 30 bales of hay. If 6 of those farmers have an average of 22 bales of hay, what is the average for the other 14 farmers?

Okay. Slow down, take a breath, and then break the question down. You know that the first thing you have to do is find the number of farmers that you are being asked to average. There are 20 farmers total, but you are being asked to find the average for only 14.

Next, you need to determine what information you have. You know that the 20 farmers averaged 30 bales of hay. If all 20 farmers averaged 30 bales of hay, you can determine that those 20 farmers had 600 bales of hay:

30 average bales × 20 farmers = 600 bales of hay

You also know that 6 of those farmers averaged 22 bales of hay per truck.

22 average bales × 6 farmers = 132 bales of hay

You need to find out what the other 14 farmers averaged.

You should next subtract the number of bales the 6 farmers had from the total number of bales all 20 farmers had:

600 total bales − 132 bales from 6 farmers = 468 bales from 14 farmers

Now you know the number of bales the other 14 farmers had. You're almost there. You know how to find the average of a list of values, right? Divide the sum of all the values by the number of values. To answer this question simply divide the number of bales these 14 farmers had by 14:

468 bales ÷ 14 farmers = 33.43 average bales

Voila! If you take these complex questions one step at a time, they usually prove to be pretty easy!

Question Type 6: EXPONENTS AND RADICALS

Bust it!

The final type of arithmetic question that you'll find on the SAT involves exponents and radicals. You must be familiar with these terms in order to do well on the SAT.

A power of a number is the product obtained by multiplying the number by itself a given number of times. To raise a given number (let's call it a base value), multiply the base value by itself as many times as the power indicates (let's call this number an exponent). It's easier to understand if we show you an example:

$$5^3 = 5 \times 5 \times 5 = 125$$

125 can be written as 5^3

The base value is 5 and the exponent is 3. The exponent indicates how many times you should multiply the base value by itself. The exponent is always a little number (or letter) placed in the upper-right hand corner.

Here's another example:

$$4^6 = 4 \times 4 \times 4 \times 4 \times 4 \times 4 = 4,096$$

4,096 can be written as 4^6

In 4^6, 4 is the base and 6 is the exponent.

Pretty simple, right? Now let's look at radicals. This is kind of the opposite process of writing a number with an exponent. A radical indicates the square root of a value.

For example:

$$5 \times 5 = 25$$

$$\sqrt{25} = 5$$

or

$$7 \times 7 = 49$$

$$\sqrt{49} = 7$$

Sometimes, a radical can indicate the cube root of a number. For example:

$$3 \times 3 \times 3 = 27$$

$$\sqrt[3]{27} = 3$$

or

$$6 \times 6 \times 6 = 216$$

$$\sqrt[3]{216} = 6$$

Testbusting Exponents and Radicals Tip #1: KNOW HOW TO MANIPULATE EXPONENTS

In order to succeed at exponent questions on the SAT, you'll need to know how to multiply them. It is easy to do, but the writers of the SAT love to make sure you know how to do it.

To multiply exponents that have the same base value, simply add the exponents:

$$2^4 \times 2^5 \times 2^9 = 2^{18}$$

Be extremely careful not to confuse multiplying exponents that have the same base with adding exponents that have the same base. $2^4 + 2^5 + 2^9$ does NOT equal 2^{18}. To add numbers with exponents, you need to determine their actual values and add those together:

$$2^4 + 2^5 + 2^9 = (2 \times 2 \times 2 \times 2) + (2 \times 2 \times 2 \times 2 \times 2) + (2 \times 2 \times 2 \times 2 \times 2 \times 2 \times 2 \times 2 \times 2)$$

$$16 + 32 + 512 = 560$$

You can divide two base values that are the same; you would simply subtract the exponents.

$$4^5 \div 4^3 = 4^2$$

Again, be sure not to confuse dividing exponents with the same base with subtracting them. To subtract exponents that have the same base, you need to determine their actual values and subtract them, similar to the process of adding exponents that have the same base. Here is an example:

$$4^5 - 4^2 = (4 \times 4 \times 4 \times 4 \times 4) - (4 \times 4) = 1024 - 16 = 1008$$

When you multiply the exponents of two or more bases, instead of adding them, you are "raising a power to a power". This is often done when exponents appear in parentheses. Here's an example:

$$(3^4)^5 = 3^{4 \times 5} = 3^{20}$$

Parentheses are very important when dealing with exponents and can be confusing. For this reason, the writers of the SAT will use parentheses often. To keep yourself on track to the correct answer, be sure to employ the distributive property when working with parentheses. The distributive property, in the case of exponents, states that anything inside parentheses must be multiplied by the exponent outside the parentheses. For example:

$$(4a)^2 + 2 = 16a^2 + 2$$

not

$$(4a)^2 + 2 = 4a^2 + 2$$

Testbusting Exponents and Radicals Tip #2:
USE YOUR CALCULATOR

Working with exponents and radicals is very simple to do on your calculator. Just make sure that you are using a scientific calculator with a y^x key and a $\sqrt{}$ key. To find the value of an exponent, simply use the y^x key. To do this, for example, to find the value of 5^4, you would punch in 5 for the y value. Next you would punch the y^x key and then punch in 4 for the x value and finally the equals key. This is an extremely good timesaving technique and will prevent many miscalculations.

Testbusting Exponents and Radicals Tip #3:
KNOW HOW EXPONENTS BEHAVE

You may remember that we warned you to be careful with fractions because they sometimes don't work the way you'd expect them to. Well, exponents do the same thing. Knowing how exponents behave before you take the SAT will give you an edge and help you avoid choosing answers that look correct but are actually wrong.

Here is a quick summary of what to learn about exponents before taking the SAT:

1. A negative number raised to an even power will become positive.

    Example: $(-3)^2 = -3 \times -3 = 9$

                              or

                      $(-3)^4 = -3 \times -3 \times -3 \times -3 = 81$

2. A negative number raised to an odd power will be negative.

    Example: $-3^3 = -3 \times -3 \times -3 = -27$

3. A number raised to a negative power implies a fraction.

    Example: $(3)^{-2} = \dfrac{1}{3^2} = \dfrac{1}{3 \times 3} = \dfrac{1}{9}$

4. If you square or cube a fraction it will become less than the base value.

    Example: $\left(\dfrac{3}{4}\right)^3 = \dfrac{27}{64}$

5. If the exponent of a base is 0, the value will be 1 (unless the base is 0, then it will be 0).

    Example: $3^0 = 1$

                      $0^0 = 0$

6. If you square or cube a value greater than 1, it will become larger than the base.

    Example: $3^2 = 9$

                      $4^2 = 16$

                      $5^3 = 125$

7.   If your base is 10, the exponent will equal the number of zeros in the number.

Example: $10^2 = 100$ (two zeroes)

$10^5 = 100,000$ (five zeroes)

 Testbusting Exponents and Radicals Tip #4: KNOW HOW RADICALS BEHAVE

Just like exponents, you'll have a leg up on the SAT if you know how radicals behave. This will help you avoid any traps laid by the question writers who want you to pick the answer choice that looks right but really isn't.

1.   No matter what, if you are being asked the square root of a number, the square root will be positive. Although 3^2 and $(-3)^2$ both equal 9, the square root of 9 is only positive 3.

2.   To multiply square roots, multiply the values inside the brackets.

Example: $\sqrt{4} \times \sqrt{9} = \sqrt{36} = 6$

3.   The square root of a positive fraction is larger than the fraction you see.

Example:

$$\sqrt{\frac{1}{9}} = \frac{1}{3}$$

$$\frac{1}{9} > \frac{1}{3}$$

Points to Remember for Busting SAT Arithmetic Questions

On Target!

✔   *Study the operations and behaviors of fractions. Know how to add, subtract, multiply, and divide fractions. Understand and know how to manipulate improper fractions, mixed numbers, and complex fractions.*

✔   *Whenever possible, convert fractions to decimals. Doing so will enable you to use your calculator to work with decimals and will enable you to more easily compare and work with fractional values.*

✔   *Always reduce fractions to their lowest form. When you run into a fraction that confuses you because of the large values involved, and you can't convert it to a decimal, always reduce it. This will enable you to look at the problem more easily.*

✔   *Use your calculator as much as possible when working with decimals. Adding, subtracting, multiplying, and dividing decimals with your calculator is usually much faster and always more accurate than working them out by hand.*

✔   *Know how to use the placement of the decimal point to compare decimal values.*

✔   Use estimation and logic to weed out answer choices in ratio problems.

✔   Know how to mathematically solve ratio problems by summing up the parts because guessing and using logic will not always get you to the correct answer.

✔   Understand that ratio questions can appear as proportion problems even if they don't include the word "ratio." Know how to identify and solve such questions.

✔   Memorize the most common percentages and their fractional and decimal equivalents.

✔   Know how to convert percentages to fractions and decimals.

On Target!

✔   When presented with a complex percentage question, slow down; take a deep breath; and attack it one step at a time. Usually, a complex question that looks intimidating turns out to be several simple problems put together.

✔   To find the mean of a set of values, your first step is to determine the number of values in the set. Only then can you begin to find the mean.

✔   Just like with complex percentage problems, if you run into a complex mean, median, or mode question, slow down; take a deep breath; and attack

On Target!

it one step at a time. Don't be intimidated by a question that is really simple if you just look at it in parts.

✔ Know how to manipulate exponents through addition, subtraction, multiplication, and division.

✔ Use your calculator whenever possible to work with exponents and radicals.

✔ Understand how exponents and radicals behave to avoid making mistakes because the correct answer "looks wrong" or an incorrect answer "looks right."

Attacking SAT Algebra Questions

The algebra questions on the SAT use letters, or variables, to represent numbers. In these questions, you will be required to solve existing algebraic expressions or translate word problems into algebraic expressions.

Sound difficult? If it does, you're not alone. Most students find algebra difficult, but in this section we'll teach you some strategies and help you review the algebraic principles that will enable you to successfully attack the algebra questions on the SAT.

All the algebra questions on the SAT fall into one of the following two question types:

1. Algebraic Expressions
2. Word Problems

There are just these two types of questions! Of course each of these question types can require you to use a wide variety of algebraic skills. But we'll tell you what skills you'll need and teach you some strategies to make working out algebra questions quicker and easier.

Let's learn more about these strategies before we go into a discussion about the types of questions. The strategies you'll learn will help you solve algebra problems faster than if you use the techniques you learned in school. "What's wrong with the way I learned in school?" you may ask. Well, to put it bluntly: it takes too long! The

Bust it!

Important Strategy

291

clock is one of your worst enemies on the SAT and the way you learned algebra in school eats up too much time.

The strategies that will help you save the most time on algebra questions are "Starting from the Choices" and "Testing Choices." As you can see from their names, both strategies involve the use of the answer choices. This is because the SAT is a multiple-choice test and you should use that to your best advantage. When you took an algebra class in school, more often than not your teacher didn't give you multiple-choice tests. This forced you to work through each problem using the algebraic functions you learned in class. But the SAT is a multiple-choice test and you can use the answer choices as a way to get the correct answer easier and quicker. Let's begin with Starting from the Choices.

Important Strategy

Testbusting Algebra Tip #1:
STARTING FROM THE CHOICES

As you probably know, algebra is a form of math that uses letters, or variables, to represent numbers. This is why so many students are afraid of algebra questions. The variables are strange and unfamiliar. Most other math problems have regular numbers that are easy to understand and work with. But the variables in algebra questions are numbers too, it's just a little harder to see them.

This is the first step to doing well in algebra: think of the variables as numbers. Most algebra problems ask you to take an equation and find the numbers that are represented by the variables. For example:

$$2x + 5 = 15$$

The x is the variable in this problem. You should read this as "what number (x) times 2 added to 5 equals 15?" You would multiply x and 2 because, in algebra, two numbers that are placed right next to one another implies that they are to be multiplied. Now, on a basic question like this it's pretty simple to figure out the right answer.

And on the SAT it would be even easier. Why? Because the test would give you the correct answer! Let's look at this example as it would appear on the SAT:

$$2x + 5 = 15$$

(A) 1   (D) 2

(B) −3   (E) 0

(C) 5

Remember that this question is asking you to find the value (or number) for *x*. Since one of the answer choices is correct, that means one of the answer choices is *x*! All you have to do is look at the answer choices, pick one that looks correct, plug it into the equation, and see if it works! That's what we mean by Starting from the Choices!

Look!

Important Strategy

Here's how to use the Starting from the Choices strategy:

First, you need to make some decisions. For our example you are being asked what number multiplied by 2 and added to 5 equals 15. From this, you need to decide which answer choice to pick and place in the equation first.

It is best to pick a number that is in the middle of all the possible choices. This is because, if the choice you pick is wrong, you'll be able to tell whether the correct answer is greater or lesser than your first choice and then your second choice is guaranteed to be closer to the correct answer. Picking the middle number first saves you time, lots of time.

Look at the answer choices again:

(A) 1   (D) 2

(B) −3   (E) 0

(C) 5

The middle number would be 1 or 2 since a negative number is given and 5 is the highest positive number. Let's use choice (D) 2:

2 times 2 plus 5 = 15

4 plus 5 = 15

9 ≠ 15

Too low. Since 2 gives you a number that is lower than 15, the next number you plug in the equation should be higher than 2. Let's look at what choices remain:

(A) 1   (D) 2

(B) −3   (E) 0

(C) 5

The only number that is higher than 2 is choice (C), 5. You could simply select (C) at this time, but it is wise to check that your assumption is correct by working the equation out using 5:

2 times 5 plus 5 = 15

10 plus 5 = 15

15 = 15

So choice (C) is correct. You only had to pick two choices and you didn't need to perform any algebra to find the right answer choice!

Using the strategy of Starting from the Choices will help you get the correct answer easier (because you won't have to do the algebra) and quicker (because you'll probably be able to eliminate wrong answer choices and plug in the remaining choices faster than it would take you to actually do the question)!

Let's do another problem, only this time a bit harder:

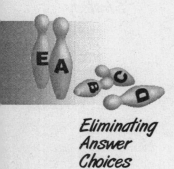

Eliminating Answer Choices

Look!

Important Strategy

Gregg wants to buy a new car but doesn't have enough money to buy one. He has $300 in savings and makes $150 a week as a gas station attendant. The car he wants is $1,200. How many weeks must he work before he can afford the car?

    (A) 3   (D) 8

    (B) 1   (E) 6

    (C) 22

"But that's not an algebra question!" Yes, it is. You just have to write the equation. So writing the equation is your first step. You know Gregg needs $1,200 to buy the car, so let's place this on one side of the equal sign:

$$= \$1,200$$

You know that he already has $300 in savings, so let's place this on the other side of the equal sign:

$$\$300 = \$1,200$$

Next, you know that he makes $150 per week as a gas station attendant. The question you need to answer is how many weeks he needs to work in order to afford the car. The number of weeks is what you need to find and, thus, is the variable. So, let's finish the equation by writing how many weeks (x) of $150, plus the $300 he already has, would give Gregg the $1,200 he needs to buy the car. We would write this equation as:

$$\$150x + \$300 = \$1,200$$

You are now ready to Start from the Choices. Let's look at the answer choices:

    (A) 3   (D) 8

    (B) 1   (E) 6

    (C) 22

As we stated earlier, it is a good idea to use the middle number first. The closest number to middle would be choice (D), 8. Plugging 8 into our equation we would get:

$$\$150(8) + \$300 = \$1,200$$

$$\$1,200 + \$300 = \$1,200$$

$$\$1,500 \neq \$1,200$$

You know $1,500 doesn't equal $1,200, so choice (B) is not correct. You can tell from the answer using 8 as *x* that the correct answer is going to be lower than 8. So, looking at our choices again, you should try choice (E), 6, the next number lower than 8:

$$\$150(6) + \$300 = \$1,200$$

$$\$900 + \$300 = \$1,200$$

$$\$1,200 = \$1,200$$

Found it! So choice (E), 6, is the correct answer. See how easy Starting from the Choices can be!

Before moving onto the Testing Choices strategy, we have a few words of advice about Starting from the Choices:

1.   *It should be pretty obvious that the algebra questions you will want to use this strategy on must have answer choices that are numbers.*

2.   *Make sure you know where you are in the math section. Remember that the questions are given to you from easiest to hardest. Be sure you understand that choices that look correct are usually correct in the easy and medium questions. So the first number you plug into the equation should be the answer choice that seems to be correct. The harder questions (the last third of the section) may have some traps waiting for you and the choices that*

On Target!

seem correct probably are not. So, if you use the Starting from the Choices strategy on the last third of a section, you may want to avoid plugging in choices that seem obviously correct since this may be a waste of time.

3.	Make sure you plug in the answer choice everywhere the variable appears. Algebra questions can use a variable in more than one place. For instance:

$$3x + 8 - \frac{3}{4}x + x = 200$$

On Target!

In this example, you must find a number that will be used in three different places in the equation and still come up with the answer of 200. When plugging in the choices, make sure that you plug the choices in all three places. If you don't, you won't find the correct answer.

4.	Don't worry if you can't tell which answer choice is exactly the middle number. Just pick one that's close and work from there. You may have to work through all the answer choices to find the correct answer, but by picking one that's close to the middle first, you should find the answer quicker than by just randomly picking a number.

Testbusting Algebra Tip #2: TESTING CHOICES

This strategy will help you attack algebra questions that don't have numbers in their answer choices (where you should use the Starting from the Choices strategy). Testing Choices is very similar to Starting from the Choices, but you use clues in the question to determine what numbers you plug into the equation instead of looking at the answer choices (as you would when using Starting from the Choices).

Questions with phrases like "solving for *y*" or "in terms of *x*" are tip-offs that you should use the Testing Choices strategy. Trying to solve questions like these using traditional algebra methods is extremely slow and the chances that you will make errors is very high. So whenever you see phrases like "solving for *y*" or "in terms of *x*", be sure to employ the Testing Choices strategy.

To use the Testing Choices strategy, you must first pick numbers to represent the variables in the question. Second, you have to use the numbers you've picked to find the answer to the question. And, third, you have to use the numbers you've picked and plug them into the answer choices to determine which choice will give you the answer to the question (which you found in Step 2).

Important Strategy

Confused? Don't be. Here's an example to clarify the steps:

Nancy scored an average of *x* number of points per game during the entire basketball season. If Nancy's team played 20 games in the season, how many points, in terms of *x*, did Nancy score?

(A) $\dfrac{2}{x}$

(B) $20x$

(C) $\dfrac{x}{2}$

(D) $20 + x$

(E) x^2

Okay, the first step is to pick numbers to represent the variables in the question. The only variable is *x*, the average number of points Nancy scored per game during the entire season. You have to pick a number for *x*, something easy to work with, like 10.

Next, work out the question using 10:

Nancy scored an average of 10 points per game during the entire basketall season. If Nancy's team played 20 games in the season, how many points did Nancy score?

The answer would be 200 since Nancy's team played 20 games and she averaged 10 points per game (20 games × 10 points per game = 200 points).

The final step would be to use 10 in the answer choices to see which one will give you the correct answer 200. Unlike Starting from the Choices questions, it doesn't really matter which answer choice you start with. If one choice looks to you to be more likely to be correct than the others, choose this one first. Here are the answer choices for our example:

Look!

Important Strategy

(A) $\dfrac{2}{x}$ (D) $20 + x$

(B) $20x$ (E) x^2

(C) $\dfrac{x}{1}$

Let's try choice (A), $\dfrac{2}{x}$, first. Remember we're substituting 10 for x:

$$\frac{2}{x} = \frac{2}{10} = \frac{1}{5}$$

Definitely not the correct answer since $\dfrac{1}{5}$ does not equal 200. Let's try choice (B) next:

$$20x = 20(10) = 200$$

Got it! Choice (B) is the correct answer because it represents the correct relationship between the average number of points Nancy scored per game and the total number of points she scored in the season.

Bust it!

Let's try another one! This time the question will not be as easy to recognize using the Testing Choices strategy:

If 500 people paid the same amount of money for 500 concert tickets, and the people spent a total of x dollars, 25 of these tickets cost how much?

(A) $\dfrac{5}{x}$ (D) $\dfrac{x}{20}$

(B) $\dfrac{x}{40}$ (E) $\dfrac{80}{x}$

(C) $10x$

There are lots of numbers here to confuse you, but the question is really not that hard if you know the correct strategy. The first step is to pick a number to use in the question. Let's pick 2. If each ticket cost $2, then 500 people spent $1,000 on 500 tickets. That means $1,000 is the value for x. Also, if each ticket costs $2, then 25 tickets would cost $50.

In order to answer this question, you need to plug–in $1,000 for x in the answer choices to find the choice that gives you $50 (what 25 tickets would cost).

Let's start with (A):

$$\frac{5}{x} = \frac{5}{1,000} = \frac{1}{200}$$

Now let's try (B):

$$\frac{x}{40} = \frac{1,000}{40} = \frac{500}{20} = \frac{250}{10} = \frac{25}{1} = 25$$

Still not it. How about choice (C)?

$$10x = 10(1,000) = 10,000$$

Nope. Let's try choice (D):

$$\frac{x}{20} = \frac{1,000}{20} = \frac{500}{10} = \frac{50}{1} = 50$$

So the correct answer is choice (D). See how easy that was!

There are many ways that the SAT will present algebra questions that can be solved using the Testing Choices strategy. Just remember, the same steps apply to every question that you can answer using this strategy. The trick is to recognize the types of problems for which you can use this strategy to solve the question. Here are some types of problems and how to solve them using the Testing Choices strategy:

Inequalities:

An inequality is an expression that doesn't have an equal sign (=) but, in its place, another sign. These types of signs include lesser than (<); greater than (>); lesser-than-or-equal ($\leq$); or greater-than-or-equal ($\geq$).

You can use the Testing Choices strategy to answer inequalities, but you have to follow some special rules: Sometimes you'll need to pick a few numbers to solve an inequality problem, and you might have to pick specific numbers to help yourself out. Picking numbers like 0 or 1, or negative numbers and fractions, will enable you to work with inequalities because those numbers behave in strange ways when they are multiplied or squared.

Sometimes you don't even have to use the Testing Choices strategy on an inequality problem if you can simplify the question. Here's an example:

$-4y + 13 \geq 21$, **so which of the following is true?**

(A) $y \leq -4$ (D) $y \geq 6$

(B) $y \leq 6$ (E) $y = 1$

(C) $y \leq -2$

Simplify the problem as much as possible:

$$-4y + 13 \geq 21$$

$$-4y \geq 8$$

$$-y \geq \frac{8}{4}$$

$$-y \geq 2$$

$$y \leq -2$$

It is extremely important that you multiply the variable $-y$ by -1 so you get a positive variable. Remember to switch the inequality sign in direction when you multiply the other side by a negative.

The correct answer choice is (C), $y \leq -2$, and you didn't have to do anything but simplify the problem!

It Cannot Be Determined:

Once in a while, you'll see a question on the SAT regular multiple-choice math that has "It Cannot Be Determined" as answer choice (E). This doesn't pose any problem to you except that if you plan to use the Testing Choices strategy, you'll need to test every answer choice just to be sure that choice (E) "It Cannot Be Determined" is not the correct choice.

Even and Odd:

Many of the questions that you encounter involving even and odd numbers will contain the word "could." If this is the case, all you have to do is pick a number, use it in the problem and find just one instance where the conditions of the problem are met. Once you've done this, you've solved the problem. Here's an example:

> **If a is an odd number and b is even, which of the following could be an even number?**
>
> (A) $a - b$ (D) $\dfrac{a}{2} - b$
>
> (B) $a + b$ (E) $\dfrac{a}{b} - \dfrac{a}{2}$
>
> (C) $a + \dfrac{b}{2}$

When dealing with questions containing even and odd numbers, it is best to pick 1 and 2 for the numbers you'll plug into the question. Using 1 for *a* and 2 for *b*, let's look at the answer choices again:

(A) $a - b = 1 - 2 = -1$

(B) $a + b = 1 + 2 = 3$

(C) $a + \dfrac{b}{2} = 1 + \dfrac{2}{2} = 1 + 1 = 2$

Having found that (C) is an even number, you can stop trying out the answer choices. Choice (C) is correct because, by using 1 and 2 for *a* and *b*, this choice could be an even number. No further searching is necessary.

Now that you know two extremely effective strategies for approaching SAT algebra questions, let's review the types of algebra questions you'll see on the regular multiple-choice math section of the SAT.

Question Type 1: ALGEBRAIC EXPRESSIONS

Problems involving algebraic expressions will often ask you to compare two expressions, or rearrange and simplify them. To successfully complete questions on algebraic expressions, you'll need to know the following skills:

Bust it!

1. **Combining like terms**

2. **Factoring an expression**

1. Combining like terms: To combine like terms you need to look at values in an expression that differ only in their numerical coefficients. Here's a quick review of terminology: You've learned that a *variable* is a letter that represents a number. However, a variable can take on several values at a given time. A *constant*, on the

Look!

Important Strategy

other hand, is a symbol which takes on only one value at a given time. A *term* is a constant, a variable, or a combination of constants and variables. For example: 7.76, 3x, xyz, $\dfrac{5z}{x}$, $(0.99)x^2$ are terms. If a term is a combination of constants and variables, the constant part of the term is referred to as the *coefficient* of the variable (such as 2x or 4x^2). If a variable is written without a coefficient, the coefficient is assumed to be 1.

So, to combine like terms, you need to combine terms which differ only in their numerical coefficients. For example:

$$P(x) = (x^2 - 3x + 5) + (4x^2 + 6x - 3)$$

By using the commutative and associative laws, you can rewrite this expression as:

$$P(x) = (x^2 + 4x^2) + (6x - 3x) + (5 - 3)$$

Then, using the distributive law, we can rewrite the expression as:

$$P(x) = (1 + 4)x^2 + (6 - 3)x + (5 - 3)$$

$$P(x) = 5x^2 + 3x + 2$$

This is combining like terms. Here's another example:

$$= (5x^2 + 4y^2 + 3z^2) - (4xy + 7y^2 - 3z^2 + 1)$$

$$= 5x^2 + 4y^2 + 3z^2 - 4xy - 7y^2 + 3z^2 - 1$$

$$= 5x^2 + (4y^2 - 7y^2) + (3z^2 + 3z^2) - 4xy - 1$$

$$= 5x^2 + (-3y^2) + 6z^2 - 4xy - 1$$

2. Factoring an expression: To factor a polynomial completely is to find the prime factors of the polynomial with respect to a specified set of numbers.

The following concepts are important while factoring or simplifying expressions:

a.   The factors of an algebraic expression consist of two or more algebraic expressions which, when multiplied together, produce the given algebraic expression.

b.   A prime factor is a polynomial with no factors other than itself and 1. The *Least Common Multiple (LCM)* for a set of numbers is the smallest quantity divisible by every number of the set. For algebraic expressions the least common numerical coefficients for each of the given expressions will be a factor.

c.   The *Greatest Common Factor (GCF)* for a set of numbers is the largest factor that is common to all members of the set.

d.   For algebraic expressions, the greatest common factor is the polynomial of highest degree and the largest numerical coefficient which is a factor of all the given expressions.

The procedure for factoring an algebraic expression completely is as follows:

STEP 1 | **First, find the greatest common factor, if there is any. Then examine each factor remaining for greatest common factors.**

Important Information!

STEP 2	Continue factoring the factors obtained in Step 1 until all factors other than monomial (consisting only of one term) factors are prime.

For example:

Factor $4 - 16x^2$:

$$4 - 16x^2 = 4(1 - 4x^2) = 4(1+2x)(1 - 2x)$$

Here's another example:

Express each of the following as a single term:

$$3x^2 + 2x^2 - 4x^2 \text{ and } 5ax^2 - 7axy^2 - 3xy^2$$

Step 1: Factor x^2 in the expression.

$$3x^2 + 2x^2 - 4x^2 = (3 + 2 - 4)x^2 = 1x^2 = x^2$$

Step 2: Factor xy^2 in the expression and the factor a.

$$5axy^2 - 7axy^2 - 3xy^2 = (5a - 7a - 3)\, xy^2$$
$$= [(5 - 7)a - 3]xy^2$$
$$= (-2a - 3)xy^2$$

Question Type 2: Word Problems

Bust it!

The vast majority of word problems found on the SAT can be easily and quickly solved using the Starting with the Choices and Testing Choices strategies. There will, however, be some problems that cannot be solved using either of these strategies. For these types of questions, you'll need to rewrite the word problem as an equation and solve it using traditional algebra.

In order to rewrite word problems as equations, you'll need to pay attention to key words in the problems. Here is a quick list of key words and what they should mean to you:

KEYWORD	EQUIVALENT
is	equals
sum	add
plus	add
more than, older than	add
difference	subtract
less than, younger than	subtract
twice, double	multiply by 2
half as many	divide by 2
increase by 3	add 3
decrease by 3	subtract 3

Important Information!

Here's an example of a word problem as you might see one on the SAT:

Adam has 50 more than twice the number of frequent flier miles that Erica has. If Adam has 200 frequent flier miles, how many does Erica have?

(A) 25

(B) 60

(C) 75

(D) 100

(E) 250

The keywords in this problem are "more" and "twice." If you let:

A = the number of frequent flier miles that Adam has

and

E = the number of frequent flier miles that Erica has

If Adam has twice the number of miles that Erica has plus 50 more you can write:

A (Adam) = 50 + 2E

Since A = 200, the solution becomes:

200 = 50 + 2E

Bust it!

Therefore,

$$200 = 50 + 2E$$

$$200 - 50 = 2E$$

$$150 = 2E$$

$$75 = E$$

So choice (C), 75, would be the correct answer.

Points to Remember for Busting SAT Algebra Questions

✔   Using the Starting from the Choices strategy to answer algebra questions will be faster and easier than using traditional algebra. To use this strategy,

    1) think of variables as numbers,

    2) pick an answer choice and use it to answer the question,

    3) if it works, that's the correct choice, and

    4) if it doesn't work, keep trying answer choices until you find the right one.

✔   When a question doesn't have numbers in its answer choices, use the Testing Choices strategy to solve it. The first step for using the Testing Choices strategy is to pick a number. Second, use the number you've picked to solve the problem. Third, use the the number you picked and plug it into the answer choices to determine which answer choice will give you the answer to the question. The answer choice that gives you the answer to the question is the correct answer.

✔   If you are being asked a question about an inequality, you can use the same Testing Choices strategy to solve the problem. But, you may be able to

On Target!

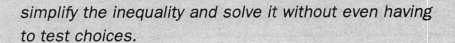

simplify the inequality and solve it without even having to test choices.

✔   If the question you are working has "It Cannot Be Determined" as its answer choice (E), be sure to test every answer choice before selecting your answer. This is the only way to be absolutely sure that (E) is not the correct answer.

✔   If the word "could" appears in the question you are working on, you only have to find one instance where the numbers you pick satisfy the conditions of the question. Once you find numbers that meet these conditions, you've found the correct answer. This applies mostly to questions that involve even and odd numbers.

✔   Know the fundamental rules and terminology of algebraic expressions. Know how to combine like terms and how to factor an expression.

✔   Understand that most word problems can be solved using the Starting with the Choices or Testing Choices strategies, but that there will be instances where you'll need to rewrite a word problem as an equation. Know how to recognize the keywords in a word problem and be able to translate those key words into equations.

On Target!

The final type of question you'll encounter on the Regular Math sections of the SAT will cover geometry. Like the arithmetic and algebra questions, you will not need to know complex formulas, theorems, or proofs to solve SAT geometry. In fact, whatever formulas you need, (such as the area of a circle or the number of degrees in a straight line) will be given to you at the beginning of the SAT math section. In this section we'll teach you:

1. Geometry rules and principles that are frequently tested on the SAT

2. How to "eyeball" a geometry question

3. How to use the strategy of Starting from the Choices to answer geometry questions

Bust it!

The Fundamental Rules of SAT Geometry

Geometry is a branch of math that deals with points, lines, angles, planes and figures. Geometry is built upon a series of defined terms. For the SAT, you should be familiar with the basic terms related to geometry. Here they are:

Important Information!

Point: A *point* is a particular and definite position. Although we represent points on paper with small dots, a point has no size, thickness, or width.

Line:	A *line* is a series of adjacent points which extends indefinitely. A line can be either curved or straight; however, unless otherwise stated, the term "line" refers to a straight line.
Plane:	A *plane* is a collection of points lying on a flat surface, which extends indefinitely in all directions.
Line Segment:	If A and B are two points on a line, then the line segment $\overline{AB}$ is the set of points on that line between the points *A* and *B*, and including *A* and *B*, which are endpoints. The line segment is referred to as $\overline{AB}$.

Once you are comfortable with these terms, you can begin to study the areas of geometry that you'll need to master for the SAT. These areas include:

1. Degrees and Angles

2. Triangles

3. Circles

4. Quadrilaterals (Squares and Rectangles)

Degrees and Angles

Important Information!

At the extreme basic level, geometry is all about degrees and angles. A *degree* is a unit that is used to measure angles. There are 360° in a circle (the little symbol after "360" denotes "degrees"). It doesn't matter how big, or how small the circle is, it will always contain 360°.

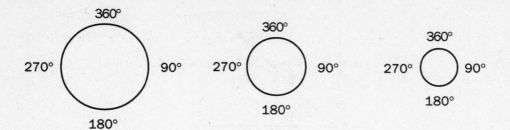

An angle is formed when two lines extend from one point. It is easier to understand angles if you think of a circle. If the point the two lines extend from is at the center of the circle, the measure of the angle is determined by the number of degrees enclosed by the lines as they cross the edge of the circle:

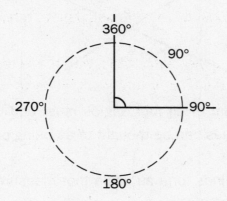

Important Information!

Angles can be referred to in any of the three following ways:

1. By a capital letter which names its *vertex* (the point where the two lines converge), for example: $\angle A$

2. By a lowercase letter or number placed inside the angle, for example: $\angle x$

3. By three capital letters, where the middle letter is the vertex and the other two letters are not on the same line, for example: $\angle CAB$ or $\angle BAC$, both of which represent the angle that follows:

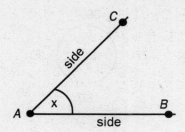

Vertical angles are formed when two lines intersect. The angles opposite to each other are equal: $\angle a = \angle c$ and $\angle b = \angle d$.

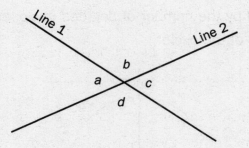

The sum of all four angles must add up to 360°. This is true because all angles can be thought of as being part of a circle:

If two lines form an angle that measures 90°, it is said to be a *right angle*. Also, the two lines making a right angle are said to be *perpendicular*. In the case of a right angle, all four angles will be 90°:

Important Information!

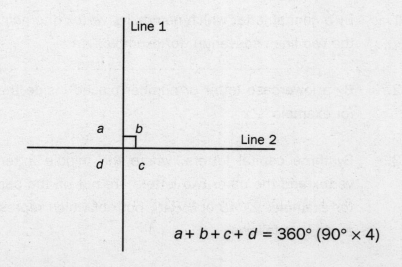

$$a + b + c + d = 360° \ (90° \times 4)$$

Two lines are called parallel lines if, and only if, they are in the same plane and DO NOT intersect. This means the two lines will run alongside one another in both directions and will never intersect. If two or more lines are perpendicular (form right angles) to the same line, then these lines are parallel to each other:

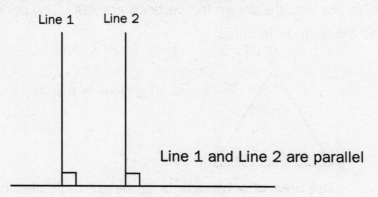

Line 1 and Line 2 are parallel

If two parallel lines (Lines 1 and 2) are cut by a transversal line (Line 3) then the following is always true:

1. The sum of the adjacent angles is equal to 180°
   (e.g. $a + b = 180°$, $b + d = 180°$, etc.)

2. $\angle a$ on Line 1 is equal to angle $\angle a$ on Line 2, $\angle b = \angle b$ and so forth

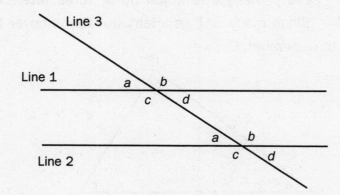

3. Opposite angles are equal (e.g. $\angle a = \angle d$, $\angle b = \angle c$)

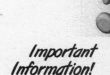

Important Information!

Triangles

Important Information!

A closed three-sided geometric figure is called a triangle. The sides of a triangle are straight lines. The points of intersection of the sides of a triangle are called the vertices of the triangle. For example, in the triangle shown the vertices are *ABC*. The perimeter of a triangle is the sum of its sides:

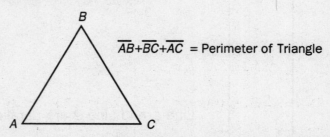

$$\overline{AB}+\overline{BC}+\overline{AC} = \text{Perimeter of Triangle}$$

The **area of a triangle** is its height multiplied by its base divided by 2.

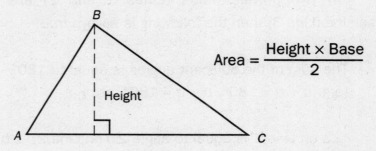

$$\text{Area} = \frac{\text{Height} \times \text{Base}}{2}$$

Every triangle is made up of three interior angles that equal 180°. Since many SAT geometry questions cover this rule, it is important to remember it.

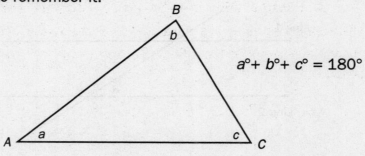

$$a° + b° + c° = 180°$$

Important Information!

There are three main types of triangles: *equilateral*, *isosceles*, and *right*. **An equilateral triangle is a triangle having three**

equal sides. Because the sides of an equilateral triangle are the same, so are the angles. This is true because angles opposite equal sides are also equal. **The angles of an equilateral triangle are always 60°.**

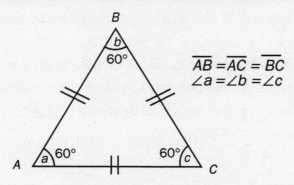

$$\overline{AB} = \overline{AC} = \overline{BC}$$
$$\angle a = \angle b = \angle c$$

An isosceles triangle is a triangle in which two of the sides are equal. And since angles opposite equal sides are equal, two of the angles in an isosceles triangle are equal:

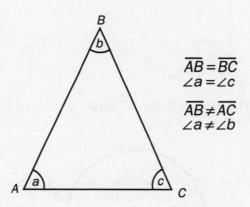

$$\overline{AB} = \overline{BC}$$
$$\angle a = \angle c$$

$$\overline{AB} \neq \overline{AC}$$
$$\angle a \neq \angle b$$

Important Information!

A triangle with a right angle (90°) is called a right triangle. The side opposite the right angle is called the hypotenuse of the right triangle. The other two sides are called the arms or legs of the right triangle.

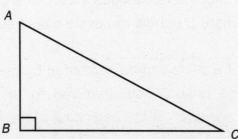

Important Information!

Circles

Important Information!

A *circle* is a set of points in the same plane equidistant (the same distance) from a fixed point, called its center.

A *radius* of a circle is a line segment drawn from the center of the circle to any point in the circle. The *diameter* of a circle is double its radius, or the length of a straight line extending from one edge of the circle to the other:

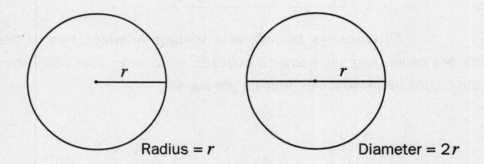

Radius = *r*   Diameter = 2*r*

A portion of a circle is called an *arc* of the circle:

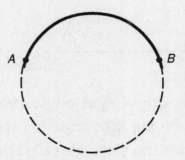

Bust it!

A circle's *circumference* equals $2\pi r$, where *r* equals the circle's radius—or πD—where *D* equals the circle's diameter.

The area of a circle can be computed by the formula πr^2, where *r* equals the circle's radius. Both formulas for the circumference and area of the circle are given at the beginning of the SAT math section.

Quadrilaterals (Squares and Rectangles)

A *quadrilateral* is a polygon with four sides. A *square* is a quadrilateral, so is a *rectangle*. The difference between a square and a rectangle is that a square has four equal sides. Each side of a rectangle is parallel to another side of equal length.

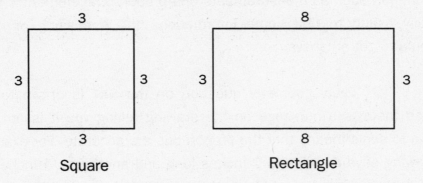

Square   Rectangle

All angles in every square or rectangle must be 90°.

Important Information!

To determine the perimeter of a quadrilateral, simply add the lengths of its sides:

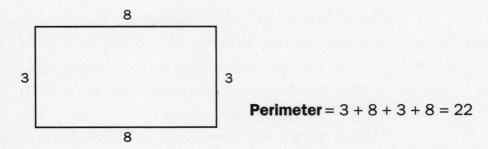

Perimeter = 3 + 8 + 3 + 8 = 22

To determine the area of a quadrilateral, multiply its length by its width:

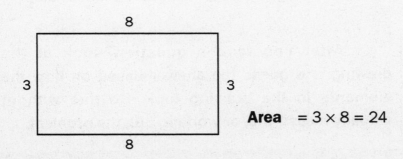

Area = 3 × 8 = 24

Bust it!

Testbusting Geometry Tip #1:
LEARNING TO "EYEBALL" GEOMETRY QUESTIONS

As with geometry you learned in school, the SAT geometry questions will give you a drawing from which you must take the necessary information to answer the question. These drawings contain information such as measurements and proportional elements. You are usually asked to find some information that is missing or apply a formula to get an answer.

Every geometry question on the SAT is drawn to scale, unless there is a message on the drawing telling you it is not. Being drawn to scale means that the proportions are accurate. For example, if a drawing says one line is 2 inches long and another is 4 inches long, the 2-inch line will be exactly half the length of the 4-inch line. "What does this mean to me?" you may ask. It means that, since the geometry drawings on the SAT are proportional and to scale, you can "eyeball" a question to get the right answer.

What's "eyeballing?" Well, "eyeballing" is another way to say *guess*. Construction workers and other workers "eyeball" when they make a decision about the size of something without actually measuring it. In other words, they are using their eyes to make a measurement.

"Eyeballing" is a very effective way to attack the geometry questions on the SAT. Not only will it help you eliminate incorrect answer choices, "eyeballing" a question will sometimes answer a question for you without doing any of the work! Here's how to do it:

STEP 1
After you read a question, look at the drawing and guess the answer based on how the elements in the drawing look. Do this without actually measuring, or working out, the problem.

STEP 2   Next, look at the answer choices, eliminate any that look obviously wrong.

STEP 3   Look at the answer choices that remain. Be more critical of the elements in the drawing, paying special attention to the proportion and relationships of those elements. Using this more critical evaluation, choose the answer choice that looks the best. It's that simple!

Let's look at an example:

If the area of the square is 50, what is its perimeter?

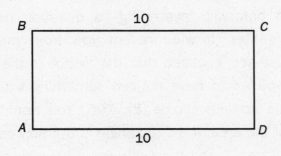

(A) 10   (D) 60

(B) 20   (E) 100

(C) 30

To use the "eyeball" strategy, you must first read the question and then look at the figure. From the question you know that you need to find the perimeter of the rectangle. Once you look at the figure, you know that you need to find the measure of the rectangle's height in order to determine its perimeter.

Look!

Important Strategy

You should notice that there isn't a note telling you the drawing is not drawn to scale. This means you can trust your eyes. You should be able to see just by looking at the drawing that height of the rectangle (lines *AB* and *CD*) is roughly half the length (lines *BC* or *AD*). Knowing that *BC* and *AD* are 10 inches in length, you can "eyeball" the rectangle and guess that *AB* is about 5 inches.

Guessing that the height of the perimeter is 5 inches, you can determine that the perimeter of the rectangle would be 30 (5 + 5 + 10 + 10 = 30). Now take a look at the answer choices. You'll see that your answer is given in choice (C).

Just to show that you've found the correct answer, let's double check. If the perimeter of the rectangle is 30 and the width of the rectangle is 10 and its height is 5, then the area would be 50. That is consistent with the question, so choice (C) is your correct answer!

Important Strategy

Not only will "eyeballing" a question help you find a correct answer faster, it will prevent you from making careless mistakes. Because you guessed that the height of the rectangle was half its length, you would have noticed something was wrong if your calculations came up with choice (E), 100. You would have stopped and thought, "but the area of the rectangle is 50, how can its perimeter be more than its area?" And then you would have recalculated, found your mistake, and entered the correct answer.

This is the secret of "eyeballing." Your guess will not be exact, but it will give you a measuring stick to go by. You will be able to eliminate choices from the very start and you will know approximately what the correct answer will be. If your calculations give you a number that is very different than your "eyeballed" figure, you'll know that you made a mistake and will recalculate in order to get the right answer.

Let's try another one, this time a little harder:

In the figure below, the perimeter of Triangle *A* is $\frac{1}{2}$ the perimeter of Triangle *B*, and the perimeter of Triangle *B* is $\frac{1}{2}$ the perimeter of *C*. If the area of Triangle *A* is 16, what is the area of Triangle *C*?

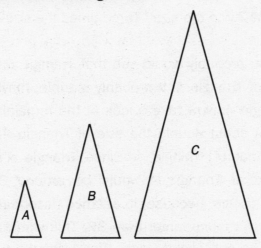

(A) 16   (D) 40

(B) 24   (E) 80

(C) 32

You should be able to see just by looking at the drawing that Triangle *C* is quite a bit larger than Triangle *A*. There isn't a note telling you the drawing is not drawn to scale. Because of this, you can trust your eyes. So, if the area of Triangle *A* is 16, the area of Triangle *C* is going to be quite a bit more than 16. By reading the question and then "eyeballing" the figure, you should be able to eliminate choices (A) 16, (B) 24, and (C) 32. You should be able to eliminate these choices because they are not that much larger than 16. This leaves you with two choices: (D) 40 and (E) 80.

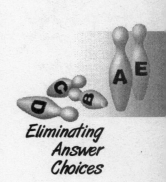

Eliminating Answer Choices

To find the correct choice, you need to think in terms of proportion. Your first "eyeball" guess was that Triangle *C* was quite a bit larger than Triangle *A*. Thus the area of Triangle *C* is going to be a lot bigger than that of Triangle *A* (16). This enabled you to eliminate three of the five choices. Now you have to choose between two choices. Look more closely at the figure, being more critical of proportion. How much bigger is Triangle *C* than Triangle *A*? Twice the size? Three times the size?

You probably would see that Triangle *C* is much more than double the size of Triangle *A*. It probably is triple, maybe even quadruple, the size of Triangle *A*. Now take a look at the remaining answer choices. If Triangle *C* was about double the size of Triangle *A*, its area would be roughly double that of Triangle *A*. Since Triangle *A*'s area is 16, that means the area of Triangle *A* would be around 32. You've already eliminated that choice because it seemed incorrect immediately. But choice (D), 40, isn't much larger than 32. This would mean that Triangle *C* would have to be only slightly more than twice the size of Triangle *A* for choice (D) to be correct. Since Triangle *C* is obviously much more than twice the size of Triangle *A*, you can eliminate choice (D) and you are left with the correct answer: choice (E), 80.

This is a good example of how "eyeballing" will enable you to solve a question that you normally wouldn't be able to. The following illustrates the complicated solution that would be necessary to solve a problem like this:

Look!

Important Strategy

First, you should remember that the area of a triangle is $\frac{b \times h}{2}$. If the area of Triangle *A* is 16 that means that

$$\frac{b \times h}{2} = 16$$

$$b \times h = 16 \times 2$$

$$b \times h = 32$$

At this point you know that the base and height are denominators of 32. They could be 8 and 4; 2 and 16; or 1 and 32. By looking at the figure, you could determine that it is probably 8 and 4, since the other two would give you a very tall and narrow triangle. Since the base and height of Triangle *A* are probably 8 and 4, the perimeter of Triangle *A* is

$$8 + 8 + 4 = 20$$

According to the question, the perimeter of Triangle *A* is $\frac{1}{2}$ the perimeter of Triangle *B*. So the perimeter of Triangle *B* must be 40. You also know from the question that the perimeter of Triangle *B* is $\frac{1}{2}$ the perimeter of Triangle *C*. So the perimeter of Triangle *C* is 80. From this you can determine that

$$\frac{b \times h}{2} = 80$$
$$b \times h = 80 \times 2$$
$$b \times h = 160$$

Now you know that the base and height of Triangle *C* are denominators of 160. They could be 10 and 16; 8 and 20; 4 and 40; 2 and 80; or 1 and 160. If the triangle had a height and base of 4 and 40; 2 and 80; or 1 and 60; it would be an extremely tall and very narrow triangle. This is not the case so you can eliminate them. This leaves us with a base and height of 10 and 16 or 8 and 20.

If the base and height of Triangle *C* were 10 and 16, its area would be 80 because:

$$\frac{10 \times 16}{2} = 80$$
$$\frac{160}{2} = 8$$
$$80 = 80$$

Bust it!

So choice (E) is your correct answer. How much faster did you get this answer by "eyeballing" the problem instead of working through it? "Eyeballing" is much faster and easier than using the traditional method. Remember that and use this strategy as much as possible on the SAT.

Tips for Better "EYEBALLING":

There are ways to "eyeball" better and certain tricks that will let you get your guesses faster and with more accuracy.

The first tip is in regards to π. You know that π equals 3.14159265... . But when you are "eyeballing" geometry problems, simply think of π as roughly 3. This will make doing calculations in your head much easier and quicker. You should also know some of the basic square roots ($\sqrt{1} = 1$; $\sqrt{2} = 1.4$; $\sqrt{3} = 1.7$; $\sqrt{4} = 2$).

Important Strategy

Second, you should be familiar with how large or small common angles are. Here are a few to work with:

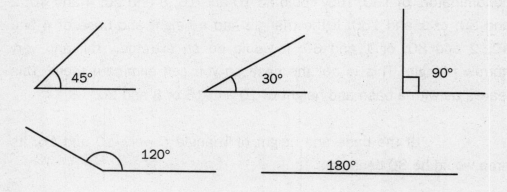

Third, you can create a ruler to use during the SAT. That's right! Any piece of paper can be a ruler if you mark down some measurements on it. In order to make a ruler, you'll need to be working on a question that has a line measurement already labeled. Simply use the bottom of your answer sheet and line it up with the line that has a measurement. Now make a mark on your answer sheet at the beginning of the measured line and one at the end. Then write down the measurement of the line you just copied. Now you have a ruler! Use it to measure other lines in the problem and even to find the correct answer!

Another way to use your answer sheet, or scrap paper, is to measure angles:

1. The corner of a piece of paper is a 90° angle.

2. If you fold a piece of paper diagonally, you'll get a 45° angle.

By using a piece of paper, you can guess the measure of almost any angle.

It is important to note that you'll need to make a new ruler for every question. The SAT drawings may be drawn to scale (unless otherwise noted), but each drawing isn't drawn to the same scale. A ruler that measures 10 in one drawing will not measure 10 in another. Also, be sure to erase your pencil marks before handing in your answer sheet because they will throw off the computer that grades your SAT.

Look!

Important Strategy

What if the Figure is not Drawn to Scale?

You will encounter at least one figure that is not drawn to scale. Don't panic, you can still "eyeball" the question. The easiest way to do this is to redraw the figure in the margin of your test booklet. You can redraw the figure using the information provided in the question. Most of the time, the SAT does not draw a figure to scale because the answer would be too obvious. If you redraw the figure exaggerating the proportions, the correct answer will sometimes jump out at you!

Here's an example:

Which line is biggest, $\overline{AB}$, $\overline{BC}$, $\overline{CD}$, $\overline{DE}$, or $\overline{EF}$?

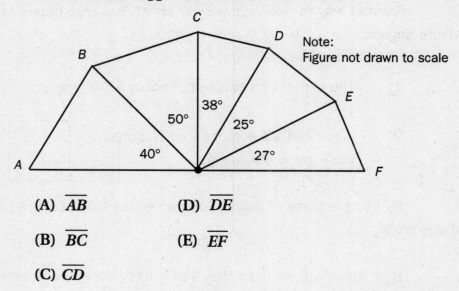

Note: Figure not drawn to scale

(A) $\overline{AB}$ (D) $\overline{DE}$

(B) $\overline{BC}$ (E) $\overline{EF}$

(C) $\overline{CD}$

Since this figure is not drawn to scale, you can't trust the way it looks. It is not proportional, so you must redraw it. To give yourself an edge, when you redraw the figure, exaggerate the differences in the measurements. Doing so will highlight the relationships of the different elements in the drawing. So, redraw the figure in the margin of your test booklet as follows:

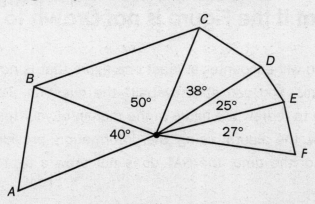

Notice how the bigger the angle, the longer the line segments are to connect the line segments? This should point you right to the correct answer. The largest angle, choice (B), 50°, is the correct answer. This figure was not drawn to scale in order to trick you into making a very easy question harder than it is.

Sometimes you may find it helpful to redraw a figure to scale. This is very time consuming, but in a complicated question it may be worth the effort. You'll need to make a ruler with your answer sheet, mark off the measurements you'll use and then recreate the figure using the exact measurements in the problem. Most times it is easier to simply eliminate as many answer choices as you can and guess, but if you have time left over, redrawing to scale may point you to the correct answer.

 Testbusting Geometry Tip #2:
STARTING FROM THE CHOICES

As you learned to do for algebra questions, Starting from the Choices can help you find the correct answer to a question faster and easier than if you used traditional methods. This is also true of geometry questions!

You should remember that there are three steps to using the Starting from the Choices strategy. Here's a summary of those steps amended to fit geometry questions:

STEP 1 | Read the question, "eyeball" the drawing, and look at the answer choices. Pick one of the answer choices that you think would most likely be the correct answer based on your "eyeball" assessment of the drawing. If this doesn't help you, pick the most likely answer quickly, just pick the number that is in the middle of all the values.

STEP 2   Use the answer choice you've picked to see if it works in the question.

STEP 3   If the answer choice you picked doesn't work, choose another answer choice. Keep trying choices until you find one that works. This is your correct answer.

This strategy will help you answer any geometry questions that ask you to find measurements or determine missing information.

Let's do an example:

What is the value of x in the triangle below?

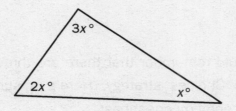

(A) 25   (D) 55

(B) 30   (E) 90

(C) 40

Looking at the choices, you should pick the number in the middle. In this case, the middle number is choice (C) 40. Your next step is to plug in that answer into the problem to see if it works.

You know that the sum of a triangle's interior angles must equal 180°. So, using 40 for *x*, see if choice (C) is the correct answer:

$$2(40)° + 3(40)° + 40° = 180°$$

$$80° + 120° + 40° = 180°$$

$$240° \neq 180°$$

Wrong! That's okay. Choice (C) gave you a number that was too big. Your next step is to go back to the answer choices and pick a choice that is less than 40. The next choice that is less than 40 would be choice (B), 30. Plug 30 into the question and see if it works:

$$2(30)° + 3(30)° + 30° = 180°$$

$$60° + 90° + 30° = 180°$$

$$180° = 180°$$

That's it! Choice (B), 30, is the correct answer. Just to be sure, let's solve the question in the traditional manner:

Bust it!

What is the value of *x* in the triangle below?

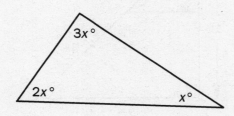

(A) 25   (D) 55

(B) 30   (E) 90

(C) 40

As you knew before, the sum of the interior angles of a triangle must equal 180°. So, let's create an equation to find *x*:

$$2x° + 3x° + x° = 180°$$

Now, combine like terms:

$$6x° = 180°$$

Finally, isolate the variable:

$$x° = 30°$$

Bust it!

So you chose the correct answer! Using the strategy of Starting from the Choices will help you get the correct answer easier (because you won't have to work out the question from scratch) and quicker (because you'll probably be able to eliminate wrong answer choices and plug in the remaining few choices faster than it would take you to actually do the question)! Let's do another problem, only this time a little harder:

If the perimeter of the larger triangle is 48, what could be the value of *x* in the triangles below?

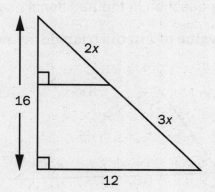

(A) 1   (D) 4

(B) 6   (E) −1

(C) 7

For this example, the answer choice you should pick first is probably (D), 4, since this is the middle number. Now plug 4 into the question:

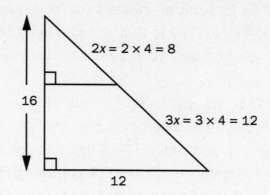

You should know that the perimeter of a triangle is the sum of its sides. So, if *x* equals 4, the hypotenuse is 20 (8 + 12). From this you can determine that the large triangle's perimeter would be 48 (12 + 16 + 20 = 48). Choice (D) is correct!

There is another strategy you can use to get the answer to this question, one that is even easier than Starting from the Choices. This alternate method can be used for any problem that contains a right triangle—and you will see a lot of right triangles on the SAT.

The reason right triangles are so special is because there is a rule that applies to them—a rule called the **PYTHAGOREAN THEOREM**. This theorem can be used to find the measure of the hypotenuse, or any leg, of a right triangle. The theorem states that the square of the length of a right triangle's hypotenuse equals the sum of the squares of the lengths of the two other sides. This equation reads as $a^2 + b^2 = c^2$:

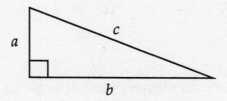

SAT geometry problems often involve right triangles with sides measuring 3, 4, and 5—or multiples of these numbers. The SAT writers do this because these measures create the smallest possible right

Important Information!

triangle with sides that are all integers (no decimals or fractions). The great part about this for you is that you can learn the multiples of the 3–4–5 right triangle and save yourself lots of time on the SAT!

"What do you mean, 'multiples of the 3–4–5 right triangle'?" Well, since the sides of a right triangle are related by their squares ($a^2 + b^2 = c^2$), a larger 3–4–5 right triangle will be proportional in its measure. For instance, the next bigger triangle based on a 3–4–5 triangle would be 6–8–10; and then 12–16–20; and then 24–32–40, etc....

Keep these relationships in mind when you are faced with a right triangle question on the SAT. If a question asks you to find the length of one of the sides of a right triangle, look at the other measures. If you recognize the triangle as a 3–4–5 triangle (or one of its multiples) you will be able to find the missing measure from memory. For example:

Find the length of *c*:

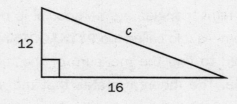

(A) 20   (D) 28

(B) 22   (E) 40

(C) 26

You should recognize this triangle as a 3–4–5 triangle and from this know that measure of the side *c* (the hypotenuse) must be a multiple of 5. The only answer choice that is a multiple of 5 is choice (A), 20. So this is the correct answer.

Try and answer this question using the 3–4–5 Triangle strategy:

If the perimeter of the larger triangle is 24, what could be the value of *x* in the triangles below?

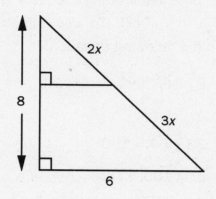

(A) 1   (D) 2

(B) 6   (E) -1

(C) 7

First, you should recognize this triangle as a 3–4–5 triangle. To answer the question through that method, you must find a value for *x* that gives us 10. You know this because, according to the 3–4–5 triangle theory, a triangle with one side that equals 6 (3 × 2) and one side that equals 8 (4 × 2), the third side must equal 10 (5 × 2). Thus, to find the value of *x*, you must use the following equation:

$$2x + 3x = 10$$

Combine like terms:

$$5x = 10$$

Isolate the variable:

$$\frac{5x}{5} = \frac{10}{5}$$

$$x = 2$$

Bust it!

So the answer to this question is choice (D), 2. Pretty simple, right?

Now let's answer the question using the Pythagorean Theorem. You remember that the Pythagorean Theorem states that the square of the hypotenuse of a right triangle equals the sum of the squares of its sides ($a^2 + b^2 = c^2$). To use this theorem in this problem, we need to set up the following equation:

$$6^2 + 8^2 = c^2$$

Simplify:

$$36 + 64 = 100$$

$$c^2 = 100$$

$$c = \sqrt{100} = 10$$

Now you know that the hypotenuse of the triangle equals 10, but you don't know the value of x (which is what the question is asking you). To find the value of x, you must use the following equation:

$$2x + 3x = 10$$

Combine like terms:

$$5x = 10$$

Isolate the variable:

$$\frac{5x}{5} = \frac{10}{5}$$

$$x = 2$$

So, once again you've found that the correct answer to this problem is choice (D), 2. And along the way you've learned three different ways to solve the problem. Some are easier than others, some are faster than the others. It really doesn't matter which technique you use ("Eyeballing", 3–4–5 Triangle, or the Pythagorean Theorem), as long as you feel comfortable and arrive at the correct answer. It is important that you feel comfortable with all of these techniques, because if you don't feel comfortable, you will take too much time to answer a question and will make careless mistakes while answering the question. So practice these techniques, figure out how to use them in different situations and how to use them when you encounter a right triangle on the SAT.

Back to the Starting with the Choices Strategy we were discussing before we introduced the Pythagorean Theorem and 3–4–5 Triangles. As with the algebra questions, there are some things you should look out for when using the Starting with the Choices strategy on geometry questions:

Important Strategy

1.   You will want to use this strategy only for questions that have answer choices that are numbers.

2.   Make sure you know where you are in the math section. Remember that the questions are given to you easiest to hardest. Make sure you understand that choices that look correct are usually correct in the easy and medium-difficulty questions. So the first number you plug into the equation should be the answer choice that seems to be correct. The harder questions (the last third of the section) may have some traps waiting for you and the choices that seem correct probably are not. So, if you use the Starting from the Choices strategy on the last third of a section, you may want to avoid plugging in choices that seem obviously correct since this may be a waste of time.

3.   Don't worry if you can't tell which answer choice is exactly the middle number. Just pick one that's close and work from there. You may have to work through all the answer choices to find the correct answer, but by picking one that's close to the middle first, you should find the answer quicker than by just randomly picking a number.

Points to Remember for Busting SAT Geometry Questions

On Target!

✔   *The most common formulas that you will need to answer geometry questions will be printed on the first page of each Regular Math section of the SAT.*

✔   *Know the basic terminology of geometry: point, line, plane, and line segment.*

✔   *Understand degrees and angles. Know the different ways to write an angle. Become knowledgeable about the different types of angles and the relationship between angles.*

✔   *Know what a triangle is and the different types of triangles. Understand that the three interior angles of a triangle must add up to 180°. Be able to determine the perimeter (the sum of the measure of its sides) and area $\left(\dfrac{base \times height}{2}\right)$ of a triangle.*

✔   *Understand what a circle is and what its parts are called and how they are measured. Be able to determine a circle's circumference ($2\pi r$ or πD) and its area (πr^2).*

✔   Know what a quadrilateral is and the difference between a square and a rectangle. Understand that all angles for any quadrilateral must be 90°. Be able to determine a quadrilateral's perimeter (the sum of the measure of its sides) and area (length × width).

✔   Learn how to "eyeball" a drawing to quickly determine which answer choices can be immediately eliminated. Know how to estimate the value of π and common square roots. Be able to recognize common angle measurements just by looking at them. And know how to use a piece of paper as a ruler and as a protractor to measure angles.

✔   Understand how a figure being drawn to scale will affect the way you answer it. Know how to redraw a figure not drawn to scale in order to highlight its proportions.

✔   Using the Starting from the Choices strategy to answer geometry questions will be faster and easier than using traditional geometry. To use this strategy, 1) pick an answer choice and use it to answer the question; 2) if it works, that's the correct choice; 3) if it doesn't work, keep trying answer choices until you find the right one.

✔   Know how to use the 3–4–5 Triangle strategy and the Pythagorean Theorem ($a^2+b^2=c^2$) when attacking questions that involve right triangles. Understanding these principles and using them to

On Target!

On Target!

answer right triangle questions will save you a lot of time and headaches on SAT geometry questions. Expect to see a lot of right triangles on the SAT, and become comfortable with both of these techniques to find the measure of their sides.

Drill: Regular Multiple-Choice Math Questions

DIRECTIONS: Choose the best answer choice and fill in the corresponding oval on the answer sheet.

1 If $8-(7-6-5)=8-7-(x-5)$, what is the value of x?

(A) −6
(B) −16
(C) −18
(D) 4
(E) 6

2 The average (arithmetic mean) volume of 4 containers is 40 liters. If 3 of these containers each has a volume of 35 liters, what is the volume in liters of the fourth container?

(A) 40
(B) 50
(C) 55
(D) 105
(E) 160

3

$$\begin{array}{r} 2\,\Diamond\,5 \\ \times\quad 7 \\ \hline 1{,}8\oplus 5 \end{array}$$

In the correctly computed multiplication problem above, if $\Diamond$ and $\oplus$ are different digits, then $\Diamond =$

(A) 2.
(B) 6.
(C) 5.
(D) 4.
(E) 7.

4 If for any number n, $[n]$ is defined as the least whole number that is greater than or equal to n, then $[-3.7]+14=$

(A) 10.3
(B) 17.7
(C) 18
(D) 10
(E) 11

5 How many tenths of a kilometer will a cyclist travel in 1 minute if she cycles at a rate of 30 km/hour?

(A) 5

(B) 1

(C) 2

(D) 10

(E) $\dfrac{1}{30}$

8 If $n \div 5 = 150 \div 25$, then $n =$

(A) 5.
(B) 6.
(C) 25.
(D) 30.
(E) 125.

6

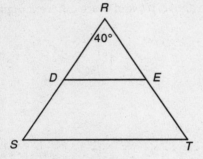

If $\overline{DE}$ is parallel to $\overline{ST}$ and triangle RST is an isoceles triangle, then $\angle E$ is

(A) 50°.
(B) 40°.
(C) 70°.
(D) 90°.
(E) 75°.

7 If 20 students share the cost equally of a gift for Coach Brown, what percent of the total cost do 5 of the students share?

(A) 5%
(B) 10%
(C) 25%
(D) 40%
(E) 50%

9 If the average (arithmetic mean) of -9 and s is -9, then $s =$

(A) -9
(B) 0
(C) 9
(D) -18
(E) -4.5

10 If $x \Diamond y = (x-3)y$, then $8 \Diamond 3 + 5 \Diamond 2 =$

(A) 34.
(B) 50.
(C) 0.
(D) -5.
(E) 19.

11 If $22 \times 3 \times R = 6$, then $R =$

(A) $\frac{1}{9}$.

(B) $\frac{1}{11}$.

(C) $\frac{1}{8}$.

(D) 11.

(E) 9.

12 What is the total area, in square meters, of two adjacent square garden plots with sides 4 meters and 1 meter, respectively?

(A) 1
(B) 4
(C) 16
(D) 17
(E) 20

13

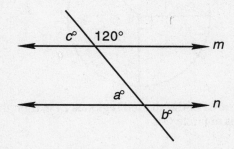

If line m is parallel to line n as shown, then $\angle b =$

(A) 30°.
(B) 45°.
(C) 55°.
(D) 60°.
(E) 120°.

14 If $\frac{6m}{9} = 4$, then $18m =$

(A) 6.
(B) 24.
(C) 36.
(D) 72.
(E) 108.

15 During a local high school track meet, all three contestants earn points. Olivia earns 12 times more points than Barbara, and Diane earns 8 times more points than Barbara. What is the ratio of Diane's points to Olivia's points?

(A) 96 : 1
(B) 8 : 1
(C) 3 : 2
(D) 2 : 3
(E) 1 : 8

16 If $x^2 - z^2 = 130$, and $x - z = 10$, then $x + z =$

(A) 10.
(B) 13.
(C) 36.
(D) 30.
(E) 120.

17

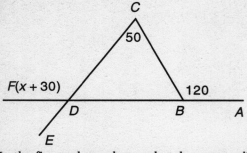

In the figure shown here, what does x equal?

(A) 80
(B) 90
(C) 100
(D) 110
(E) 120

18 In triangle ABC, $\angle ABC$ is 53° and $\angle BCA$ is 37°,

$\overline{BC}$ = 5 inches and $\overline{AC}$ = 4 inches, what is the

length of the shortest side?

(A) 2 inches
(B) 3 inches
(C) 4 inches
(D) 5 inches
(E) 6 inches

19 If 22 is the average of n, n, n, 15, and 35, then n =

(A) 16.
(B) 18.
(C) 20.
(D) 50.
(E) 110.

20 If $7x + 18 = 16x$, then $x =$

(A) – 2.

(B) $\dfrac{18}{23}$.

(C) $\dfrac{23}{18}$.

(D) 2.

(E) 36.

21 A circular design with a radius of 5 inches is inscribed in a square piece of tile. What is the area in square inches of the tile?

(A) 25
(B) 78.5
(C) 50
(D) 10
(E) 100

22

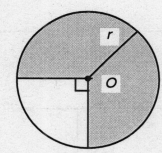

If the area of the shaded region is 24 π, then the radius of circle O is

(A) 4.

(B) 16.

(C) $2\sqrt{6}$.

(D) $4\sqrt{2}$.

(E) $2\sqrt{2}$.

23

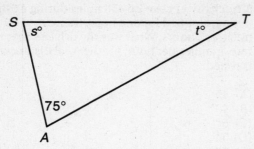

If, in the triangle shown here, $\overline{AS} < \overline{ST}$, which of the following <u>cannot</u> be the value of t?

(A) 20
(B) 36
(C) 65
(D) 71
(E) 80

24 If $R \# S = \dfrac{R+2}{S}$, then $(4 \# 3) \# k =$

(A) $\dfrac{5}{4}$.

(B) 2.

(C) $\dfrac{2}{k}$.

(D) $\dfrac{4}{k}$.

(E) $4k$.

25 If $48x - 6y = 1$, then $16x - 2y =$

(A) -3.

(B) 0.

(C) $\dfrac{1}{3}$.

(D) $\dfrac{1}{2}$.

(E) 1.

26 Sam is 5 years older than Marcia, and Marcia is 6 years older than Jack. How many years older than Jack is Sam?

(A) 11
(B) 9
(C) 7
(D) 6
(E) 2

27 A cat ate $\dfrac{1}{2}$ of the food in its dish in the morning, and 2 ounces of food in the afternoon. The cat's owner came home to find $\dfrac{2}{5}$ of the original amount of food in the dish. How many ounces of food were in the dish at the start of the day?

(A) 4 ounces
(B) 5 ounces
(C) 8 ounces
(D) 16 ounces
(E) 20 ounces

28 The average value of A, B, and C is 8, and $2(A + C) = 24$. What is the value of B?

(A) 0
(B) 3
(C) -16
(D) 32
(E) 12

29 If S is the sum of the positive integers from 1 to n, inclusive, then the average (arithmetic mean), k, of these integers can be represented by the formula

(A) $S \times n$.

(B) $\dfrac{S}{n}$.

(C) $\dfrac{k}{n}$.

(D) $S + n$.

(E) $n + 1$.

30 If $3a + 4a = 14$, and $b + 6b = 21$, then $7(a + b) =$

(A) 21.
(B) 28.
(C) 35.
(D) 40.
(E) 42.

31 The perimeter of an equilateral triangle is 18. What is the altitude of the triangle?

(A) 3

(B) 6

(C) 9

(D) $\sqrt{3}$

(E) $3\sqrt{3}$

32 A truck driver covered 450 miles during a 9-hour period, stopped for one hour, then drove 90 miles in 2 hours. What was the driver's average rate, in miles per hour, for the total distance traveled?

(A) 45
(B) 49
(C) 50
(D) 54
(E) 60

33 If $x + y = 7$ and $x - y = 3$, then $x^2 - y^2 =$

(A) 4.
(B) 10.
(C) 16.
(D) 21.
(E) 40.

34 If $\sqrt{x - 1} = 2$, then $(x - 1)^2 =$

(A) 4.
(B) 6.
(C) 8.
(D) 10.
(E) 16.

35 If $m < n < 0$, which expression must be < 0?

(A) The product of m and n

(B) The square of the product of m and n

(C) The sum of m and n

(D) The result of subtracting m from n

(E) The quotient of dividing n by m

36

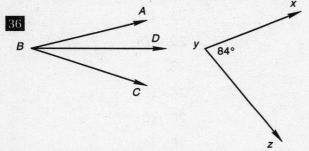

In the figure shown, if $\overline{BD}$ is the bisector of angle ABC, and angle ABD is one-fourth the size of angle XYZ, what is the size of angle ABC?

(A) 21°
(B) 28°
(C) 42°
(D) 63°
(E) 168°

37 A cube of volume 8 cubic centimeters is placed directly next to a cube of volume 125 cubic centimeters. What is the perpendicular distance in centimeters from the top of the larger cube to the top of the smaller cube?

(A) 7
(B) 5
(C) 3
(D) 2
(E) 0

38 The length of a rectangle is four more than twice the width. The perimeter of the rectangle is 44 meters. Find the length.

(A) 6 m
(B) 8 m
(C) 11 m
(D) 16 m
(E) 22 m

39 If $21 - (a - b) = 2(b + 9)$, and $a = 8$, what is the value of b?

(A) 31

(B) 13

(C) 4

(D) $-\dfrac{5}{3}$

(E) -5

40 Five years ago, Tim's mom was three times Tim's age today. Now their combined ages are 50. How old is Tim's mom today?

(A) 40
(B) 35
(C) 45
(D) 50
(E) 30

Regular Multiple-Choice Math Questions Drill

ANSWER KEY

1. (A)	21. (E)
2. (C)	22. (D)
3. (B)	23. (E)
4. (E)	24. (D)
5. (A)	25. (C)
6. (C)	26. (A)
7. (C)	27. (E)
8. (D)	28. (E)
9. (A)	29. (B)
10. (E)	30. (C)
11. (B)	31. (E)
12. (D)	32. (A)
13. (D)	33. (D)
14. (E)	34. (E)
15. (D)	35. (C)
16. (B)	36. (C)
17. (A)	37. (C)
18. (B)	38. (D)
19. (C)	39. (D)
20. (D)	40. (B)

Attacking Quantitative Comparison Questions

In the Quantitative Comparison section of the SAT you are asked to compare two quantities. Since you only need to compare quantities, the questions in this section usually take less time to solve than regular multiple-choice questions. That's good news for you since working quickly is a key to beating the SAT.

There are many techniques you can use to aid you in successfully attacking the Quantitative Comparison section of the SAT. We'll teach you seven in this chapter:

Bust it!

- **How to identify the five types of Quantitative Comparison questions**

- **Avoiding working through addition problems by comparing individual quantities**

- **Changing the way quantities look to make it easier to compare them**

- **Looking at the properties of numbers to save time in solving the problem**

- **Substituting variables for numbers to aid in comparing values**

- **Using estimates to approximate values**

- **Ignoring figures that are not drawn to scale or don't look accurate**

Important Information!

You'll notice that Quantitative Comparison questions look much different than the questions you've encountered on the SAT thus far. In Quantitative Comparison questions, the two quantities are always presented in two columns, Column A and Column B. Here's an example:

Column A

23

Column B

22

Your job is to determine which quantity, if either, is greater. You will be given the same four answer choices for every Quantitative Comparison question:

(A)   if the quantity in Column A is greater;

(B)   if the quantity in Column B is greater;

(C)   if the two quantities are equal;

(D)   if the relationship cannot be determined from the information given.

Bust it!

Let's look at the example again:

Column A   # Column B

23   22

What would the correct choice be? Since the quantity in Column A is equal to 23 and the quantity in Column B is equal to 22, and 23 > 22, the correct choice is (A). That's all there is to it! So let's get started....

About the Directions

Now that you have seen some of the directions, let's go over the rest of them. It's important to become familiar with the directions before the test so you don't waste time reading them during the test. You will also see the same reference information that appeared before the regular multiple-choice problems. Become familiar with this material before you take the SAT. If you have to refer to any part of this page during the test, you are taking away valuable time needed to solve the problems.

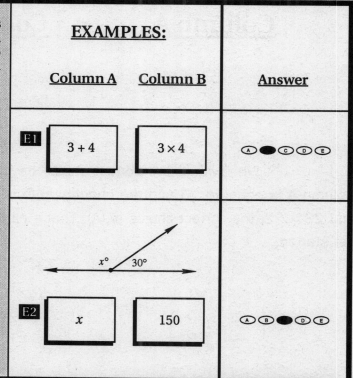

__DIRECTIONS__: Each of the following questions consist of two quantities, one in Column A and one in Column B. You are to compare the two quantities and on the answer sheet blacken space

(A) if the quantity in Column A is greater;
(B) if the quantity in Column B is greater;
(C) if the two quantities are equal;
(D) if the relationship cannot be determined from the information given.

NOTES:

1. In certain questions, information concerning one or both of the quantities to be compared is centered above the two columns.
2. In a given question, a symbol that appears in both columns represents the same thing in Column A as it does in Column B.
3. Letters such as x, n, and k stand for real numbers.

__EXAMPLES:__

Column A	Column B	Answer
E1 $3 + 4$	3×4	Ⓐ ● Ⓒ Ⓓ Ⓔ
E2 x	150	Ⓐ Ⓑ ● Ⓓ Ⓔ

About the Questions

The following section will take you through the different types of Quantitative Comparison questions that you will encounter on the SAT. Five main types exist and will be described here.

Important Information!

Question Type 1: CALCULATIONS

This type of question will ask you to perform addition, subtraction, multiplication, or division. The question may ask you to perform one or more of these operations in order to compare the quantities in columns A and B.

 PROBLEM

Column A	Column B
$(13 + 44)(37 - 40)$	$(13 - 44)(37 - 40)$

Look!

Important Strategy

 SOLUTION

You could do the addition and subtraction in each column, but if you use your number knowledge, you can get the right answer in a matter of seconds! Try working with just signs. Remember that a smaller number minus a larger number yields a negative result so the answers to all the subtractions are negative. You'll get:

$$(+)\,(-) \quad \text{and} \quad (-)\,(-)$$

which becomes

$$(-) \quad \text{and} \quad (+)$$

The correct choice is (B).

Question Type 2: CONVERSIONS

This type of question may require you to convert the quantities given by asking you to find a percentage of a number, find a fraction of a number, or find the area if given length and width, etc., in order to compare the quantities in columns A and B.

 PROBLEM

Column A	Column B
60% of $\dfrac{3}{4}$	75% of $\dfrac{3}{5}$

Important Strategy

SOLUTION

Change the way the quantities look; change the percents to fractions. You'll get:

$$60\% = \frac{60}{100} = \frac{3}{5} \qquad\qquad 75\% = \frac{3}{4}$$

$$\left(\frac{3}{5}\right)\left(\frac{3}{4}\right) \qquad\qquad \left(\frac{3}{4}\right)\left(\frac{3}{5}\right)$$

You can now *compare parts*. The correct choice is (C).

Question Type 3: EXPONENTS AND ROOTS

This type of question will ask you to determine a number's value, and then may ask you to use the value to perform an indicated operation in order to compare the quantities in columns A and B.

? PROBLEM

Column A	Column B
$\sqrt{.81}$	$\sqrt[3]{.81}$

Look!

Important Strategy

! SOLUTION:

In this problem, $\sqrt{.81}$ is easy to compute with your calculator—it's 0.9. The problem is finding $\sqrt[3]{.81}$. There is no procedure to find $\sqrt[3]{.81}$ except estimating and multiplying. Since you are really concerned with seeing how $\sqrt[3]{.81}$ compares to 0.9 and not finding out exactly what it is, try 0.9 as an estimate. That means you have to cube 0.9. 0.9^3 is .729. Since .729 is less than .81, then $\sqrt[3]{.81}$ must be greater than 0.9. The correct choice is (B).

Question Type 4: VARIABLES

This type of question will present you with variables of unknown quantities. You will be provided with additional information which must be applied in order to compare the quantities in columns A and B.

? PROBLEM

Column A	Column B
$y^* = y(y+1)$ if y is even	
$y^* = y(y-1)$ if y is odd	
7^*	6^*

Look!

Important Strategy

SOLUTION

Change the way the quantities look by applying the rules that appear between the two columns:

7* = (7) (7 − 1)	6* = 6(6 + 1)
7* = (7) (6)	6* = (6) (7)
= 42	= 42

The factors are identical in the two columns. The correct choice is (C).

Question Type 5: FIGURES

This type of question will include a figure. You will be asked to use the figure provided to compare the quantities in columns A and B. The figures may or may not be drawn to scale.

PROBLEM

<u>**Column A**</u>   <u>**Column B**</u>

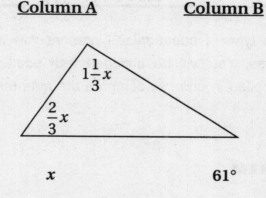

x 61°

SOLUTION

The sum of the three angles of a triangle equals 180°. Therefore, we can add together the angles in the triangle above and set them equal to 180° to solve for x.

$$1\frac{1}{3}x + \frac{2}{3}x + x = 180$$

If we multiply this equation by three, we can eliminate the fractions.

$$3\left(\frac{4}{3}x + \frac{2}{3}x + x = 180\right)$$

$$4x + 2x + 3x = 540$$

Simplifying the equation, we obtain

Look!

Important Strategy

$$9x = 540$$
$$x = 60$$

Therefore, the correct choice is (B), since 60° is less than 61°.

As you attempt to answer Quantitative Comparison questions, it is not completely necessary that you be able to classify each question. However, you should be familiar with how to handle each question type. The remainder of this review will teach you how to approach and attack the questions.

Points to Remember

On Target!

✔ Always examine **both columns and** the information in the **center**, if there is any, before you begin to work. By doing this, you won't overlook any information and you will be able to decide upon the appropriate strategy to use.

✔ If a problem seems to involve a lot of calculations, there is probably a faster way to do it. The numbers that are used in the problems are not selected to make you do a lot of calculations; they are selected so that, if you are aware of certain mathematical relationships or properties, you can do the problems relatively quickly.

✔ Since you only have to compare quantities, don't work out the problems completely once you have enough information to make the comparison.

✔ Keep your work neat and in the appropriate columns so it will be easier to make comparisons.

✔ Be suspicious of problems with obvious answers if they occur toward the end of the section. The problems at the end of the section are always the more difficult ones. If the answer seems obvious, you have probably overlooked something important.

✔ If you have to guess, remember if a problem contains only numbers in both columns, the answer cannot be (D). If a problem contains only numbers, you can get an exact value for the quantities in each column and a comparison can be made.

Answering Quantitative Comparison Questions

As you go through Quantitative Comparison questions, some seem to require a lot of calculations. On the other hand, there are some questions for which the answer seems immediately obvious. Often neither is the case. Excessive calculations can often be avoided and questions for which the answer seems obvious are often tricky.

The following steps will help guide you through answering Quantitative Comparison questions. These steps will cover strategies for every situation that you may encounter. Therefore, you may not need to go through every step for every question.

STEP 1 | When you are presented with an addition or multiplication problem, you can often avoid these calculations just by comparing individual quantities.

Look!

Important Strategy

? **PROBLEM**

<u>Column A</u>	<u>Column B</u>
$\dfrac{1}{3}+\dfrac{1}{6}+\dfrac{1}{12}$	$\dfrac{1}{4}+\dfrac{1}{8}+\dfrac{1}{16}$

Bust it!

SOLUTION

Both columns contain an addition problem. Don't bother to add! Compare the fractions in each column:

Column A		Column B
$\dfrac{1}{3}$	$>$	$\dfrac{1}{4}$
$\dfrac{1}{6}$	$>$	$\dfrac{1}{8}$
and $\dfrac{1}{12}$	$>$	$\dfrac{1}{16}$

For each fraction in Column B, there is a greater fraction in Column A. Therefore, the sum in Column A must be greater than the sum in Column B. The correct choice is (A).

Bust it!

PROBLEM

Column A	Column B
The area of a rectangle with a base of 3 and a height of 4	**The area of a circle with a radius of 2**

SOLUTION

You have to compare the area of a rectangle to the area of a circle. Your two columns will look like:

Area of rectangle	Area of circle
(3) (4)	$\pi 2^2 = 4\pi$

Both columns contain a multiplication problem with positive numbers. Don't multiply! Compare the factors in each column:

3	$<$	π
and 4	$=$	4

Bust it!

The factors in Column B are greater than or equal to the factors in Column A so the product in Column B (the area of the circle) must be greater than the product in Column A (the area of the rectangle). The correct choice is (B).

STEP 2 Sometimes you are faced with problems in which comparing parts seems to apply but you can't compare the quantities the way they are presented in the problem. If you change the way the quantities look, you may be able to compare parts.

Look!

Important Strategy

? PROBLEM

Column A	Column B
20% of 368	$\frac{1}{4}$ of 368

Bust it!

! SOLUTION

Both columns contain multiplication of positive quantities:

$$(20\%)(368) \qquad \left(\frac{1}{4}\right)(368)$$

This means that you can compare individual quantities to avoid multiplication. Both columns contain 368 but Column A contains a percent and Column B contains a fraction. You can either change the percent to a fraction or the fraction to a percent.

If you change 20% to a fraction, the columns will look like:

$$\left(\frac{1}{5}\right)(368) \qquad \left(\frac{1}{4}\right)(368).$$

Now you can compare quantities:

$$\frac{1}{5} \quad < \quad \frac{1}{4}$$

$$368 \quad = \quad 368$$

or

If you change $\frac{1}{4}$ to a percent, the columns will look like:

$$(20\%)(368) \qquad (25\%)(368)$$

Now you can compare quantities in the two columns:

$$20\% \quad < \quad 25\%$$

$$368 \quad = \quad 368$$

Using either approach, the product in Column B is greater than the product in Column A. The correct choice is (B).

 PROBLEM

Column A	Column B
The area of a rectangle with length of 2.5 feet and width of 2 feet	The area of a rectangle with length of 27 inches and width of 23 inches

 SOLUTION

Since you multiply length by width to find the area of a rectangle, both columns contain multiplication of positive quantities:

$$(2.5)(2) \qquad (27)(23)$$

If you write the problem this way and forget about the units, you have:

Bust it!

2.5 < 27

2 < 23

The product in Column B seems to be greater than the product in Column A. But this is **wrong!** Column A contains feet and Column B contains inches. Make sure you change feet to inches or inches to feet before you make the comparisons!

Let's change the feet to inches and see what happens. 2.5 feet equals 30 inches and 2 feet equals 24 inches. Now all the quantities are in inches so you can make the comparisons. Your two columns look like:

<u>Column A</u>	<u>Column B</u>
(30) (24)	(27) (23)

The product in Column A is greater than the product in Column B. The correct choice is (A).

PROBLEM

<u>Column A</u>	<u>Column B</u>
The number of ounces in 2 pints	The number of pints in 2 gallons

SOLUTION

In this problem you must make sure to convert to the units specified in each column.

1 pint = 16 ounces	1 gallon = 8 pints
2 pints = 32 ounces	2 gallons = 16 pints

There are more *ounces* in 2 pints (Column A) than there are *pints* in 2 gallons (Column B). The correct choice is (A).

Bust it!

Bust it!

? PROBLEM

Column A	Column B
(4.37) (125)	(437) (1.25)

! SOLUTION

Each column contains a multiplication problem with positive numbers but comparing parts doesn't work since:

Column A		Column B
4.37	<	437
but 125	>	1.25

Even if you switch the numbers around, it still won't help:

125	<	437
but 4.37	>	1.25

You may think that you are forced to multiply, but you don't have to if you notice that all the digits are the same. The only differences between the quantities in the two columns are where the decimal points are. You can move the decimal points to try to get some or all of the numbers to look the same and then make the comparisons. When you move the decimal points, you are really multiplying or dividing by powers of 10 and what you do in one column must be done in the other column.

You can move the decimal point in 4.37 to the right 2 places in Column A (you're really multiplying by 100). You must then move the decimal point in Column B two places to the right.

Column A	Column B
(4.37) (125)	(437) (1.25)

becomes

$$(437)(125) \qquad (437)(125)$$

Now you have identical factors in both columns. The correct choice is (C).

PROBLEM

Column A	Column B
$\dfrac{(14)(15)}{(35)(8)}$	1

Bust it!

SOLUTION

Sometimes changing the way quantities look won't help you compare parts, but it will make the arithmetic a lot easier!

Column A contains multiplication and division of positive numbers. Factor and reduce and you will make the problem a lot easier to solve.

When you factor,

Column A	Column B
$\dfrac{(14)(15)}{(35)(8)}$	1

becomes

$\dfrac{(2)(7)(3)(5)}{(2)(7)(4)(5)}$	1

When you reduce, you get:

$$\frac{3}{4} \qquad\qquad\qquad 1$$

The quantity in Column B is greater than the quantity in Column A so the correct choice is (B).

Important Strategy

STEP 3 | Make sure to look at the numbers presented. Numbers have important properties that can be used to save time. There are many properties that will be useful to know for the SAT. We'll highlight a few here.

 PROBLEM

Column A	Column B
(17) (15) (13)	(18) (16) (14) (0)

 SOLUTION

Bust it!

You may be tempted to compare factors in this problem, but you don't have to if you remember to look at both columns before you do any work. Notice that 0 is a factor in Column B. The quantity in Column B is equal to 0 since 0 times any number is 0. The quantity in Column A is greater than 0 since all the factors are positive. The correct choice is (A).

 PROBLEM

Column A	Column B
$(2)^5 + (-2)^5$	$(3)^5 + (-3)^5$

SOLUTION

When you first look at this problem, you probably want to compare parts. To do that, you might think that you have to find the values of each part, but you don't! Getting the values involves a lot of multiplication so there must be a faster way and there is. Analyze the numbers in each column:

Bust it!

$(2)^5$ = some positive number
$(-2)^5$ = the same as $(2)^5$ but with a negative sign

$(3)^5$ = some positive number
$(-3)^5$ = the same as $(3)^5$ but with a negative sign

The two numbers in each column are the same but opposite in sign. What does that mean when you add the two numbers in each column? The sum in each column is 0. The quantities in the two columns are equal. The correct choice is (C).

PROBLEM

Column A	Column B
$\dfrac{(-1)^7 + (-1)^9}{(-1)^4 + (-1)^6}$	1

Bust it!

SOLUTION

When -1 is raised to an odd power, the result is -1. When -1 is raised to an even power, the result is $+1$. Using that information, you get the following:

$\dfrac{(-1)+(-1)}{(+1)+(+1)}$	1
$\dfrac{-2}{+2}$	1
-1	1

The correct choice is (B).

Important Strategy

STEP 4   Try substituting values for the variables, in particular 0, 1, − 1, and fractions between 0 and − 1. Sometimes you can use values that appear in the problem. To get a better understanding of how this will help you solve problems, let's look at a few.

Bust it!

 PROBLEM

Column A	Column B
x is positive	
2^x	2^3

 SOLUTION

In order to compare the two quantities, you have to know the value of *x*. According to the information centered above the two columns, *x* can be any positive number. You could try different values for *x*, but where do you begin? Column B gives you a starting point. What happens if *x* = 3? The quantities in the two columns would be equal. Now that you have tried one value for *x* and established that the two quantities can be equal, try another value to see if you can make one quantity greater than the other. What if *x* > 3? Then the quantity in Column A would be greater than the quantity in Column B (you shouldn't have to do the arithmetic!). By making these two comparisons, you have determined that:

the quantity in Column A = the quantity in Column B

or

the quantity in Column A > the quantity in Column B

The correct choice is (D).

(It's unnecessary to check values for $x < 3$ since you have already determined that (D) is the correct choice.)

PROBLEM

Column A   **Column B**

The average of a, b, and c is 10.

$a > b > c$

$a - b$ $b - c$

Bust it!

SOLUTION

Try some values for a, b, and c. The choice of numbers is up to you, but keep it simple. If you have 3 numbers with an average of 10, then their sum is 30. This may help you choose numbers.

You could start with $a = 11$, $b = 10$, and $c = 9$. Then you would have:

$$a - b = 11 - 10 = 1 \quad \text{and} \quad b - c = 10 - 9 = 1$$

The quantities in the two columns can be equal. But can there be some other relationship? Try some more numbers.

What if $a = 12$, $b = 11$, and $c = 7$? Then you would have:

$$a - b = 12 - 11 = 1 \quad \text{and} \quad b - c = 11 - 7 = 4$$

In this case, the quantity in Column B is greater than the quantity in Column A.

You have determined that:

the quantity is Column A = the quantity in Column B

or

the quantity in Column A < the quantity in Column B

The correct choice is (D).

Bust it!

 PROBLEM

Column A	Column B

x is positive
$x \neq 1$

| x | x^2 |

 SOLUTION

Once again you have to try different values for x. Keep the arithmetic as simple as possible.

If $x = 2$, then you get:

| 2 | 4 |

If $x = 3$, then you get:

| 3 | 9 |

The answer seems obvious, doesn't it! Column B > Column A.

But if you try $x = \dfrac{1}{2}$, you get:

| $\dfrac{1}{2}$ | $\dfrac{1}{4}$ |

Column A > Column B!

Depending upon the value selected for x, the quantity in Column A can be greater or less than the quantity in Column B. The correct choice is (D).

Bust it!

 PROBLEM

Column A	Column B

A pound of apples costs 89 cents.
A pound of pears costs 99 cents.

| The number of apples in a pound | The number of pears in a pound |

SOLUTION

Although a pound of pears costs more than a pound of apples, that does not mean that there are more pears than apples in a pound. There is no way to know how many pears or apples make up a pound. The correct choice is (D).

PROBLEM

Column A	Column B

A rectangle has an area of 8.

The perimeter of the rectangle	12

Bust it!

SOLUTION

The centered information tells you the area of the rectangle. Since the area is 8, the length could be 4, and if the length is 4, the width would be 2. If these are the measurements, then the perimeter would equal 12. But could the length and width have other values? What if the length is 8 and the width is 1? The area would still be 8 but the perimeter would be 18. We have found one set of values which make the quantities in Column A and Column B equal (4 and 2) and another set which make the quantities not equal (8 and 1). The correct choice is (D).

STEP 5 | Estimation is useful when the numbers in the problem are close to any number that is easy to work with like $\frac{1}{2}$ or 1, or when an approximation will do.

Look!

Important Strategy

Bust it!

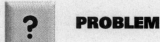 **PROBLEM**

Column A	Column B
$\dfrac{3}{8}+\dfrac{3}{7}$	1

SOLUTION

In this problem, you have to compare the sum of two fractions, with different denominators, to 1. One way to do this is to change both fractions so that they have a common denominator and then do the arithmetic. A faster way is to estimate values. In Column A, $\dfrac{3}{8}$ is close to $\dfrac{1}{2}$, but a little less. $\dfrac{3}{7}$ is also close to $\dfrac{1}{2}$, but a little less. Since both numbers are each a little less than $\dfrac{1}{2}$, their sum must be less than 1, the quantity in Column B. The correct choice is (B).

PROBLEM

Column A	Column B
(16.8) (.51)	(8.4) (.99)

Bust it!

SOLUTION

Each column contains a multiplication problem with positive numbers but comparing parts doesn't work since:

	Column A		Column B
	16.8	>	8.4
but	.51	<	.99

Even if you switch the numbers around, it still won't help:

	16.8	>	.99
but	.51	<	8.4

You may think that you are forced to multiply, but you don't have to if you notice that .51 is a little more than .5 and .99 is a little less than 1. Using these estimates will help you work out the problem without doing all the multiplication in the original problem! (You may find it faster to use $\frac{1}{2}$ instead of .5 to multiply 16.8 by.)

Using these estimated values in the columns, you get:

Column A	**Column B**
$(16.8)\left(\dfrac{1}{2}\right)$	$(8.4)(1)$

which becomes

8.4	8.4

But remember that you are using estimated values! The real value in Column A is a little more than 8.4 since you really had to multiply 16.8 by .51. The real value in Column B is a little less than 8.4 since you really had to multiply 8.4 by .99. The correct choice is (A).

STEP 6 If figures are not drawn to scale or do not look accurate, do not use them to help you solve the problem. These types of figures can throw you off and cause you to select the wrong answer.

Look!

Important Strategy

? PROBLEM

Column A	**Column B**
Line $\ell\,1$ is parallel to line $\ell\,2$.	
Line $\ell\,2$ is parallel to line $\ell\,3$.	
The distance between $\ell\,1$ and $\ell\,2$	The distance between $\ell\,2$ and $\ell\,3$

SOLUTION

This problem involves parallel lines but there is no figure. Draw a figure that fits the description in the problem, and then try to draw another figure that also fits the description but shows a different relationship. Two acceptable figures for this problem follow. Note that if you draw only one figure, you will get an incorrect answer.

In this first figure, the lines are evenly spaced so the distance between lines $\ell 1$ and $\ell 2$ is the same as the distance between lines $\ell 2$ and $\ell 3$ If this is the only figure you draw, you would choose (C) as your answer.

$$\ell 1$$
$$\ell 2$$
$$\ell 3$$

Bust it!

In this second figure, the distance between lines $\ell 1$ and $\ell 2$ is greater than the distance between lines $\ell 2$ and $\ell 3$ If this is the only figure you draw, you would choose (B) as your answer.

$$\ell 1$$
$$\ell 2$$
$$\ell 3$$

But if you draw both figures, you will choose the correct answer. The correct choice is (D).

The following questions should be completed to further reinforce what you have just learned. After you have completed all of the questions, check your answers against the answer key. Make sure to refer back to the review for help.

Drill: Quantitative Comparisons

		EXAMPLES:	

DIRECTIONS: Each of the following questions consist of two quantities, one in Column A and one in Column B. You are to compare the two quantities and on the answer sheet blacken space

    (A) if the quantity in Column A is greater;
    (B) if the quantity in Column B is greater;
    (C) if the two quantities are equal;
    (D) if the relationship cannot be determined from the information given.

NOTES:
1.   In certain questions, information concerning one or both of the quantities to be compared is centered above the two columns.
2.   In a given question, a symbol that appears in both columns represents the same thing in Column A as it does in Column B.
3.   Letters such as x, n, and k stand for real numbers.

EXAMPLES:

	Column A	Column B	Answer
E1	$3 + 4$	3×4	Ⓐ ● Ⓒ Ⓓ Ⓔ
E2	x	150	Ⓐ Ⓑ ● Ⓓ Ⓔ

(E2 figure: angle with $x°$ and $30°$)

	Column A	**Column B**
1	The average of 560, 374, and 241	The average of 560, 364, and 251

$$a > b > c > d$$

	Column A	**Column B**
2	$a + c$	$b + d$
2	The number of months in 7 years	The number of days in 12 weeks

	Column A	**Column B**
3	$\left(\dfrac{1}{4}\right)\left(\dfrac{3}{5}\right)\left(\dfrac{9}{8}\right)$	$\left(\dfrac{4}{3}\right)\left(\dfrac{1}{3}\right)\left(\dfrac{10}{7}\right)$
5	(5) (7) (9) (11)	(8) (10) (4) (6)
6	The distance a car travels in 30 minutes at 60 mph	The distance a car travels in 2 hours at 30 mph

<u>Column A</u>	<u>Column B</u>		<u>Column A</u>	<u>Column B</u>
7 $(1.75)(24)$	$(175)(2.4)$	**13** $\dfrac{(5)(0)}{(19)(3)(21)}$	$(-3)^7 + (9)(3)^5$
8 $\dfrac{(14)(21)}{(49)(6)}$	1	**14** $\dfrac{(-2)^4(-5)^3}{(-3)^2}$	$\dfrac{(174-356)}{(97-132)}$
9 $(3)^2(4)^3$	$(\pi)^2(2)^6$	**15** $-\dfrac{7}{8}$	$-\dfrac{8}{87}$
10 $(2.17)(682)$	$(196)(6.7)$			

$$\frac{x}{y} = 7$$

	<u>Column A</u>	<u>Column B</u>
16	x	y

11 $\dfrac{\dfrac{1}{2}+\dfrac{1}{4}}{\dfrac{1}{3}+\dfrac{1}{5}}$	1

There are 40 students in Class A.
There are 30 students in Class B.
There are more boys in each class than girls.

12 $\dfrac{(78-94)}{(35-41)}$	$\dfrac{(175-123)}{(134-167)}$	**17** The number of boys in Class A	The number of boys in Class B

Column A	Column B	Column A	Column B

$a > b,\ c > d,\ c \neq 0,\ d \neq 0$

18 $\dfrac{a}{c}$ $\dfrac{b}{d}$

24 $\dfrac{1}{\sqrt{2}} + \dfrac{1}{\sqrt{3}}$ $\dfrac{1}{\sqrt{6}}$

$|X| > 1$

19 X^3 X^2

25 $(6.9)(8.9)$ $\sqrt{(50)(82)}$

$XY = 1,\ X > 0$

20 X Y

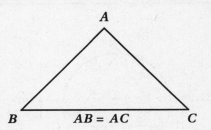

$AB = AC$

Note: Figure not drawn to scale.

26 $\angle A$ $\angle B$

21 $\dfrac{9}{10} \times \dfrac{12}{13}$ $\dfrac{5}{9} \times \dfrac{6}{11}$

22 $\sqrt{37} + \sqrt{27}$ $\sqrt{37 + 27}$

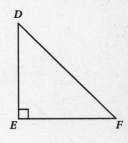

$S_1 = S_2$

Note: S_1 and S_2 are the areas of the two triangles.

23 $\sqrt{\dfrac{7}{3} \times \dfrac{1}{5} \times \dfrac{11}{5}}$ $\sqrt{\dfrac{5 \times 2}{6}}$

27 AC DF

Column A	**Column B**	**Column A**	**Column B**

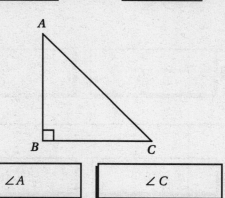

28   ∠A   ∠C

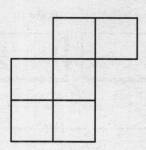

6 congruent squares. The area of the figure is 150.

31   The perimeter of the figure   65

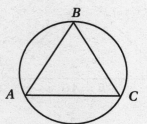

29   AB   AC

$$A + B = 18$$

32   The maximum value of AB   70

$$x = \left(.03 \div \frac{3}{5}\right)$$

33   x   .0025

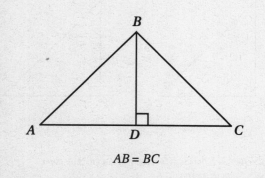

AB = BC

30   AD   DC

All lines are perpendicular or parallel.

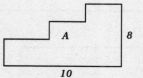

34   The perimeter of A   The perimeter of B

Column A	Column B

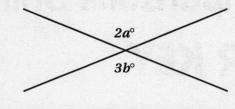

$2a°$

$3b°$

35 | a | b |

$N > 0$

36 | N^{10} | N^{12} |

It takes a motorist 1 minute and 40 seconds to go 1 mile.

37 | The motorist's speed in m.p.h. | 35 m.p.h. |

Column A	Column B

$$N = \frac{7}{12}$$

38 | The value of $\dfrac{N^{12}}{N^{10}}$ | $\dfrac{1}{2}$ |

---

39 | The average of all numbers ending in 8 between 200 and 310 | 250 |

A bell rings every 5 minutes.
A light flashes every 6 minutes.
A buzzer buzzes every 8 minutes.

40 | If the 3 of them start together, the number of minutes the 3 happen again together | 110 minutes |

Quantitative Comparisons Drill
ANSWER KEY

1. (C)	21. (A)
2. (A)	22. (A)
3. (C)	23. (A)
4. (B)	24. (A)
5. (A)	25. (B)
6. (B)	26. (D)
7. (B)	27. (D)
8. (C)	28. (D)
9. (B)	29. (D)
10. (A)	30. (C)
11. (A)	31. (B)
12. (A)	32. (A)
13. (C)	33. (A)
14. (B)	34. (C)
15. (A)	35. (A)
16. (D)	36. (D)
17. (D)	37. (A)
18. (D)	38. (B)
19. (D)	39. (A)
20. (D)	40. (A)

Attacking
Grid-In
Questions

The Student-Produced Response math questions (Grid-ins) are different from the other sections on the SAT. **Instead of seeing multiple-choice answer choices, you will be asked to calculate the correct solutions to the problems and then enter them into a grid.** This grid has been constructed so that a solution can be given in either decimal or fraction form. You can use whichever form you feel most comfortable with unless otherwise stated.

While the format is different, many of the techniques and strategies you have learned to answer SAT math questions in the preceding chapters will still be helpful.

The questions in the Student-Produced Response section have been written to reflect real-world situations. The questions also try to emphasize data interpretation. In keeping with this emphasis, **you**

Bust it!

are allowed to use a calculator during this section. But use the same caution with using your calculator as you do for Regular Math questions.

In this chapter, you will learn how to successfully attack Grid-Ins. We'll teach you to do this through the following skills and techniques:

> - **Becoming familiar with the test format and understanding how Grid-Ins differ from the rest of the SAT and how to use these differences to your advantage**
>
> - **Learning the types of questions that you'll encounter in the section**
>
> - **Understanding how to use the math strategies which apply to each type of question**
>
> - **Making sure that your solution can be properly entered in the answer grid**
>
> - **Understanding how to properly enter your answer into the grid**

Important Information!

By learning the format of the section and knowing how to properly enter your solutions, you will be prepared for any Grid-In.

Scoring Grid-Ins

The scoring on Grid-Ins is also different than the rest of the SAT. You don't lose any points if you get a wrong answer on Grid-Ins (unlike the rest of the SAT where you lose a quarter of a point for an incorrect answer). So, just like the rest of the SAT, **you are not penalized for guessing the answers of Grid-Ins**. It's true that you won't lose any points for leaving a grid blank, but if you don't lose any points for guessing the wrong answer, what can it hurt? At least by guessing there's a chance that you'll enter the correct answer and gain points.

So be sure to fill in every grid, but try not to guess blindly. Blindly guessing the correct answer to a Grid-In is nearly impossible (you don't have answer choices to look at and eliminate). You should devote as much time as you can to working through the problems. A good technique is to work through all the problems first and then go back and check your work. This way you've entered answers for all the questions before you run out of time. If you still have time when you've finished answering all the questions, then you can go back and check your work.

About the Directions

Each Grid-In requires you to solve the problem and enter your answer in a grid. There are specific rules you'll need to know for entering your solutions. **If you enter your answers in an incorrect way, you won't receive credit, even if you solved the problem correctly.** Therefore, you should carefully study the following rules now, so you don't have to waste valuable time during the actual test:

<u>DIRECTIONS</u>: Each of the following questions requires you to solve the problem and enter your answer in the ovals in the special grid:

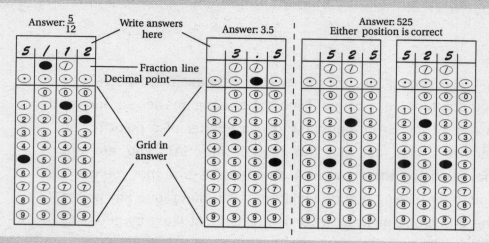

- You may begin filling in your answer in any column, space permitting. Columns not needed should be left blank.

- Answers may be entered in either decimal or fraction form. For example, $\frac{3}{12}$ or .25 are equally acceptable.

- A mixed number, such as $4\frac{1}{2}$, must be entered either as 4.5 or $\frac{9}{2}$. If you entered 41/2, the machine would interpret your answer as $\frac{41}{2}$, not $4\frac{1}{2}$.

- There may be some instances where there is more than one correct answer to a problem. Should this be the case, grid only one answer.

- Be very careful when filling in ovals. Do not fill in more than one oval in any column, and make sure to completely darken the ovals.

- It is suggested that you fill in your answer in the boxes above each column. Although you will not be graded incorrectly if you do not write in your answer, it will help you fill in the corresponding ovals.

- If your answer is a decimal, grid the most accurate value possible. For example, if you need to grid a repeating decimal such as 0.6666, enter the answer as .666 or .667. A less accurate value, such as .66 or .67, is not acceptable.

- A negative answer cannot appear for any question.

 SAMPLE QUESTION

How many pounds of apples can be bought with $5.00 if apples cost $.40 a pound?

 SOLUTION

Converting dollars to cents we obtain the following equation:

$$x = 500 \div 40$$
$$x = 12.5$$

The solution to this problem would be gridded as

1	2	.	5

Taking Advantage of the Format of Grid-Ins

Because of limitations in the format, **certain types of questions cannot appear in the Grid-Ins section.** For example, negative values cannot be accepted by the computer used to score the Grid-Ins. **This means that there will be no correct answers that are negative values.** If you solve a problem and get an answer that is a negative, check your work because you did something wrong. This is an important tool when answering Grid-Ins.

Bust it!

There is another limitation in the test format that can be used to your advantage: **Answers with algebraic variables, or letters, cannot be used in this section** (but variables may be used in the questions). So, if you get an answer with a variable in it, you know to check your work because it's wrong.

The format of these questions restricts the writers of the SAT so much that the questions you'll encounter on the Grid-Ins will be mostly arithmetic. And arithmetic is very easy to do with a calculator (remember, you're able to use a calculator in this section of the SAT). But, as always, be careful using a calculator. Make sure you've set the problem up properly (using your booklet as scratch paper) and carefully enter the numbers into the calculator.

Entering Your Answers Into the Grid

Important Information!

Because the Grid-In questions are so different from the other SAT questions, special care must be made to following the directions. **Entering your answers in the grid can cause many problems if you don't understand how to do it properly.** In fact, if done incorrectly, entering your answer can cause you to lose points. Read the following tips and strategies and be sure to apply them while gridding the answers to all Grid-In questions.

Take a look at one of the grids. You'll see four columns. Because of the way the computer used to score your grids is set up, **a decimal can appear in any of those four columns.** If your answer is 5, you could enter just the 5 or you could enter 5., or even 5.0. But just entering 5 will get you the points for answering the question correctly. Also, as you read in the directions, answers to Grid-In questions can be in fraction or decimal form. It doesn't matter. Just grid the answer in the form that takes the least amount of time to solve. The only types of numbers you cannot grid are mixed fractions or negative numbers.

Mixed fractions are a common occurrence in math problems. **If you get a mixed fraction as an answer, you'll have to do one of two things in order to enter it in the grid.** First, you can convert a mixed fraction to an improper fraction. For example, 2 and 2/3 would become 8/3. Or second, you can convert a mixed fraction to a decimal. For example, 2 and 2/3 would become the repeating decimal 2.66666... (You must run a repeating decimal out as far as the number of columns remaining, see below.) Whichever method you feel most comfortable with should be the one you use.

Special attention should be paid to the fact that a decimal point can appear anywhere. A decimal point is very important to the value of an answer. For example, if you convert your answer of 2/3 to a decimal, you will get a repeating (.666666666 ...). If you were to enter this answer in decimal form, you must be careful and NOT put a zero in the ones place (0.666666666 ...) and you must carry the repeating decimal out as far as the number of columns available. In this example, the column on the far left would have the decimal point and the remaining three columns would have 6's in them.

Look!

Important Strategy

You can round up a repeating decimal. This is allowed, but we don't recommend it. You see, rounding up takes time. And wasting time takes points away from your score. So if a repeating decimal is acceptable, don't waste the time to round up.

Another way entering your answer in the grid can cause problems is the column in which you start gridding your answer. It doesn't matter which column you start with, as long as you can fit your answer in the remaining columns. This means you can enter a short answer, like .5, in any two consecutive columns on the grid. **To get yourself used to gridding your answers with the least amount of problems, we suggest you always begin gridding your answer in the column on the far left.** This way, you won't waste time erasing and re-entering an answer if you run out of columns to fit your answer.

If the question you're working on contains dollar signs or percent signs, be sure to eliminate these signs when gridding your answer. You will not be able to input symbols. When you encounter a question that contains dollar signs or percent signs, you must convert your answer into a decimal form.

Don't use more than one oval in any column. We know, that's common sense. But gridding answers can be confusing. Be sure you only fill in one oval per column or your answer will be scored as incorrect (even if you wrote in the correct answer at the top).

Once you've arrived at your answer, enter it at the top of the grid using the columns before filling in the ovals. Writing in your answer at the top of the columns will lessen the chances of you filling in the wrong oval.

Finally, any grid with no ovals filled in will be scored "no answer", even if you wrote the correct answer in the spaces above the columns. So be sure to fill in the ovals.

About the Questions

Important Information!

Within the SAT Grid-In section you will be given 10 questions. You will have 30 minutes to answer these questions in addition to 15 Quantitative Comparison questions. This means you will be required to answer 25 questions in 30 minutes. Therefore, you should work quickly.

The Grid-In questions will come from the areas of arithmetic, algebra, and geometry. There is an emphasis on word problems and on data interpretation, which usually involves reading tables to answer questions. Many of the geometry questions will refer to diagrams or will ask you to create a figure from information given in the question.

The following will detail the different types of questions you should expect to encounter on the Grid-Ins.

ARITHMETIC QUESTIONS

These arithmetic questions test your ability to perform standard manipulations and simplifications of arithmetic expressions. For some questions, there is more than one approach. There are six kinds of arithmetic questions you may encounter on Grid-Ins. For each type of question, we will show how to solve the problem and grid your answer.

Important Information!

Question Type 1: PROPERTIES OF A WHOLE NUMBER *N*

This type of problem tests your ability to find a whole number with a given set of properties. You will be given a list of properties of a whole number and asked to find that number.

 PROBLEM

The properties of a whole number *N* are

(A)   *N* is a perfect square.

(B)   *N* is divisible by 2.

(C)   *N* is divisible by 3.

Grid in the second smallest whole number with the above properties.

 SOLUTION

What is the smallest number divisible by 2 and 3? The smallest number with properties (B) and (C) is 6. Since property (A) says the number must be a perfect square, the smallest number with properties (A), (B), and (C) is 36.

$6^2 = 36$ is the smallest whole number with the above properties. The second smallest whole number (the solution) is

$$(2^2)(6^2) = 4 \times 36 = 144.$$

The correct answer entered into the grid is

Bust it!

Question Type 2: SIMPLIFYING FRACTIONS

This type of question requires you to simplify fractional expressions and grid the answer in the format specified. By canceling out terms common to both the numerator and denominator, we can simplify complex fractional expressions.

PROBLEM

Change $\frac{1}{2} \times \frac{3}{7} \times \frac{2}{8} \times \frac{14}{10} \times \frac{1}{3}$ to decimal form.

SOLUTION

The point here is to cancel out terms common to both the numerator and denominator. Once the fraction is brought down to lowest terms, the result is entered into the grid as a decimal.

After cancellation we are left with the fraction $\frac{1}{40}$.

Equivalently,

$$\frac{1}{\cancel{2}} \times \frac{\cancel{3}}{\cancel{7}} \times \frac{\cancel{2}}{8} \times \frac{\overset{2}{\cancel{14}}}{10} \times \frac{1}{\cancel{3}} = \frac{2}{80} = \frac{1}{40}$$

Now use your calculator to divide 40 into 1 = .025

Hence, in our grid we enter

Bust it!

Note: If "decimal" was not specified, any correct version of the answer could be entered into the grid.

Question Type 3:
PRIME NUMBERS OF A PARTICULAR FORM

Here, you will be asked to find a prime number with certain characteristics. Remember—a prime number is a number that can only be divided by itself and 1.

 PROBLEM

What is the least prime number which is a divisor of

$7^9 + 11^{25}$?

 SOLUTION

This problem tests both your knowledge of prime numbers and your knowledge of exponents.

Since 7^9 and 11^{25} are both odd numbers (any number with an exponent that is an odd number will also be an odd number), their sum will have to be even. This is because any two odd numbers added together will give you an even number.

Since their sum must be even, they must be divisible by 2. And because 2 is a prime number, and also the smallest prime number besides 1, this is your answer.

Bust it!

You would enter the answer in the grid as

$$\begin{array}{|c|c|c|c|}
\hline
\mathcal{2} & & & \\
\hline
& \oslash & \oslash & \\
\odot & \odot & \odot & \odot \\
& 0 & 0 & 0 \\
\textcircled{1} & \textcircled{1} & \textcircled{1} & \textcircled{1} \\
\bullet & \textcircled{2} & \textcircled{2} & \textcircled{2} \\
\textcircled{3} & \textcircled{3} & \textcircled{3} & \textcircled{3} \\
\textcircled{4} & \textcircled{4} & \textcircled{4} & \textcircled{4} \\
\textcircled{5} & \textcircled{5} & \textcircled{5} & \textcircled{5} \\
\textcircled{6} & \textcircled{6} & \textcircled{6} & \textcircled{6} \\
\textcircled{7} & \textcircled{7} & \textcircled{7} & \textcircled{7} \\
\textcircled{8} & \textcircled{8} & \textcircled{8} & \textcircled{8} \\
\textcircled{9} & \textcircled{9} & \textcircled{9} & \textcircled{9} \\
\hline
\end{array}$$

Question Type 4: ORDER OF OPERATIONS

The following question type tests your knowledge of the arithmetic order of operations. Always work within the parentheses or with absolute values first, while keeping in mind that multiplication and division are carried out before addition and subtraction.

 PROBLEM

Find a solution to the equation $x \div 3 \times 4 \div 2 = 6$.

 SOLUTION

The key here is to recall the order of precedence for arithmetic operations. After simplifying the expression one can solve for x.

Since multiplication and division have the same level of precedence, we simplify the equation from left to right to obtain:

Bust it!

$$\frac{x}{3} \times 4 \div 2 = 6$$

$$\frac{4x}{3} \div 2 = 6$$

$$\frac{\overset{2}{\cancel{4x}}}{2} \times \frac{1}{\cancel{2}} = \frac{2x}{3} = 6$$

$$x = \frac{3}{2} \times \frac{6}{1}$$

$$x = 9$$

As 9 solves the above problem, our entry in the grid is

Question Type 5: SOLVING FOR RATIOS

This type of question tests your ability to manipulate ratios given a set of constraints.

? **PROBLEM**

The ratio of two numbers is 3 to 4. The larger number is 132. Find the smaller number. Let the common factor be x.

SOLUTION

The first step is to set up an equation to find the larger number such as follows:

$$4x = 132$$

so

$$x = 33$$

Now we have to find the smaller number by setting up an equation, substituting x

$$3x = 3 \times 33 = 99$$

The correct answer is 99. In the following grid we would enter

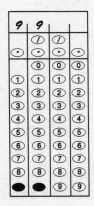

Bust it!

ALGEBRA QUESTIONS

Within the Grid-In section, you will also encounter algebra questions which **will test your ability to solve algebraic expressions in the setting of word problems.** You may encounter the following six types of algebra questions on the SAT. As in the previous section, we provide methods for approaching each type of problem.

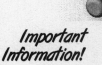

Important Information!

Question Type 1: SOLVING A SYSTEM OF LINEAR EQUATIONS

This is a standard question which will ask you to find the solution to a system of two linear equations with two unknowns.

 PROBLEM

Consider the system of simultaneous equations given by

$$y - 2 = x - 4$$

$$y + 3 = 6 - x$$

Solve for the quantity $6y + 3$.

 SOLUTION

This problem can be solved by taking the first equation given and solving for x. This would yield

$$x = y + 2.$$

Next, we plug this value for x into the second equation, giving us

$$y + 3 = 6 - (y + 2).$$

Solve this equation for y and we get

$$y = \frac{1}{2}.$$

We are asked to solve for $6y + 3$, so we can plug our value for y in and get

$$6\left(\frac{1}{2}\right) + 3 = 6.$$

Bust it!

Our answer is 6 and gridded correctly it is

Question Type 2: WORD PROBLEMS INVOLVING AGE

When dealing with this type of question, you will be asked to solve for the age of a particular person. The question may require you to determine how much older one person is, how much younger one person is, or the specific age of the person.

? **PROBLEM**

Tim is 2 years older than Jane and Joe is 4 years younger than Jane. If the sum of the ages of Jane, Joe, and Tim is 28, how old is Joe?

! **SOLUTION**

Define Jane's age to be the variable x and work from there.

Bust it!

Let

$$\text{Jane's age} = x$$
$$\text{Tim's age} = x + 2$$
$$\text{Joe's age} = x - 4$$

Summing up the ages we get

$$x + x + 2 + x - 4 = 28$$
$$3x - 2 = 28$$
$$3x = 30$$
$$x = 10$$
$$\text{Joe's age} = 10 - 4 = 6.$$

Hence, we enter into the grid

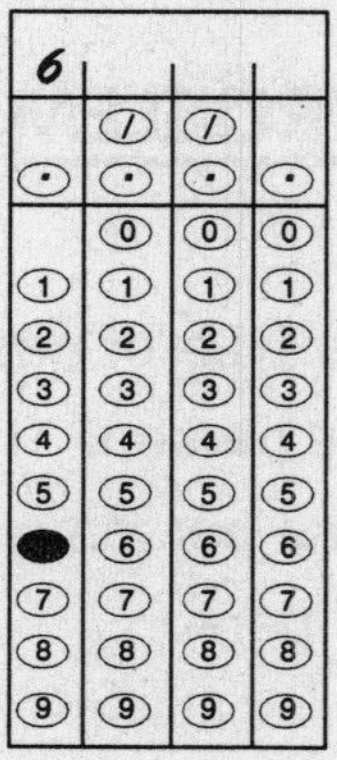

Question Type 3: WORD PROBLEMS INVOLVING MONEY

Word problems involving money will test your ability to translate the information given into an algebraic statement. You will also be required to solve your algebraic statement.

? PROBLEM

After receiving his weekly paycheck on Friday, a man buys a television for $100, a suit for $200, and a radio for $50. If the total money he spent amounts to 40% of his paycheck, what is his weekly salary?

! SOLUTION

Simply set up an equation involving the man's expenditures and the percentage of his paycheck that he used to buy them.

Let the amount of the man's paycheck equal x. We then have the equation

$$40\% \, x = 100 + 200 + 50$$

$$0.4x = 350$$

$$x = \$875$$

In the grid we enter

Bust it!

Question Type 4: SYSTEMS OF NON-LINEAR EQUATIONS

This type of question will test your ability to perform the correct algebraic operations for a given set of equations in order to find the desired quantity.

 PROBLEM

Consider the system of equations

$$x^2 + y^2 = 8$$

$$xy = 4$$

Solve for the quantity $3x + 3y$.

 SOLUTION

Solve for the quantity $x + y$ and not for x or y individually.

First, multiply the equation $xy = 4$ by 2 to get $2xy = 8$. Adding this to $x^2 + y^2 = 8$ we obtain

$$x^2 + 2xy + y^2 = 16$$
$$(x + y)^2 = 16$$
$$x + y = 4$$

or $$x + y = -4$$

Bust it!

Hence, $3x + 3y = 12$ or $3x + 3y = -12$. We enter 12 for a solution since -12 cannot be entered into the grid.

Question Type 5: WORD PROBLEMS INVOLVING HOURLY WAGE

When dealing with this type of question, you will be required to form an algebraic expression from the information based on a person's wages. You will then solve the expression to determine the person's wages (i.e., hourly, daily, annually, etc.).

 PROBLEM

> Jim works 25 hours a week earning $10 an hour. Sally works 50 hours a week earning *y* dollars an hour. If their combined income every two weeks is $2,000, find the amount of money Sally makes an hour.

 SOLUTION

Be careful. The combined income is given over a two-week period.

Simply set up an equation involving income. We obtain

Bust it!

$$2[(25)(10) + (50)(y)] = 2,000$$
$$[(25)(10) + (50)(y)] = 1,000$$
$$250 + 50y = 1,000$$
$$50y = 750$$
$$y = \$15 \text{ an hour}$$

We enter in the grid

Question Type 6: WORD PROBLEMS INVOLVING CONSECUTIVE INTEGERS

In this type of question, you will need to set up an equation involving consecutive integers based on the product of the integers, which is given.

?   **PROBLEM**

When 8 consecutive integers are multiplied, their product is 0. What would their largest possible sum be?

SOLUTION

If a series of numbers is to have a product of 0, one of those numbers must be 0. Thus, one of the 8 consecutive integers must be 0. We now want the largest set of 8 consecutive integers, having 0 as one of those integers. This would be

0, 1, 2, 3, 4, 5, 6, and 7.

When these are added together, the sum is 28. You would enter in the grid

Bust it!

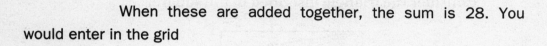

GEOMETRY QUESTIONS

In this section, we will explain how to solve questions which **test your ability to find the area of various geometric figures.** There are six types of questions you may encounter.

Important Information!

Question Type 1: AREA OF AN INSCRIBED TRIANGLE

This type of question asks you to find the area of a triangle which is inscribed in a square. By knowing certain properties of both triangles and squares, we can deduce the necessary information.

 PROBLEM

Consider the triangle inscribed in the square.

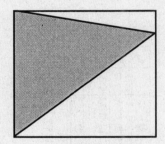

If the area of the square is 36, find the area of the triangle.

 SOLUTION

Find the height of tne triangle.

Let x be the length of the square. Since the four sides of a square are equal, and the area of a square is the length of a side squared, $x^2 = 36$. Therefore, $x = 6$.

The area of a triangle is given by

$$\frac{1}{2} (\text{base}) (\text{height}).$$

Here x is both the base and height of the triangle. The area of the triangle is

Bust it!

$\frac{1}{2}$ (6) (6) = 18.

This is how the answer would be gridded.

Question Type 2: LENGTH OF THE SIDE OF A TRIANGLE

For this type of question, one must find the length of a right triangle given information about the other sides. The key here is to apply the Pythagorean Theorem, which states that the square of the hypotenuse of a right triangle is equal to the sum of the squares of the other two sides.

? PROBLEM

Consider the line given below

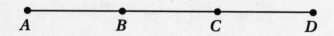

where $\overline{AD}$ = 30 and $\overline{AB}$ = 5. What length is $\overline{BC}$ if the sides $\overline{AB}$, $\overline{BC}$, and $\overline{CD}$ form the sides of a right triangle?

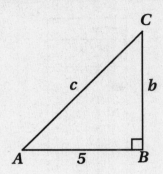

SOLUTION

Draw a diagram and fill in the known information.

Next, apply the Pythagorean Theorem ($a^2 + b^2 = c^2$), filling in the known variables. Here, we are solving for *BC* (*b* in our equation). We know that $a = 5$, and since $AD = 30$ and $AB = 5$, $BD = 25$. Filling in these values, we obtain this equation:

$$5^2 + x^2 = (25 - x)^2$$
$$25 + x^2 = 625 - 50x + x^2$$
$$50x = 600$$
$$x = 12$$

Bust it!

This is one possible solution. If we had chosen $x = CD$ and $25 - x = BC$, one obtains $BC = 13$, which is another possible solution. The possible grid entries are shown here.

or

Question Type 3: SOLVING FOR THE DEGREE OF AN ANGLE

Here you will be given a figure with certain information provided. You will need to deduce the measure of an angle based both on this information, as well as other geometric principles. The easiest way to do this is by setting up an algebraic expression.

 PROBLEM

Find the angle *y* in the diagram shown here.

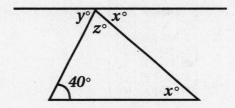

 SOLUTION

Use the fact that the sum of the angles on the bottom side of the box is 180°.

Let *z* be the angle at the top of the triangle. Since we know the sum of the angles of a triangle is 180°,

$$40 + z + x = 180$$

Isolate the variables

$$z + x = 140$$

Isolate z

$$z = 140 - x$$

Bust it!

Looking at the top of the triangle, we know that the three angles added together must equal 180°, so

$$y + z + x = 180$$

We can now substitute for z in this equation to get

$$y + (140 - x) + x = 180$$
$$y + 140 - x + x = 180$$
$$y + 140 = 180$$
$$y = 40$$

In the grid we enter

Question Type 4: SOLVING FOR THE LENGTH OF A SIDE

For this type of question, you will be given a figure with certain measures of sides filled in. You will need to apply geometric principles to find the missing side.

? PROBLEM

Consider the figure below.

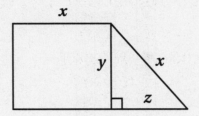

In the figure let *x* and *y* be whole numbers where $xy = 65$. Also assume the area of the whole figure is 95 square inches. Find *z*.

! SOLUTION

The key point here is that x and y are whole numbers. Using the figure we only have a finite number of possibilities for z.

The equation for the area of the above figure is

$$xy + yz = 95.$$

Substituting $xy = 65$ into the above equation we get

$$yz = 30.$$

Bust it!

Using the fact that $xy = 65$ we know y can be either 1, 5, or 13. As $y = 13$ does not yield a factorization for $yz = 30$, y is either 1 or 5. If $y = 1$ this implies $x = 65$ and $z = 60$ which contradicts the Pythagorean Theorem (i.e., $1^2 + 60^2 = 13^2$). If $y = 5$ this implies $x = 13$ and $z = 12$ which satisfies $y^2 + z^2 = x^2$; hence, the solution is $y = 5$.

In our grid we enter

Question Type 5: SOLVING FOR THE AREA OF A REGION

Here, you will be given a figure with a shaded region. Given certain information, you will need to solve for the area of that region.

PROBLEM

Consider the concentric squares drawn below.

Assume that the side of the larger square is length 1. Also assume that the smaller square's perimeter is equal to the diameter of the larger square. Find the area of the shaded region.

SOLUTION

The key here is to find the length of the side for the smaller square.

By the Pythagorean Theorem the diameter of the square is

$$d^2 = 1^2 + 1^2$$

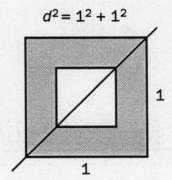

1

1

Bust it!

which yields $d = \sqrt{2}$. Similarly, the smaller square's perimeter is $\sqrt{2}$. Since the perimeter is equal to the sum of the four sides, one side of the smaller square $= \dfrac{\sqrt{2}}{4}$.

Calculating the area for the shaded region we get

$$A = A_{large} - A_{small}$$

The area of the larger square is

$$\text{side} \times \text{side} = \text{area}$$
$$1 \times 1 = 1$$

$$A = 1 - \left(\frac{\sqrt{2}}{4}\right)^2$$

$$A = 1 - \frac{2}{16}$$

$$A = \frac{16}{16} - \frac{2}{16} = \frac{14}{16}$$

$$A = \frac{7}{8}$$

In the grid we enter

Question Type 6: SOLVE FOR A SUM OF LENGTHS

The question type here involves solving for a sum of lengths in the figure given knowledge pertaining to its area.

? PROBLEM

Consider the figure below.

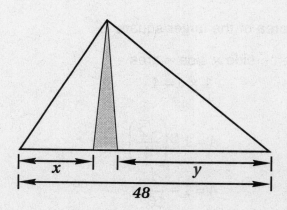

Assume that $\dfrac{\text{Total Area}}{\text{Shaded Area}} = 16$. Solve for $x + y$.

! **SOLUTION**

Solve for $x + y$ and not for x or y individually. Use s to denote the base of the shaded triangle. Then

$$48 - s = x + y.$$

From the information given

$$\frac{\frac{48h}{2}}{\frac{sh}{2}} = 16$$

$$\frac{48h}{2} = 16\left(\frac{sh}{2}\right)$$

Simplify

$$24h = 8sh$$

$$24 = 8s$$

$$3 = s$$

Inserting the value for s into our original equation for $x + y$:

$$48 - s = x + y$$

$$48 - 3 = 45$$

$$45 = x + y$$

We enter in the grid

Bust it!

Points to Remember

On Target!

✔   Be careful when using your calculator. While a calculator is helpful in computing large sums and decimals, you must be sure that you set up your problem properly before calculating the numbers. Also, some problems, such as those involving common denominators, would be more efficiently solved without a calculator.

✔   Immediately plug the values of all specific information into your equation.

✔   To visualize exactly what the question is asking and what information you need to find, draw a sketch of the problem.

✔   Even though you may think you have the equation worked out, make sure your result is actually answering the question. For example, although you may solve an equation for a specific variable, this may not be the final answer. You may have to use this answer to find another quantity.

✔   Make sure to work in only one unit, and convert if more than one is presented in the problem. For example, if a problem gives numbers in decimals and fractions, convert one in terms of the other and then work out the problem.

Answering Grid-In Questions

When answering Grid-In questions, you should follow these steps.

STEP 1 | Identify the type of question with which you are presented (i.e., arithmetic, algebra, or geometry).

STEP 2 | Once you have determined if the question deals with arithmetic, algebra, or geometry, further classify the question. Then, try to determine what type of arithmetic (or algebra or geometry) question is being presented.

Important Information!

STEP 3 | Solve the question using the techniques explained in this review. Make sure your answer can be gridded. For example, if your answer has a percent sign, it must be converted to a decimal form.

STEP 4 | Grid your answer in the question's corresponding answer grid. Make sure you are filling in the grid correctly.

The drill questions which follow should be completed to help reinforce all of the material you've just read. Be sure to refer back to this review if you need help answering the questions. Good luck!

Drill: Grid-In

(An answer sheet appears at the end of this book.)

DIRECTIONS: Each of the following questions requires you to solve the problem and enter your answer in the ovals in the special grid:

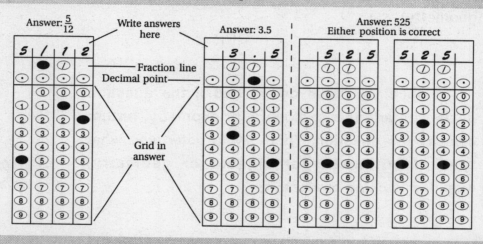

- You may begin filling in your answer in any column, space permitting. Columns not needed should be left blank.

- Answers may be entered in either decimal or fraction form. For example, $\frac{3}{12}$ or .25 are equally acceptable.

- A mixed number, such as $4\frac{1}{2}$, must be entered either as 4.5 or $\frac{9}{2}$. If you entered 41/2, the machine would interpret your answer as $\frac{41}{2}$, not $4\frac{1}{2}$.

- There may be some instances where there is more than one correct answer to a problem. Should this be the case, grid only one answer.

- Be very careful when filling in ovals. Do not fill in more than one oval in any column, and make sure to completely darken the ovals.

- It is suggested that you fill in your answer in the boxes above each column. Although you will not be graded incorrectly if you do not write in your answer, it will help you fill in the corresponding ovals.

- If your answer is a decimal, grid the most accurate value possible. For example, if you need to grid a repeating decimal such as 0.6666, enter the answer as .666 or .667. A less accurate value, such as .66 or .67, is not acceptable.

- A negative answer cannot appear for any question.

1 At the end of the month, a woman pays $714 in rent. If the rent constitutes 21% of her monthly income, what is her hourly wage given the fact that she works 34 hours per week?

2 Find the largest integer which is less than 100 and divisible by 3 and 7.

3 The radius of the smaller of two concentric circles is 5 cm while the radius of the larger circle is 7 cm. Determine the area of the shaded region.

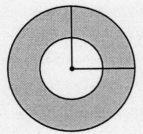

4

$$\frac{1}{6} + \frac{2}{3} + \frac{1}{6} - \frac{1}{3} + 1 - \frac{3}{4} - \frac{1}{4} =$$

5 The sum of the squares of two consecutive integers is 41. What is the sum of their cubes?

6 Find x.

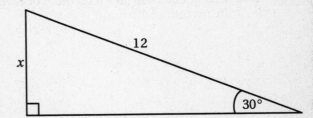

7

$$| -8 - 4 | \div 3 \times 6 + (-4) =$$

8 A class of 24 students contains 16 males. What is the ratio of females to males?

9 At an office supply store, customers are given a discount if they pay in cash. If a customer is given a discount of $9.66 on a total order of $276, what is the percent of discount?

10 Let $\overline{RO} = 16$, $\overline{HM} = 30$. Find the perimeter of rhombus *HOMR*.

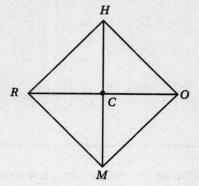

11 Solve for x.
$$x + 2y = 8$$
$$3x + 4y = 20$$

12 Six years ago, Henry's mother was nine times as old as Henry. Now she is only three times as old as Henry. How old is Henry now?

14 Find the area of the shaded triangles.

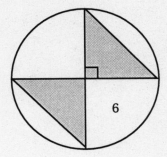

6

13 Find a prime number less than 40 which is of the form $5k + 1$.

15

$$\frac{7}{10} \times \frac{4}{21} \times \frac{25}{36} =$$

16 Find the solution for *x* in the pair of equations.

$$x + y = 7$$
$$x = y - 3$$

18 △*MNO* is isosceles. If the vertex angle, ∠ *N*, has a measure of 96°, find the measure of ∠ *M*.

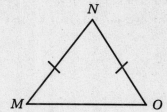

17 Given the square *RHOM*, find the length of the diagonal $\overline{RO}$ with side $\overline{OM} = 17$.

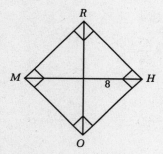

19

Simplify $\dfrac{\dfrac{1}{2} + \dfrac{1}{3}}{\dfrac{1}{6}}$.

20 In the diagram shown, *ABC* is an isosceles triangle. Sides $\overline{AC}$ and $\overline{BC}$ are extended through *C* to *E* and *D* to form triangle *CDE*. What is the sum of the measures of angles *D* and *E*?

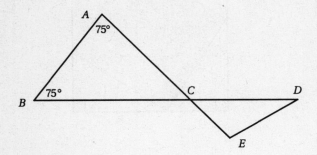

21

Number of Muffins	Total Price
1	$0.55
Box of 4	$2.10
Box of 8	$4.00

According to the information in the table above, what would be the *least* amount of money needed to purchase exactly 19 muffins? (Disregard the dollar sign when gridding your answer.)

22 Several people rented a van for $30, sharing the cost equally. If there had been one more person in the group, it would have cost each $1 less. How many people were there in the group originally?

23 For the triangle pictured below, the degree measures of the three angles are *x*, 3*x*, and 3*x* + 5. Find *x*.

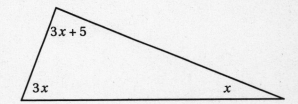

24 △*PQR* is a scalene triangle. The measure of ∠ *P* is 8 more than twice the measure of ∠ *R*. The measure of ∠ *Q* is two less than three times the measure of ∠ *R*. Determine the measure of ∠ *Q*.

25 A mother is now 24 years older than her daughter. In 4 years, the mother will be 3 times as old as the daughter. What is the present age of the daughter?

26 John is 4 times as old as Harry. In six years John will be twice as old as Harry. What is Harry's age now?

27 What is the area of the shaded region?

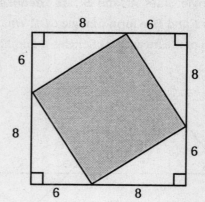

28 In an apartment building there are 9 apartments having terraces for every 16 apartments. If the apartment building has a total of 144 apartments, how many apartments have terraces?

29 Solve the equation $2x^2 - 5x + 3 = 0$.

32 Solve the proportion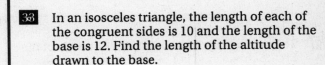

30 Find the length of a side of an equilateral triangle whose area is $4\sqrt{3}$.

33 In an isosceles triangle, the length of each of the congruent sides is 10 and the length of the base is 12. Find the length of the altitude drawn to the base.

31 Solve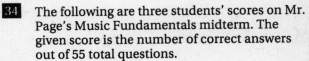

34 The following are three students' scores on Mr. Page's Music Fundamentals midterm. The given score is the number of correct answers out of 55 total questions.

      Liz   48
      Jay   45
      Carl   25

What is the *average* percentage of questions correct for the three students?

35 Reserved seat tickets to a football game are $6 more than general admission tickets. Mr. Jones finds that he can buy general admission tickets for his whole family of five for only $3 more than the cost of reserved seat tickets for himself and Mrs. Jones. How much do the general admission tickets cost?

38 The mean (average) of the numbers 50, 60, 65, 75, x, and y is 65. What is the mean of x and y?

36 The sum of three numbers is 96. The ratio of the first to the second is 1 : 2 and the ratio of the second to the third is 2 : 3. What is the third number?

39 The ages of the students enrolled at XYZ University are given in the following table:

Age	Number of students
18	750
19	1,600
20	1,200
21	450

What percent of students are 19 and 20 years old?

37 What is the smallest even integer n for which $(.5)^n$ is less than .01?

40 Find the larger side of a rectangle whose area is 24 and whose perimeter is 22.

Grid-In Drill
ANSWER KEY

1. 2 5

2. 8 4

3. 7 5 . 4

4. 2 / 3

5. 1 8 9

6. 6

7. `2 0`

8. `1 / 2`

9. `3 . 5`

10. `6 8`

11. `4`

12. `8`

13. `1 1`   or   `3 1`

14. `3 6`
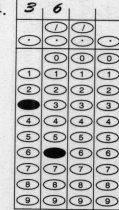

15.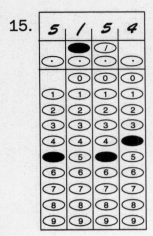

16.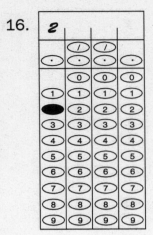

17.

18.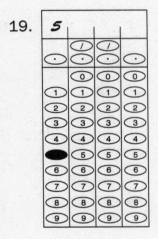

19.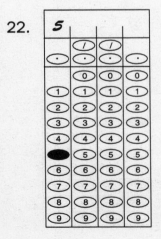

20.

21.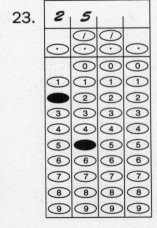

22.

23.

24. 8 5

25. 8

26. 3

27. 1 0 0

28. 8 1

29. 1

30. 4

31. 3

32. 4

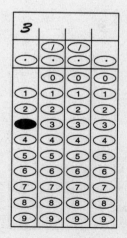

33. **8**

34. **7 1 . 5**

35. **5**

36. **4 8**

37. **8**

38. **7 0**

39. **7 0**

40. **8**

SAT Practice Test Answer Sheet

SECTION 1

1. Ⓐ Ⓑ Ⓒ Ⓓ Ⓔ
2. Ⓐ Ⓑ Ⓒ Ⓓ Ⓔ
3. Ⓐ Ⓑ Ⓒ Ⓓ Ⓔ
4. Ⓐ Ⓑ Ⓒ Ⓓ Ⓔ
5. Ⓐ Ⓑ Ⓒ Ⓓ Ⓔ
6. Ⓐ Ⓑ Ⓒ Ⓓ Ⓔ
7. Ⓐ Ⓑ Ⓒ Ⓓ Ⓔ
8. Ⓐ Ⓑ Ⓒ Ⓓ Ⓔ
9. Ⓐ Ⓑ Ⓒ Ⓓ Ⓔ
10. Ⓐ Ⓑ Ⓒ Ⓓ Ⓔ
11. Ⓐ Ⓑ Ⓒ Ⓓ Ⓔ
12. Ⓐ Ⓑ Ⓒ Ⓓ Ⓔ
13. Ⓐ Ⓑ Ⓒ Ⓓ Ⓔ
14. Ⓐ Ⓑ Ⓒ Ⓓ Ⓔ
15. Ⓐ Ⓑ Ⓒ Ⓓ Ⓔ
16. Ⓐ Ⓑ Ⓒ Ⓓ Ⓔ
17. Ⓐ Ⓑ Ⓒ Ⓓ Ⓔ
18. Ⓐ Ⓑ Ⓒ Ⓓ Ⓔ
19. Ⓐ Ⓑ Ⓒ Ⓓ Ⓔ
20. Ⓐ Ⓑ Ⓒ Ⓓ Ⓔ
21. Ⓐ Ⓑ Ⓒ Ⓓ Ⓔ
22. Ⓐ Ⓑ Ⓒ Ⓓ Ⓔ
23. Ⓐ Ⓑ Ⓒ Ⓓ Ⓔ
24. Ⓐ Ⓑ Ⓒ Ⓓ Ⓔ
25. Ⓐ Ⓑ Ⓒ Ⓓ Ⓔ
26. Ⓐ Ⓑ Ⓒ Ⓓ Ⓔ
27. Ⓐ Ⓑ Ⓒ Ⓓ Ⓔ
28. Ⓐ Ⓑ Ⓒ Ⓓ Ⓔ
29. Ⓐ Ⓑ Ⓒ Ⓓ Ⓔ
30. Ⓐ Ⓑ Ⓒ Ⓓ Ⓔ

SECTION 2

1. Ⓐ Ⓑ Ⓒ Ⓓ Ⓔ
2. Ⓐ Ⓑ Ⓒ Ⓓ Ⓔ
3. Ⓐ Ⓑ Ⓒ Ⓓ Ⓔ
4. Ⓐ Ⓑ Ⓒ Ⓓ Ⓔ
5. Ⓐ Ⓑ Ⓒ Ⓓ Ⓔ
6. Ⓐ Ⓑ Ⓒ Ⓓ Ⓔ
7. Ⓐ Ⓑ Ⓒ Ⓓ Ⓔ
8. Ⓐ Ⓑ Ⓒ Ⓓ Ⓔ
9. Ⓐ Ⓑ Ⓒ Ⓓ Ⓔ
10. Ⓐ Ⓑ Ⓒ Ⓓ Ⓔ
11. Ⓐ Ⓑ Ⓒ Ⓓ Ⓔ
12. Ⓐ Ⓑ Ⓒ Ⓓ Ⓔ
13. Ⓐ Ⓑ Ⓒ Ⓓ Ⓔ
14. Ⓐ Ⓑ Ⓒ Ⓓ Ⓔ
15. Ⓐ Ⓑ Ⓒ Ⓓ Ⓔ
16. Ⓐ Ⓑ Ⓒ Ⓓ Ⓔ
17. Ⓐ Ⓑ Ⓒ Ⓓ Ⓔ
18. Ⓐ Ⓑ Ⓒ Ⓓ Ⓔ
19. Ⓐ Ⓑ Ⓒ Ⓓ Ⓔ
20. Ⓐ Ⓑ Ⓒ Ⓓ Ⓔ
21. Ⓐ Ⓑ Ⓒ Ⓓ Ⓔ
22. Ⓐ Ⓑ Ⓒ Ⓓ Ⓔ
23. Ⓐ Ⓑ Ⓒ Ⓓ Ⓔ
24. Ⓐ Ⓑ Ⓒ Ⓓ Ⓔ
25. Ⓐ Ⓑ Ⓒ Ⓓ Ⓔ

SECTION 3

1. Ⓐ Ⓑ Ⓒ Ⓓ Ⓔ
2. Ⓐ Ⓑ Ⓒ Ⓓ Ⓔ
3. Ⓐ Ⓑ Ⓒ Ⓓ Ⓔ
4. Ⓐ Ⓑ Ⓒ Ⓓ Ⓔ
5. Ⓐ Ⓑ Ⓒ Ⓓ Ⓔ
6. Ⓐ Ⓑ Ⓒ Ⓓ Ⓔ
7. Ⓐ Ⓑ Ⓒ Ⓓ Ⓔ
8. Ⓐ Ⓑ Ⓒ Ⓓ Ⓔ
9. Ⓐ Ⓑ Ⓒ Ⓓ Ⓔ
10. Ⓐ Ⓑ Ⓒ Ⓓ Ⓔ
11. Ⓐ Ⓑ Ⓒ Ⓓ Ⓔ
12. Ⓐ Ⓑ Ⓒ Ⓓ Ⓔ
13. Ⓐ Ⓑ Ⓒ Ⓓ Ⓔ
14. Ⓐ Ⓑ Ⓒ Ⓓ Ⓔ
15. Ⓐ Ⓑ Ⓒ Ⓓ Ⓔ
16. Ⓐ Ⓑ Ⓒ Ⓓ Ⓔ
17. Ⓐ Ⓑ Ⓒ Ⓓ Ⓔ
18. Ⓐ Ⓑ Ⓒ Ⓓ Ⓔ
19. Ⓐ Ⓑ Ⓒ Ⓓ Ⓔ
20. Ⓐ Ⓑ Ⓒ Ⓓ Ⓔ
21. Ⓐ Ⓑ Ⓒ Ⓓ Ⓔ
22. Ⓐ Ⓑ Ⓒ Ⓓ Ⓔ
23. Ⓐ Ⓑ Ⓒ Ⓓ Ⓔ
24. Ⓐ Ⓑ Ⓒ Ⓓ Ⓔ
25. Ⓐ Ⓑ Ⓒ Ⓓ Ⓔ
26. Ⓐ Ⓑ Ⓒ Ⓓ Ⓔ
27. Ⓐ Ⓑ Ⓒ Ⓓ Ⓔ
28. Ⓐ Ⓑ Ⓒ Ⓓ Ⓔ
29. Ⓐ Ⓑ Ⓒ Ⓓ Ⓔ
30. Ⓐ Ⓑ Ⓒ Ⓓ Ⓔ
31. Ⓐ Ⓑ Ⓒ Ⓓ Ⓔ
32. Ⓐ Ⓑ Ⓒ Ⓓ Ⓔ
33. Ⓐ Ⓑ Ⓒ Ⓓ Ⓔ
34. Ⓐ Ⓑ Ⓒ Ⓓ Ⓔ
35. Ⓐ Ⓑ Ⓒ Ⓓ Ⓔ

SECTION 4

1. Ⓐ Ⓑ Ⓒ Ⓓ Ⓔ
2. Ⓐ Ⓑ Ⓒ Ⓓ Ⓔ
3. Ⓐ Ⓑ Ⓒ Ⓓ Ⓔ
4. Ⓐ Ⓑ Ⓒ Ⓓ Ⓔ
5. Ⓐ Ⓑ Ⓒ Ⓓ Ⓔ
6. Ⓐ Ⓑ Ⓒ Ⓓ Ⓔ
7. Ⓐ Ⓑ Ⓒ Ⓓ Ⓔ
8. Ⓐ Ⓑ Ⓒ Ⓓ Ⓔ
9. Ⓐ Ⓑ Ⓒ Ⓓ Ⓔ
10. Ⓐ Ⓑ Ⓒ Ⓓ Ⓔ
11. Ⓐ Ⓑ Ⓒ Ⓓ Ⓔ
12. Ⓐ Ⓑ Ⓒ Ⓓ Ⓔ
13. Ⓐ Ⓑ Ⓒ Ⓓ Ⓔ
14. Ⓐ Ⓑ Ⓒ Ⓓ Ⓔ
15. Ⓐ Ⓑ Ⓒ Ⓓ Ⓔ

16. Grid-in answer space (fraction bar, decimal point, digits 0–9)

17. Grid-in answer space (fraction bar, decimal point, digits 0–9)

18. Grid-in answer space (fraction bar, decimal point, digits 0–9)

19. Grid-in answer space (fraction bar, decimal point, digits 0–9)

20. Grid-in answer space (fraction bar, decimal point, digits 0–9)

21. Grid-in answer space (fraction bar, decimal point, digits 0–9)

22. Grid-in answer space (fraction bar, decimal point, digits 0–9)

23. Grid-in answer space (fraction bar, decimal point, digits 0–9)

24. Grid-in answer space (fraction bar, decimal point, digits 0–9)

25. Grid-in answer space (fraction bar, decimal point, digits 0–9)

SECTION 5

1. (A) (B) (C) (D) (E)
2. (A) (B) (C) (D) (E)
3. (A) (B) (C) (D) (E)
4. (A) (B) (C) (D) (E)
5. (A) (B) (C) (D) (E)
6. (A) (B) (C) (D) (E)
7. (A) (B) (C) (D) (E)
8. (A) (B) (C) (D) (E)
9. (A) (B) (C) (D) (E)
10. (A) (B) (C) (D) (E)
11. (A) (B) (C) (D) (E)
12. (A) (B) (C) (D) (E)
13. (A) (B) (C) (D) (E)

SECTION 6

1. (A) (B) (C) (D) (E)
2. (A) (B) (C) (D) (E)
3. (A) (B) (C) (D) (E)
4. (A) (B) (C) (D) (E)
5. (A) (B) (C) (D) (E)
6. (A) (B) (C) (D) (E)
7. (A) (B) (C) (D) (E)
8. (A) (B) (C) (D) (E)
9. (A) (B) (C) (D) (E)
10. (A) (B) (C) (D) (E)

DRILL: STUDENT-PRODUCED RESPONSE

DRILL: STUDENT-PRODUCED RESPONSE

13.

14.

15.

16.

17.

18.

19.

20.

21.

22.

23.

24.

25.

26.

27.

28.

29.

30.

31.

32.

33.

34.

35.

36.

37.

	/	/	
.	.	.	.
	0	0	0
1	1	1	1
2	2	2	2
3	3	3	3
4	4	4	4
5	5	5	5
6	6	6	6
7	7	7	7
8	8	8	8
9	9	9	9

38.

	/	/	
.	.	.	.
	0	0	0
1	1	1	1
2	2	2	2
3	3	3	3
4	4	4	4
5	5	5	5
6	6	6	6
7	7	7	7
8	8	8	8
9	9	9	9

39.

	/	/	
.	.	.	.
	0	0	0
1	1	1	1
2	2	2	2
3	3	3	3
4	4	4	4
5	5	5	5
6	6	6	6
7	7	7	7
8	8	8	8
9	9	9	9

40.

	/	/	
.	.	.	.
	0	0	0
1	1	1	1
2	2	2	2
3	3	3	3
4	4	4	4
5	5	5	5
6	6	6	6
7	7	7	7
8	8	8	8
9	9	9	9

REA's Test Preps
The Best in Test Preparation

- REA "Test Preps" are **far more** comprehensive than any other test preparation series
- Each book contains up to **eight** full-length practice tests based on the most recent exams
- **Every** type of question likely to be given on the exams is included
- Answers are accompanied by **full** and **detailed** explanations

REA has published over 60 Test Preparation volumes in several series. They include:

Advanced Placement Exams (APs)
Biology
Calculus AB & Calculus BC
Chemistry
Computer Science
English Language & Composition
English Literature & Composition
European History
Government & Politics
Physics
Psychology
Statistics
Spanish Language
United States History

College-Level Examination Program (CLEP)
Analyzing and Interpreting Literature
College Algebra
Freshman College Composition
General Examinations
General Examinations Review
History of the United States I
Human Growth and Development
Introductory Sociology
Principles of Marketing
Spanish

SAT II: Subject Tests
American History
Biology E/M
Chemistry
English Language Proficiency Test
French
German

SAT II: Subject Tests (cont'd)
Literature
Mathematics Level IC, IIC
Physics
Spanish
Writing

Graduate Record Exams (GREs)
Biology
Chemistry
Computer Science
Economics
Engineering
General
History
Literature in English
Mathematics
Physics
Psychology
Sociology

ACT - ACT Assessment

ASVAB - Armed Services Vocational Aptitude Battery

CBEST - California Basic Educational Skills Test

CDL - Commercial Driver License Exam

CLAST - College Level Academic Skills Test

ELM - Entry Level Mathematics

ExCET - Exam for the Certification of Educators in Texas

FE (EIT) - Fundamentals of Engineering Exam

FE Review - Fundamentals of Engineering Review

GED - High School Equivalency Diploma Exam (U.S. & Canadian editions)

GMAT - Graduate Management Admission Test

LSAT - Law School Admission Test

MAT - Miller Analogies Test

MCAT - Medical College Admission Test

MSAT - Multiple Subjects Assessment for Teachers

NJ HSPT- New Jersey High School Proficiency Test

PPST - Pre-Professional Skills Tests

PRAXIS II/NTE - Core Battery

PSAT - Preliminary Scholastic Assessment Test

SAT I - Reasoning Test

SAT I - Quick Study & Review

TASP - Texas Academic Skills Program

TOEFL - Test of English as a Foreign Language

TOEIC - Test of English for International Communication

REA's Test Prep Books Are The Best!

(a sample of the <u>hundreds of letters</u> REA receives each year)

" I am writing to congratulate you on preparing an exceptional study guide. In five years of teaching this course I have never encountered a more thorough, comprehensive, concise and realistic preparation for this examination. "
Teacher, Davie, FL

" I have found your publications, *The Best Test Preparation...* to be exactly that. "
Teacher, Aptos, CA

" I am writing to thank you for your test preparation... your book helped me immeasurably and I have nothing but praise for your GRE preparation."
Student, Benton Harbor, MI

" Your GMAT book greatly helped me on the test. Thank you. "
Student, Oxford, OH

" I recently got the French SAT II Exam book from REA. I congratulate you on first-rate French practice tests."
Instructor, Los Angeles, CA

" The REA LSAT Test Preparation guide is a winner! "
Instructor, Spartanburg, SC

" This book is great. Most of my friends that used the REA AP book and took the exam received 4's or 5's (mostly 5's which is the highest score!!) "
Student, San Jose, CA

(more on front page)